Beckett and Zen

Beckett and Zen

A Study of Dilemma in the
Novels of Samuel Beckett

Paul Foster

Wisdom Publications · London

First published in 1989

WISDOM PUBLICATIONS
23 Dering Street, London W1, England; and
361 Newbury Street, Boston MA 02115, USA

© Paul Foster 1989

British Library Cataloguing in Publication Data
Foster, Paul
  Beckett and Zen: a study of dilemma in
  the novels of Samuel Beckett
  (A wisdom east-west book; Grey series).
  1.   Fiction in English. Beckett, Samuel,
  1906−   −Critical studies
  I.   Title
  823'.912
Library of Congress Catalog Card Number
  88−40563

ISBN 0 86171 059 2

Set in Palatino 10½ on 12½ point by Setrite Typesetters
of Hong Kong, and printed and bound by Eurasia Press
of Singapore.

For Suzuki Sochu Roshi

Contents

Preface

Those familiar with Beckett's novels will know that they are not novels in the usual sense of the word. They do not speak of human experience but about the experience of being human. Readers expecting aesthetic satisfaction, well-developed characterization, plot, progression, and literary refinement will be disappointed. They will find themselves saddled with a 'gallery of moribunds' pursuing what appears to be nothing in particular with the intensity of a lunatic. Exasperation follows and the whole is dismissed as absurd, a term frequently employed in the past by critics either in denunciation or to describe a form of literary entertainment. In truth there is nothing absurd about Beckett. Neither is his work simple entertainment. Both the elements of absurdity and entertainment to be found in his work are in fact a guise for the expression of the deepest spiritual anguish. This anguish reveals problems of an ontological nature, which, in turn, expose the depth of Beckett's feeling. The intensity of these feelings in Beckett's work is based on certain observations, observations that we generally describe as 'religious' although they do not subscribe to any particular religious viewpoint. They are observations on the nature of existence and the suffering associated with it; they concern the meaning of existence and whether there is a God that can lend significance to life. These observations deal with the nature of consciousness and personal identity; they consider whether anything can be truly known and whether there can ever be communication between God and his creature. All these matters could be discussed either from a religious or a philosophical point of view, but Beckett rejects both and has said as much. The problem remains, nevertheless. It is here that Buddhism as a tool to interpretation can be of considerable help since, strictly speaking, it is neither exclusively a religion nor a philosophy. It contains something of both yet remains essentially a means of liberation from just those spiritual knots that Beckettian characters find themselves in and from the distress that such entanglement brings.

I have resorted to the illustrative material of Zen Buddhism because it is immediately concerned with the above problems and the feelings that attend them. The work falls into three main parts. The first deals with what has so far been said about Beckett with regard to the metaphysical aspect of his work. The second part then attempts to outline what is meant by 'the human condition,' a term that is used by many critics in reviewing Beckett's work. Finally, Beckett's novels are examined in the light of the arguments of the preceding parts. For Buddhists there may be little that is new. They may find interest, however, in Beckett's individual, passionate and meticulous expression of '*dukkha*' or suffering as he understands it. The non-Buddhist could well discover quite a new interpretation of the critical problems that Beckett's work discloses.

It must be said at once that the author is not the first to have found connections between the dilemmas that Beckett's work reveals and Buddhism or to challenge the terms 'absurd' and 'nihilist' in reference to Beckett's writing. Among others, such distinguished critics as R.N. Coe, John Pilling, Michael Robinson Steven Rosen, Ross Chambers and David Hesla have all discussed the matter, but no-one, as far as I am aware, has attemped a full-length account in Buddhist terms of what I have chosen to call the Beckettian impasse, which might be summed up as: There is no God and yet there must be one.

Whatever merit the work may have is owing to the kindly encouragement of several people. I would like most sincerely to thank Professor Kurt Otten of the University of Heidelberg's English Department for his friendship and guidance. His erudition and support were an unfailing source of inspiration while writing this book. My warmest thanks are also due to Professor Werner Habicht of the University of Würzburg. Not one word would have been written had he not first shown interest many years ago in the project. Equal acknowledgement must go to Professor Dietrich Seckel of the University of Heidelberg's East Asian Department and to Professor Günther Debon of the Department of Chinese Studies, both of whom gave unstintingly of their time to read the proofs and supervise the Buddhistic content of the work. I should also like to thank Frau Ingeborg Seefelder, who, during our many conversations, insisted on answers to practical questions and who provided a necessary spur to my procrastination. Finally, equally warm thanks are due to my wife whose good-natured indulgence, innumerable acquiescences and assistances helped enormously in smoothing the way while the work was in preparation.

PAUL FOSTER
Germersheim am Rhein, 1988

Part One
Clearing the Ground

1 *The Nature of the Impasse*

The amount of work produced by Samuel Beckett during the period 1929 to 1972 is comparatively small. It consists of nineteen plays, eight novels, three works of criticism, three short dialogues, some poetry, several short stories and a film. Only eleven of the plays are recognizably full length. Two of these, *Le Kid* and *Eleuthéria*, remain unpublished. Of the novels, *A Dream of Fair to Middling Women* and *Mercier and Camier* have not been published. Two of the works of criticism, *Proust* (1931) and *Dante..Bruno. Vico..Joyce* (1929), as well as the novel *Murphy* (1938) and the greater part of the short stories are preparatory in nature and find fuller expression in the mature Beckett's works that have been published since 1945. It is highly unlikely that any of Beckett's work written before this date would find an echo today on its own merits. As part of a metamorphosis, however, it continues to be of interest. Critical assessment of Beckett is, nevertheless, voluminous and continues to grow to such an extent that it has often been referred to as an 'industry.' Moreover, Beckett's name can be found in any account of modern literature. This leads one to assume that Beckett's writing must contain something that is of peculiar and perhaps universal interest.

Beckett himself warns us from drawing inferences from his work. He is, he says, concerned only with a 'few fundamental sounds.'[1] He observes that if people wish to acquire headaches with what he calls the 'overtones' in his work, that is not his business. 'My little exploration is that whole zone of being that has always been set aside by artists as something unusable – as something by definition incompatible with art.'[2] His concern, he announces, is with the theme of 'impotence.' At the end of the novel *Watt* we are warned once more: 'No symbols where none intended.' To those who would collate his work with established systems of thought, Beckett quite succinctly counters: 'I am not interested in any system. I can't see any trace of any system anywhere.'[3]

In tart reply to Gabriel d'Aubarède, who asked him about his possible debt to philosophical thought, Beckett said:

> 'I never read philosophers.'
> 'Why not?'
> 'I never understand anything they write.'
> 'All the same, people have wondered if the existentialists' problem of being may afford a key to your works.'
> 'There's no key or problem. I wouldn't have any reason to write my novels if I could have expressed their subject in philosophical terms.'

Critics, nevertheless, continue to analyze Beckett's material, thereby running the risk of what Swift once called 'scholastic midwifery' – the critics 'having delivered themselves of meanings that the Authors themselves never conceived...' We too should take Beckett's injunctions seriously. Criticism of his work may not carelessly assume that the author is either wrong or not in earnest. If the author himself would be 'quite incapable of writing a critical introduction to my works,'[4] then we should be doubly circumspect.

AN UNFAMILIAR WORLD

The first matter for consideration, in view of the vast amount of material written on Beckett in recent years, is whether there is anything more to be said. Moreover, Beckett's own statements that there are no hidden meanings in his work cause us to wonder whether we are justified in

saying anything at all. This would imply that we take
Beckett's work at face value, that we ask no questions and
draw no conclusions. This would be possible if we were
concerned here only with matters that relate to our daily
experience. Beckett's writing, however, engenders unease
and presents us with an unfamiliar world. The questions we
would ask are implicit in the material. An unquestioning
audience to his plays, for example, would assume that its
members are of the same level of intellectual sophistication
as Beckett himself or perhaps in the same condition of
spiritual distress.

Fletcher and Spurling support the view that, as Beckett
once said, 'It means what it says' and aver:

> ...a play is not a simulation of life outside, any
> more than football is, or the circus, or a game of
> chess, but an activity in itself...[5]

In quoting Beckett's youthful dictum on the work of Joyce in
his *Dante...Bruno. Vico..Joyce* (1929), Fletcher and Spurling
say that Beckett's writing is not '*about* something; it *is* that
something itself,' using Beckett's italics.[6] Later in the same
work:

> There is no key to *Endgame* any more than there is
> to Beckett's own life or the life of anyone else.
> Rather, there is a mass of detail lodged together
> whose general effect is likely to seem different to
> every comer simply because every comer will
> naturally pick out some details at the expense of
> others.[7]

With regard to the first quotation, Fletcher and Spurling
may be right as far as Beckett's work is concerned. However, most plays, ancient and modern, do simulate life
'outside.' The second quotation that Beckett's writing is not
about something but is that something itself immediately
gives rise to the question: What is that something? Is
Waiting for Godot simply an exercise full of words and
portentous pauses just to signify merely waiting? It may
have what Yfor Winters calls 'imitative form' (i.e. the form

of the play is imitative of its content) but that this constitutes the whole of the play is debatable. There is enough
philosophical innuendo to fill several volumes of disquisition. Mere waiting does not necessarily involve us in
suggestions about the nature of human identity:

> Estragon: We always find something, eh Didi, to
> give us the impression that we exist?

Furthermore, waiting is not necessarily associated with
anguish at God's righteousness or lack of righteousness:

> Vladimir: Two thieves crucified at the same time
> as our Saviour.
> Estragon: Our what?
> Vladimir: Our Saviour. Two thieves. One is
> supposed to have been saved and the
> other...damned.[8]

In addition to the above observation, there is considerable
evidence[9] to show that Beckett has, for most of his life, been
interested in St. Augustine's admonition:

> Do not despair; one of the thieves was saved. Do
> not presume; one of the thieves was damned.

In an interview with Tom Driver in 1961, Beckett alludes
again to this exhortation when speaking of the content of his
work:

> Take Augustine's doctrine of grace given and grace
> withheld: have you ever pondered the dramatic
> qualities in this theology? Two thieves are
> crucified with Christ, one is saved and the
> other damned. How can we make sense of this
> division?'[10]

DILEMMA IN BECKETT'S WORK

Beckett states that he is 'interested in the shape of ideas'
and this is what Fletcher and Spurling would no doubt seize
upon in order to justify their position. Like Beckett, they

might assert that it is the 'shape that counts,' thereby throwing form into prominence at the expense of content. However, as Steven Rosen remarks in his book *Samuel Beckett and the Pessimistic Tradition*,[11] St. Augustine's warning 'appears, reformulated, in most of Beckett's works [and] also suggests Beckett's most compulsive themes.' Augustine's admonition is Beckett's dilemma however appealing its 'shape' may be.

This dilemma is not the only one implied in Beckett's writing. There is the dilemma of human reason confronted with organized, implacable irrationality, with a universe spawning forth its spectacle of life, of which the attributes are suffering and death. There is the problem of Time, of which the concomitants are decay and oblivion. There is the problem of and lack of certainty about personal identity associated with Time's progression. Because of all of this, there is an overwhelming sense of isolation in a world that appears to be informed not by an all-loving God but by a monstrous taskmaster. Not to be aware of these concerns and to speak superficially of a 'mass of detail lodged together,' from which the reader may pick out whatever appeals to him, is not only to miss the point of Beckett's writing but also to be deaf — and in a critic this shows reprehensible insensitivity — to the howl of pain and desperation that pervades Beckett's work. This desperate cry is the 'fundamental sound' of which the author speaks.[12] Furthermore, it is what may be regarded as the 'content' of Beckett's art. Perfunctory concerns with mere shape, therefore, can be immediately dismissed. 'Shape' (or 'form') in the sense that Beckett uses the word will be considered later.

The consistency of Beckett's assertions over nearly three decades that one should not look for deep meanings in his work should be acknowledged. However, without distorting what he purports, we must look at his assertions in context. For example, in the interview with d'Aubarède, Beckett says: 'There's no key or problem' in referring to the novels and plays. In speaking to Tom Driver in Paris (see note 10), however, he says: 'The key word in my plays is "perhaps".'[13] This may not be the contradiction that it seems if we consider the circumstances of the interviews. In the first, Beckett is under the grilling lights of the television studio where he is unlikely to expose to several million people the inmost thoughts that inspired his work. Beckett is by nature an extremely retiring person. This, no doubt, is the reason for the terseness of his replies throughout the interview and especially his evasion in answering questions that attempt to explore his psycho-religious feelings. In the second interview, he is alone with Tom Driver, whom he took into his confidence. The word 'perhaps,' as will be shown later, has a religious meaning but it does not, I hasten to add, refer to any acknowledged religious belief.

In the same interview, Driver asks Beckett what he thinks about those who find religious significance in his plays. To this he replies:

> Well, there is none at all. I have no religious feel-
> ing. Once I had religious emotion...[14]

and goes on to speak of the shallow effects of established religious practice on his mother and brother at the time of their deaths. This, the abandonment of religion from the master's lips as it were, can be accepted as gospel. In his introduction to *Samuel Beckett* (London, 1971) p.15, Francis Doherty does in fact do so. Admittedly, Doherty is comparing Beckett with Joyce and, at the same time, demonstrating that Beckett, unlike Joyce, has no religious axe to grind. I do not take issue with him on his point. However, in calling Beckett a 'man without belief'[15] and by quoting at length the above unfinished statement about Beckett's rejection of Protestant belief, Doherty automatically categorizes him as someone with no interest in religion. This is far from the truth as can be seen in the interview with Driver: 'But do the plays deal with some facets of experience religion must also deal with?' Beckett replies: 'Yes, for they deal with distress.' He proceeds to illustrate the ubiquity of distress.

Distress is at the core of Beckett's work. I believe this to be so not only because Beckett was more communicative during the Driver interview but also because there is a large consensus of critical opinion that has recognized this fact in his work. Moreover, Deidre Bair's biography of Beckett shows clearly that Beckett's personal awareness of distress, like Dostoyevsky's, is very highly developed. Distress can be of various kinds. Physical distress that is due to deprivation; distress that is owing to an inability to deal with the circumstances of one's environment; distress that arises from social intercourse. All of these are alluded to in Beckett's writing. We may take the play *Waiting for Godot* and the novels *Moran* and *Molloy* by way of example.

The dominant theme of distress in Beckett, however, is that which arises from mental and spiritual perplexity, from the recognition of dilemma. The guileless humour that Beckett's characters display, the 'excrement and the caperings' as well as the apparent scatology scattered through the plays and novels intensify the feeling of impotence in the face of an impasse that defeats rational solution. In the moment of realization, philosophical sandcastles succumb to the incoming tide of what Beckett has often referred to as the 'mess' of irrationality.

In the play *Endgame*, Hamm says:

> Moment upon moment, pattering down, like the millet grains of . . . (he hesitates) that old Greek, and all life long you wait for that to mount up to a life.[16]

The image of the grains of millet is, as most critics have pointed out, taken from Zeno's *Paradoxes*. If one takes from a pile of millet one half to make a second pile and then again the half of what was taken before and then half of this and so on, one never actually completes the task. It corresponds to finding the centre of the circle or reaching the end of the digits of pi. But what for Zeno was a speculative quibble is for Beckett an agonizing inner distress that admits no relief. So much so that Hamm, in the next sentence and after a pause indicating disgust with further comment, says impatiently: 'Ah, let's get it over!'

There are no solutions to the dilemma of existence and the irrationality of suffering; death appears to be a preferable alternative. The entire play is an expression of frustration and disgust. In *Waiting for Godot*, there is the manifest expression of the 'perhaps' that Beckett intimated to Driver, the possibility of divine order in the 'matrix of surds' that existence poses; in *Endgame* there is contempt for any such principle:

> Nagg: (clasping his hands etc) Our Father which art −
>
> Hamm: Silence! In silence! Where are your manners? (pause) Off we go. (Attitudes of prayer. Silence. Abandoning his attitude, discouraged.) Well?
>
> Clov: What a hope! And you? (abandoning his attitude)
>
> Hamm: Sweet damn all! (To Nagg) And You?
>
> Nagg: Wait! (Pause. Abandoning his attitude) Nothing doing!
>
> Hamm: The bastard! He doesn't exist![17]

But the dilemma persists. The statement 'He doesn't exist!' is ambiguous. It is not a statement of absolute conviction but an expression of frustration that That which should exist apparently does not; the epithet is not wholly one of contempt (for how can one condemn an absence?) but is, again, the agonized realization of dilemma. This recognition is composed of (1) an acknowledgement of the senselessness of life and particularly an existence without God, (2) an inability to change the situation, i.e. the situation of impotence in which humans find themselves, and (3) despite the above, the need to 'live it out' since there is a suspicion that death may not bring relief. The three components of Beckett's dilemma appear throughout his work. It is perhaps sufficient at this point to give only a brief example. *How It Is* is the tortured expression of the frustration arising from the first component, the senselessness of life. The second point above, impotence, can be seen very clearly in *Waiting for Godot*. The third realization summarizes the attitude that appears throughout *The Unnamable*, the last words of which are: '. . . in the silence you don't know, you must go on, I can't go on, I'll go on.'

It should be noted that all the examples cited above are also at the same time examples of the other two components. It is simply suggested here that one or other of the elements might dominate. For example, all three factors are present in *Endgame*:

> Clov: (fixed gaze, tonelessly) Finished, it's finished, nearly finished. (Pause) Grain upon grain, one by one, and one day, suddenly, there's a heap, a little heap, the impossible heap...(Pause) I'll go now to my kitchen, ten feet by ten feet, and wait for him to whistle me...I'll lean on the table, and look at the wall, and wait for him to whistle me.[18]

and while Hamm for his part:

> Hamm: No, all is a (he yawns) absolute, (proudly) the bigger a man is the fuller he is. (Pause. Gloomily) And the emptier...(Pause) Enough, it's time it ended, ...(Pause) And yet I hesitate, I hesitate to...to end. Yes, there it is, it's time it ended and yet I hesitate to − (he yawns) − to end.[19]

and in counterpoint:

> Hamm: Have you not had enough?
> Clov: Yes! (Pause) Of what?
> Hamm: Of this...this...thing.
> Clov: I always had. (Pause) Not you?
> Hamm: (Gloomily) Then there's no reason for it to change.
> Clov: It may end. (Pause) All life long the same questions, the same answers.
> Hamm: Get me ready. (Clov does not move) Go and get the sheet. (Clov does not move) Clov!
> Clov: Yes.
> Hamm: I'll give you nothing more to eat.
> Clov: Then we'll die.

Hamm: I'll give you just enough to keep you
         from dying. You'll be hungry all the time.
Clov: Then we shan't die. (Pause) I'll go and
         get the sheet.[20]

In saying that this three-pronged dilemma is present in all Beckett's writing, I do not wish to convey the impression that his work can be reduced to a convenient formula. Such an attitude would be committing just that sin that is an anathema to Beckett, the sin of creating a system. Apropos of this, I might be forgiven for citing a delightful story both to illustrate what I mean by the word 'system' in the sense that I use it here and to support Beckett's view that there is no system in his work.

One day the devil and a friend were walking down a certain street when they both saw a man stoop down and pick up something which he immediately put into his pocket. The friend asked the devil what the man had picked up. The devil replied that it was a piece of Truth. 'That's a bad business for you then, my friend,' said the devil's companion. 'Oh, not at all,' answered the devil, 'I'm going to let him organize it.'

The aim here in pointing out that the three-pronged dilemma can be found throughout Beckett's work is not to categorize but to elucidate by suggesting that these are the themes around which Beckett weaves his narratives and plays. Both forms of writing are an expression of dilemma. This is what Beckett's work is about. Moreover, the clarification that I am aiming for is not an 'interpretation' but is rather a desire to show, as Susan Sontag declares, 'how it is what it is, even that it is what it is rather than to show what it means.'[21] Herein lies my justification in embarking on yet another critical study of Beckett.

Although the problem of dilemma and the impasse to which the dilemma has led the author has been frequently alluded to in critical studies,[22] it has not been as thoroughly considered as it deserves. If the core of Beckett's work indeed lies in the components of dilemma as we have outlined above and in the associated problems, such as personal identity (nature of the self), the origin of suffering (awareness of change, death and decay), and yet the ever-present desire to seek fulfilment in a condition or in a God, which may or may not exist, then we are concerned with an issue that is universal among all thinking persons, especially at the present time. In speaking of Beckett's 'search for a dimension of the self outside both time and words,' of the *angoisse* recognizable in his work, Michael Robinson[23] alludes to Heidegger's observation that:

> It (i.e. our age) is the time of the gods that have fled and of the god that is coming. It is the time of need because it lies under a double Not: the No-more of the gods that have fled and the Not-yet of the god that is coming.[24]

However this may be, the fact remains that Beckett has reopened the ontological question of the meaning of existence. He has given voice in artistic form to the root existential question: What am I? By a process of elimination, he has gone deeper into the 'mud' of the unconscious than his literary predecessors (Kafka and Dostoyevsky) and certainly deeper than any of his literary existentialist compatriots. The ontological question is open to a dialogue in which Beckett's work can serve as illustration, particularly so if no attempt is made to align it with preconceived systems of thought that would cause it to fall into the devil's trap in the anecdote above. As Steven Rosen says:

> Thus Beckett's critics distort the spirit of his writing when their interpretations confine his lament to a particular intellectual system or psychological condition.[25]

Beckett's works are 'not social commentaries nor are they philosophical treatises, they are works of fiction.'[26] Although his writings possess what could be called philosophical 'overtones,' it is doubtful whether western philosophy is an appropriate tool to deal with the psychoreligious considerations of which Beckett writes. Western philosophy has become a highly sophisticated, specialized discipline directed mainly at elucidating particulars and not generalities; it is, as a result, akin today to mathematics, its methods and conclusions accessible to only a few. Perhaps that is what Beckett meant in the d'Aubarède interview when he announced that he never understood philosophers. Earlier philosophies are either parodied or rejected in Beckett's work as it progresses.[27] Beckett's indebtedness to philosophy as part of his intellectual background has been exhaustively treated elsewhere.[28]

The same objections apply to psychology.[29] There is little doubt that the plight of Beckett's heroes is psychological in nature. Indeed Beckett himself has both been subject to psychological treatment[30] and spent some time as an observer of the mentally sick.[31] Literary excursion has already been made into the connection between the clinical conception of schizophrenia and the Beckettian hero in G.C. Barnard's *Samuel Beckett, A New Approach.*[32] Although Mr. Barnard's contribution to Beckett criticism is undoubtedly valuable, the reservation I would make is that schizophrenia is not, as it were, a common denominator in Beckett's work and, therefore, of secondary, albeit revealing, interest. If psychology is to be applied to all, it must be applied in a general sense, a sense that implies wisdom or the knowledge of human, healthy human, behaviour. Moreover, both disciplines, philosophy and psychology, suffer from diversification and controversialism.

Finally, too much rigour in analyzing Beckett is also out of place as a means of approaching the problems that Beckett's work insinuates.[33] A too rigorous approach is already an attempt to organize that which cannot be organized in the way that the material of scientific investigation can. All too frequently such a method is simply the recrystallization of Beckett's material into a system, for which he reserves his most damning invective. For example, one may recall the caustic satire of Lucky's speech in *Waiting for Godot* or, for that matter, any of Beckett's sneers at organized religion, which, he feels, is dissective murder of the truth as he sees it.

In view of the above, the question naturally arises of what

yardstick could one apply to a clarification of the Beckettian dilemma. It would have to (1) be relevant, (2) be neither philosophy nor psychology and yet embrace both, (3) be free from dogma, (4) not be divided by controversial schools of thought and (5) allow the subject to 'breathe.'

We are, in fact, concerned directly with Buddhism. This is clear if we allow that Beckett's work deals with the question of personal identity (*Molloy*), the problem of suffering (*How It Is*), the search for fulfilment (*Moran*), lack of satisfaction in existence while waiting for fulfilment (*Waiting for Godot*), abandonment of the search for fulfilment (*Endgame*), the quest for self (*The Unnamable*), the problem of Time, of age and decay (*Krapp's Last Tape*, *Malone Dies*), the apprehension of an abyss behind what is taken for reality (*The Unnamable*, *Happy Days*), the problem of the nature of mind (*Molloy*, *Watt*) and the springs of desire, the 'pernicious will to live' of *Proust* (*Not-I*, *Proust* and *Three Dialogues*). Buddhism is primarily involved in these issues. Buddhism deals essentially with just that concern which is described in criticism of Beckett as 'the human condition.'[34]

Some exploratory work into the possible connections between Beckett and Buddhism has been done by R.N. Coe, David Hesla, Eugene Webb, Steven Rosen as well as G.C. Barnard and Ruby Cohn. Only Coe and Rosen, however, go into scholastic detail. Coe, for his part, draws parallels, makes correct assumptions, supports these with accurate, authentic examples, but goes no further.[35] The appetite has .been whetted. Rosen provides a good deal of information with regard to the convergence of Beckett's conceptions and those of Buddhism, going so far as to say: 'Indeed, a whole complex of Buddhist ideas is reproduced by Beckett.'[36]

This is not to say, of course, that Beckett is inclined to Buddhism or that, necessarily, he has read the subject. He does, however, mention Buddhism explicitly in his little-known essay *Henri Hayden; homme peintre*. There he affirms a Buddhist principle when he says 'Gautama...said that one is fooling oneself if one says that the "I" exists, but in saying it does not exist, one is fooling oneself no less.'[37]

Since this doctrine, the 'non-existence of the "I",' is at the heart of Buddhist teaching, one wonders whether there is liberty to assume that Beckett has taken no interest in the subject, especially since the passage from which this quotation is taken reveals considerable insight. Nor is this the only hint of Buddhist teaching to be found in Beckett's work.

What is required, I feel, is an explanation of Buddhism that begins with first principles. This elucidation should be attempted because firstly it is basic to a fuller understanding of Beckett's writing and secondly it reveals, by implication, some of the inadequacies in the outlook of people today, especially in the West. If Beckett deals with what is generally described as the 'human condition,' which may be taken to mean the ego's experience of suffering[38] (Beckett's distress), of being and dying (Sanskrit, *samsara*), then this is the province of Buddhism.

THE PRINCIPLES OF BUDDHISM

But what is Buddhism? It is neither a religion nor a philosophy. It is a path of liberation. It is liberation from precisely those dilemmas from which Beckett's characters, and perhaps also Beckett himself, suffer. In this respect and in its universality, Buddhism resembles mathematics in being a tool, a means to an end. By 'universality' I mean that Buddhist methods are applicable to all human beings and to the spiritual situation in which they find themselves. Buddhism maintains that the experience of life for all is one that is involved in suffering (Sanskrit, *dukkha*).[39]

The situation of suffering and dissatisfaction is brought about by desire (Beckett's hypothetical imperative). It can be described as a thirst (Sanskrit, *tanha*), the basic motivation in all human beings for seeking satisfaction. But this thirst for satisfaction, Buddhism claims, is misdirected. It fastens upon the wrong objects for relief, wrong because they are misguided. They are misguided since in the end they do not bring the lasting satisfaction that the mind craves. Moreover, they are frequently injurious. Knowing this but not being able to find a way out or to find peace of mind results in frustration, a dilemma resulting from our ignorance (Sanskrit, *avidya*). Buddhism maintains that these situations are demonstrable wherever human beings are to be found. They comprise the first two of the Four Noble Truths, which are the basis of Buddhist teaching. The third truth is often posed as a question: Recognizing the first two to be true, can we do anything to change the situation? In extended commentaries on the third truth, the contents of the first truth (*dukkha*) and the second truth (cause of *dukkha* = *tanha*) are thoroughly treated so that one naturally asks: If this is so, what hope is there for us? The answer Buddhism gives is: Yes, there is hope. An escape from the dilemma is achieved by abandoning desire.

The first three truths are directed to those desirous of obtaining liberation from the state of *dukkha* and are concerned, respectively, with a correct understanding[40] of the situation in which we as human beings find ourselves. The fourth Noble Truth is concerned with the ethical prerequisites to liberation and with the means, both mental and spiritual, whereby this may be achieved.[41] In this essay, I shall be concerned primarily with showing how the first two truths are relevant to the Beckettian impasse. I shall touch upon the third truth from time to time while the fourth will be mentioned only occasionally as a point of reference.

Various schools of Buddhism have been set up during the last two-and-a-half thousand years. The devil's prediction in the anecdote above has never been realized to the exclusion of the Four Noble Truths. These have remained at the core of every Buddhist's path. Although several Buddhist 'philosophies' have developed, they have never lost sight of the fact that Buddhism is something to do and not simply something upon which to cogitate. Heinrich Zimmer sums up this point:

> Indian, like Occidental philosophy, imparts information concerning the measurable structure and powers of the psyche, analyzes man's intellectual faculties and the operations of the mind, evaluates

various theories of human understanding, estab-
lishes methods and laws of logic, classifies the
senses and studies the processes by which experiences are apprehended and assimilated, interpreted and comprehended. Hindu (and Buddhist)
philosophers, like those of the West, pronounce on
ethical values and moral standards ...But the primary concern − in striking contrast to the interests
of the modern philosophers of the West − has
always been, not information, but transformation:
a radical changing of man's nature and therewith, a
renovation of his understanding both of the outer
world and his own existence; a transformation as
complete as possible, such as will amount when
successful to a total conversion or rebirth.[42]

Buddhist philosophy, for its part, is always associated
with what we would call today a 'psychological' component,
using this word in its most general sense. It concerns itself
with the workings of the mind. It looks at ways to understand the mind for purposes of liberating it from the
bondage of suffering. The end is always practical and is
finally a matter of realized experience in the practice of
meditation. Buddhism is ultimately a state of mind. It is the
completion of a process of disentangling the mind from
craving and its associated snares. In other words, Buddhism
does not seek to establish anything more than what an
individual can prove from his or her own experience. Once
satisfied that the situation does in fact correspond with that
described in Buddhist teaching, the individual can then be
shown how to abandon all attachments. Buddhism is, therefore, at once 'psychological' and 'philosophical' in that it
deals with the mind on the one hand and with the accumu-
lation of practical wisdom on the other. It is not, however,
concerned with evolving systems of knowledge.

Two main schools of Buddhism developed so that the
basic teaching could be provided both to those who were
able to receive the substance of its thought at once and to
those who were able to receive it only obliquely. These

schools, respectively, were called the Mahayana or Great Vehicle and Hinayana or Lesser Vehicle, the word 'vehicle' meaning a method of conveying the student of Buddhist teaching from one state of mind to another.

From its beginnings in India, Buddhism spread to Tibet, China, Korea, South-East Asia and Japan, adapting itself in the process to the character of the people it reached. However, in doing so, it did not develop in the same way that Christianity did, with its superstructure of a Church and its carefully organized hierarchical body of priests, bishops, archbishops and cardinals, culminating in the person of a supreme pontiff.[43] There were monasteries and temples where training was undertaken and religious activity took place. Those aspiring to be teachers of Buddhism had to undergo lengthy training not only — and this is perhaps the principal difference between the western and eastern approach — of the intellect but also of the character and mind.

A ZEN APPROACH TO BECKETT

From this we can see that Buddhism fulfils the requirements for clarifying the Beckettian dilemma that were set out above.[44] Buddhism is relevant to our discussion; it is neither philosophy nor religion exclusively, nor psychology, yet it embraces them all; it is free from dogma since it does not have a code of divinely inspired rules to explain the circumstances of our existence; and it is not divided into mutually exclusive schools of thought. Lastly, individual development is possible since Buddhism is a path and not a system.

Before turning to how Buddhist tenets are pertinent to the Beckettian impasse, I should add that the particular frame of reference in this elucidation will be that of the Zen stream of Buddhism (Chinese Ch'an Buddhism). There are two reasons for selecting Zen: first, it is a teaching with which the writer is thoroughly familiar and second, its particular method of tackling existential dilemma — what Alan Watts

once called its 'flavour' — is much more in the spirit of the
West than that of other forms of Buddhism and for this
reason it is more readily understood. Furthermore, there are
no mysteries in Zen. The theory is not difficult: the practice
is difficult but that is another matter.[45]

What follows is an interdisciplinary exercise. It will not
attempt to be exclusively analytical and thereby separative
but will be seminal and unifying. The main objective is
to consider Beckett's plays and novels as expressions of
dilemma. It assumes, as has been implied above, that a
proper appreciation of Beckett's work is impossible without
careful attention to the nature of the problems that Beckett
incorporates in his work. It is further assumed that the
problems and dilemmas that he presents are neither intellectual, philosophical nor sociological but what I would call
'spiritual.' Since Buddhism has dealt scientifically with such
dilemmas over the centuries, I feel that it provides an
apposite frame of reference and in this case a sharp critical
tool, with which to expose the nature of the Beckettian
ontological impasse.

The novels that will be considered for examination in the
study will be principally those works published after 1945.
Reference will also be made to the novel *Murphy* (1938). In
addition, careful consideration will be given to Beckett's
major critical work *Proust* (1931), in which there are many
elements that find expression elsewhere. For the same
reason, the *Three Dialogues* (1949) will also be considered. The
minor criticism[46] will be assessed only in passing. I will not
look at Beckett's poetry even although it, too, contains much
of what I have referred to as the 'Beckettian dilemma' since
this work has been exhaustively treated by Lawrence
Harvey.[47]

Principal emphasis will be given to Beckett's major novels:
Watt; the trilogy, *Molloy, Malone Dies*, and *The Unnamable*;
and to *How It Is*. At the same time, reference will be made to
Beckett's plays as illustrative material. Of these, the principal ones will be: *Waiting for Godot, Endgame, Happy Days*,
and *Krapp's Last Tape*.

Critical endeavour dedicated to Beckett amounts to some

sixty full-length books and seven thousand essays, scholarly treatises, articles, reviews and extended references to his work. Selection has been made from the latter, the essays. I have chosen the work on the basis of whether the article, essay or other short work is essentially concerned with what is regarded as the Beckett preoccupation, that is, the epistemological issues referred to above. This has not been an easy task. Apart from the fact that the title may not always be an indication of the main burden of the essay in question, a great many pieces of work included in this legion refer to the theme under consideration although they may not deal principally with it. I have excluded from this study criticism at second hand as well as analysis that attempts to force Beckett's work into some established system of thought whether philosophical, political, psychological or sociological. Similarly, none of the criticism that deals exclusively with linguistic problems, which have no wider reference than an interest in words and their syntactic relationships, has been considered here.

Finally, in considering Beckett's work as the expression of dilemma, the essay attempts to abide by Beckett's own observation that his work is 'not about philosophy but about situations.'[48] It assumes that these 'situations' are not simply figurative, that they are not mere literary artefacts for the purposes of entertainment, but that they indicate actual mental — spiritual — conditions. This assumption is in accord with Eugene Webb's remark that the plays (and I might add, the novels) 'are explorations into the meaning of human life' and that this meaning 'is not an abstract idea of the kind that can be known objectively with the intellect, but a mystery that is lived in with the whole self.'[49] The study will try to show how Beckett's 'excavatory and immersive'[50] techniques toward a definition of self are similar to those found in Buddhist practice and that the dilemmas encountered in the quest for identity are those that the Buddha formulated and solved two-and-a-half thousand years ago. The study is concerned above all with demonstrating the nature of the Beckettian dilemma. The dilemmas inherent in Beckett's work disclose an impasse, which is an embarrassment both to literature and philosophy. The solution in Buddhist terms to this quandary is not outlined in specific detail in the study although it is implicit. The reason is that the study acknowledges as axiomatic that we are dealing primarily with literature and not religious philosophy.

The study is an empirical one. It does not proceed from any literary or philosophical theory. It will demonstrate by comparison and analysis how the dilemmas evident in Beckett's work coincide with those that Buddhism enunciates as life's dilemmas. The study will also show that Beckett's work contains a clearly traceable line of development, which indicates a growth in complexity and depth of the dilemmas. I shall assess critical reaction to his work in this connection and, in particular, attempt to define clearly the omnipresent term 'human condition.' In doing so, I shall introduce the Buddhist approach as a tool to better understanding.

What is meant by the word 'dilemma'? *The Shorter Oxford English Dictionary*[51] defines it as follows: '1. in *Rhet.* A form of argument involving an adversary in choice between two (or, *loosely*, more) alternatives, both equally unfavourable to him. (The alternatives are the 'horns' of the dilemma). Hence in *Logic.* A hypothetical syllogism having one premise conjunctive and the other disjunctive. 2. Hence popularly: A choice between two (or, *loosely*, several) alternatives, which are equally unfavourable; a position of doubt or perplexity.'

The root dilemma in Beckett is the desire to express, checked by the impossibility of expression. Beckett sums this up in his conversation with Georges Duthuit when he says in referring to artistic expression that there is 'nothing to express, nothing with which to express, nothing from which to express, no power to express, no desire to express together with the obligation to express.'[52] The 'obligation to express,' which is Beckett's 'hypothetical imperative.' is the drive to seek understanding and a solution to such problems as, What am I? This is the energy behind the quest that Watt, Molloy and Pim undertake, behind the urge to go on

talking in *Malone Dies* and *The Unnamable*, behind the need
to wait in *Waiting for Godot*, and even behind the desire to
end everything in *Endgame*. In each case, the energy is
checked by the knowledge that what is sought cannot be
expressed, what is talked about is in fact ineffable and what
is desired is unattainable. Graphic examples of this situation
are to be seen everywhere in Beckett's work but a few
notable instances might be cited. In *Waiting for Godot*, the
following scene occurs repeatedly:

> Estragon: What do we do now?
> Vladimir: I don't know.
> Estragon: Let's go.
> Vladimir: We can't.
> Estragon: Why not?
> Vladimir: We're waiting for Godot.
> Estragon: Ah![53]

At the conclusion of *The Unnamable* (also cited earlier):

> ...you must go on, I can't go on, I'll go on.

In the novels, the complete breakdown of the situation can
be seen in the disintegration of form in *The Unnamable*, in
the sudden, apparently senseless, savagery in *Molloy*,
Malone Dies and in *Watt*,[54] and in the violent outbursts of
frustration, which occur throughout *How It Is*:

> and all this business of above yes light yes skies
> yes a little blue yes a little white yes the earth
> turning yes bright and less bright yes little scenes
> yes all balls yes the women yes the dog yes the
> prayers yes the homes yes all balls yes
>
> and this business of a procession no answer this
> business of a procession yes never any procession
> no nor any journey no never any Pim no nor any
> Bom no never anyone no only me no answer only
> me yes so that was true yes it was true about me
> yes and what's my name no answer WHAT'S MY
> NAME screams good[55]

In this way, Beckett himself voices his dilemma. There is grappling with the problem of identity — WHAT'S MY NAME? he screams. The poles of the dilemma are the alternatives of going on to find out who he is (in the ontological sense) and the agony of receiving no answer. It is the situation that Alan Watts describes as 'That of fleas on a hot griddle...for the flea who falls must jump and the flea who jumps must fall.'[56] It is a dilemma for Beckett because it is not only frustration; the situation of not-knowing (Beckett's term: man as a non-knower: see the interview with Driver, op.cit.) is intolerable and the situation of not being able to know (his 'impotence') is equally intolerable.[57]

One of the principal dilemmas constantly alluded to in Beckett's work is that of Time. Clearly, this is a subject of great importance to both philosophy and psychology. The implications of this subject have far-reaching effects, which touch many aspects of scientific endeavour as well as impinging on every facet of our existence.[58] Thus, in speaking of Time in connection with Beckett, it is necessary to circumscribe the limits of the enquiry to the experience of time as expressed by Beckett's characters. An example is given below from the second act of *Happy Days*:

> Winnie: The bag is there, Willie, as good as ever, the one you gave me that day...to go to market. (Pause. Eyes front) That day (Pause.) I say I used to pray (Pause.) Yes, I must confess I did. (Smile) Not now. (Smile broader) No, no. (Smile off. Pause.) Then...now...what difficulties here, for the mind. (Pause.) To have always been what I am — and so changed from what I was. (Pause.) I am the one, I say the one, then the other. (Pause.) There is so little one can say, one says it all. (Pause.) All one can. (Pause.) And no truth in it anywhere.[59]

As with all Beckett's plays, the stage directions are punctilious almost to the point of being tiresome. They have been included here in their entirety so that the whole effect of the passage can be conveyed. It is clear that Beckett wishes the effect of what Winnie says to be correctly understood, the technique being similar to that of the close-up camera shot, which gives significance to every nuance of facial expression. Timing too is important. The pause in each case lends emphasis to what is said. What is in fact being said here that deserves such punctuation? The dilemma in this dramatic statement is clearly uttered: 'To have been always what I am – and so changed from what I was.' It is a recognition of change and constancy at the same time. She is the same yet, paradoxically, different. Logically, this is impossible, hence perhaps the 'difficulties here, for the mind.' Logically, too, it should be either 'I am still what I have always been' or 'I am different from what I was.'

A more useful attack on the problem from the point of view of this study is to consider Winnie as the apprehending subject, which can see itself as it 'was' and, by comparison, see itself as it 'is' now. The dilemma arises from the question: Am I what I was then, or, Am I what I am now? This I cannot accept either because I feel that I am now what I was then. This cannot be true because the body tells me that I am not what I was then but despite this I feel that I must be in some sense what I was then and am now. The system begins to waver, to become unstable.

The problem in essence is one of self-identification. Winnie sees herself as the object of a perceiving subject. I see myself as 'I' was then and as 'I' am now. This object of Winnie's perception is a projection of memory, that is to say, it is a compound of selected memories of past experience, carefully preserved by the mind as an identification of itself. The perceiving mind, the subject, is in general so fused with this imaginary extension of itself that it acquires in time a sense of permanence. Thus, it thinks of itself (or more accurately, the self thinks) that what it was it must also be now.

In this way, we speak of ourselves as we were and as we are, having the body and our present consciousness of ourselves to support us in the illusion: 'I am the one, I say the one, then the other. (Pause.) Now the one, then the other. (Pause.)' During this pause there is time to consider. Indeed, what else can one say? It is all merely a convention. We are not expected to go into abstractions or to investigate the real nature of perception every time we meet another individual. And so: 'There is little one can say, one says it all. (Pause.)' Here again there is pause for reflection. Such is the convention. Very well. But what of the truth of the situation? Winnie sees Time in the generally acknowledged way of a 'something,' which flows from the future, past the subject, and into a conceptual past. The subject, apprehending this movement, understands the present to be nothing more than a hair's breadth of momentariness as it recedes into the past and is lost. From Winnie's point of view, she cannot logically be the same person that she was. She cannot in fact be the same person from minute to minute. There is, she says, 'No truth in it anywhere.'

There is no truth in it, Buddhism would concur, because Winnie is looking in the wrong direction. The idea of Time, according to Buddhist experience, is a subjective conception, which develops, as the child becomes adult, with the formation of the ego and the notion of self. Its attributes of past, present and future are wholly bound up with the idea of ourselves as 'object.' Indeed, our conception of such a three-faceted phenomenon is merely our memory, our idea of the present in terms of the past and future, and our anticipations. All three, Buddhism urges, are self-orientated. But more of this later.

Let us turn to another example of dilemma as illustrated by Beckett, this time from one of his novels, from *Watt*. Watt contemplates a pot in Mr Knott's house:

> Looking at a pot...it was in vain that Watt said, Pot, pot. Well, perhaps, not quite in vain, but very nearly. For it was not a pot, the more he looked, the more he reflected, the more he felt sure of that, that it was not a pot at all. It resembled a pot, it was almost a pot, but it was not a pot of which one could say, Pot, pot, and be comforted. It was in vain that it answered, with unexceptionable

adequacy, all the purposes, and performed all the offices, of a pot, it was not a pot. And it was just this hair-breadth departure from the nature of a true pot that so excruciated Watt.[60]

We are informed of a dilemma involving recognition of an object. The object appears not to be what it is; its deviation from what Watt would normally cognize as pot is a 'hair-breadth departure from the nature of a true pot' and 'excruciating.' One might suppose that the observer were about to have a fit or that he is suffering from the effects of drug-induced hallucination, or that he is simply mad. This, it might be argued, is not a true situation of dilemma because it involves a perverted point of view. It is, therefore, not a situation of dilemma that has general relevance. For that reason, it has no validity. It is merely a lunatic's conundrum, a piece of tomfoolery. Perhaps.

In resolving the problem by splitting it into the elements of subject and object, however, the dilemma assumes plausibility. Watt observes the pot. He is the subject obeserving the object. But Watt-subject is himself the object; he is aware of himself as a 'something' looking at a 'something else.' Thus Watt-subject is itself Watt-object. But one object cannot be the subject of another object. Confusion arises: What is doing the looking? I-as-object cannot look and neither, of course, can the object of my looking. It becomes clear, therefore, that both object (pot) and I-as-object are the manifestation of an antecedent subjectivity, which may be termed here as awareness or consciousness. This clearly cannot be known by our intellect in the way that things are usually known, that is, as objects (of our knowing). For 'knowing' or 'seeing' to arise, however, this awareness or consciousness must necessarily be there. Wherever it is, the objects of the awareness will also be there; if it is not there, the objects will vanish. Subjectivity involves objectivity and vice-versa. What we have called subjectivity is, in fact, mind. We can, therefore, say: where mind is, there too are the objects of perception. Mind gives rise to objects as objects imply mind (subjectivity).

This is well illustrated by the Zen example of the moon's

reflection in the water. The water is likened to the subject and the moon the object. When there is no water, there is no moon since the reflection cannot take place. The same is true when there is no moon. But, where there is moon and water, the reciprocity of the two can be seen.

If there are no objects (phenomena) without mind, no pot without Watt, the idea of 'pot,' which we understood with such certainty in our everyday sense and rarely doubted 'lest we be thought mad,' is no longer secure in its 'pot-ness.' We realize that it is a product of our mind. Watt recognizes this and it worries him. It is only slightly 'off-centre,' 'but it was not a pot of which one could say, Pot, pot, and be comforted.' The fact that the pot functions as a pot quite unexceptionally is no comfort either. We can now see why.

Watt's experience can be found expressed as a well-known Zen adage. It runs as follows:

> Before I studied Zen, mountains were mountains and rivers were rivers. When I became a monk, mountains were no longer mountains and rivers no longer rivers. On enlightenment, mountains were again mountains and rivers rivers.

In our familiar, everyday world, mountains are simply mountains and rivers are rivers. Our looking is outwardly directed and the existence of phenomena is not doubted. We give a name to what we see. When we discover the existence of subjectivity, however, either by our own efforts or with the assistance of a teacher, who has understood the nature of 'Reality,' then things are no longer as they were before. The reality of their existence is doubted. They become mere products of the mind and are, therefore, only relatively real for the struggling student. Buddhism is an aid in transcending this condition, however. It attains a state where both subjectivity and objectivity are erased. One can then accept the mountains and the rivers as they are without (1) the ignorance of our familiar, everyday world and (2) the insecurity that results when one first discovers the existence of subjectivity.

It may be doubted that this is indeed Watt's dilemma. However, there are two cogent reasons for endorsing the view that it is. First, the consideration of subject and object as represented above is familiar material in Beckett's work. The idea of seeing and being seen occupies his thoughts in the creation of *Film* (written in 1963 and filmed in mid-1964). The introduction to the script[61] headed 'General' and sub-headed with an abbreviated Latin quotation (from Bishop Berkeley) '*Esse est percipi*' — to be is to be perceived — leaves little doubt that Beckett had considered the theory of subject-object. The following sentences outline the content of the film:

> All extraneous perception suppressed, animal, human, divine, Self-perception maintains in being.

> Search of non-being in flight from extraneous perception breaking down in inescapability of self-perception.

He then adds:

> No truth value attaches to above, regarded as of merely structural and dramatic convenience.

> In order to be figured in this situation, the protagonist is sundered into object (O) and eye (E), the former in flight, the latter in pursuit. It will not be clear until the end of film that pursuing perceiver is not extraneous, but self.

The second reason for believing that the subject-object question is Watt's dilemma is the text of *Watt* itself. After consideration of the pot, the next paragraph begins:

> Then, when he turned to reassurance to himself, who was not Mr. Knott's, in the sense that the pot was, who had come from without and whom the without would take again, he made the distressing discovery that of himself too he could no longer affirm anything that did not seem as false as if he had affirmed it of a stone...but he found it a

> help...to be able to say, with some appearance of
> reason, Watt is a man, all the same, Watt is a man
> or, Watt is in the street, with thousands of fellow-
> creatures within call. And Watt was greatly troub-
> led by this tiny little thing more troubled perhaps
> than he had ever been by anything.[62]

Watt is unsure not only of the object of his perception but
also of himself. In Buddhist terms, this is the beginning of
wisdom and heralds the breakthrough to apprehending
what Buddhism calls the true Self (i.e. subjectivity). The
word 'apprehending' is not used here in an accusative
sense. As we have shown, the true subject cannot be
thought of as object in any sense, whether actually (as
tangible object) or abstractly (as mental conception).

In the passage above, Watt has perceived the fact that the
I-as-object has no validity and that the subject of such
perception is thereby implied. He admits that the discovery
is a distressing realization — often, when that fact is discovered accidentally, the experience can be a considerable
shock[63] — for nothing could be affirmed as real, that is, not
bearing the stamp of the conceiving part of the mind. He
describes phenomena in this moment of realization as 'false'
and adds that he finds the experience more disturbing than
anything else that had affected him.

The aim of the ancient Zen masters of China was to
precipitate this profoundly distressing experience, that of
pulling the ego-fabricated false self from under one.[64] They
did this by means of a short exchange, which is generally
referred to today by its Japanese name, '*mondo.*' During such
a 'barbed' encounter, the master would ask questions,
which his counterpart (usually a monk) would be obliged to
answer.

In the early days of Zen Buddhism in China, such encounters were a natural part of daily life within the monastery.
Later, they became formalized interviews (Japanese,
dokusan), especially in Japanese Zen. This was often a tricky
situation for the monk. The master wished to know what
stage of discernment the monk had reached. The monk, for
his part, was expected to respond in the same terms that the

master used, in the manner that we would describe today as repartee. Failure to answer the master's questions in the spirit of deep discernment in which they were asked resulted in either a sharp slap or an admonitory blow with the master's stick (Japanese, *kyosaku*), which the master usually carried with him for this purpose. Sometimes, the master would leave in silent contempt. If he were satisfied with the answer, the master would generally conclude the session by withdrawing, indicating his satisfaction in some way. Sometimes he would leave the monk in a state of stupefaction and acute mental strain, similar to that experienced by Watt. This indicates a half-way point to what is described in Buddhism as the Enlightenment experience, that is, full awareness — *not* intellectual awareness — of subjectivity. An example of such a *mondo* is given below:

> Wen-chun (1061–1115) came to the master Chen-ching dissatisfied with the expositions of traditional Buddhist teaching, his mind no doubt chock-full of intellectual concepts. The master asked him:
>
> 'Where is your native town?' to which the young man replied:
> 'Hsing-yuan Fu.'
> 'Where do you come from now?' pursued the master.
> 'Tai-yang.'
> 'Where did you pass the summer?'
> 'At Wei-shan.'
>
> Thereupon, Ching held up his hand and in the same manner demanded to know why his hand so much resembled the Buddha's. Wen-chun was speechless. But Ching probed further: 'So far you have been fluent in answering my questions, so what's the matter now?'
>
> But Chun was dumbfounded.[65]

Two things can be presumed from this. First, the young Chun had anticipated intellectual instruction. Faced suddenly with a demand to clear up the matter of the

Buddha's hand left him flabbergasted as the question was entirely unexpected. This, however, was only the start of a process of bringing his mind to the state that Watt reached, apparently single-handedly. Second, Chun's mind worked strenuously on the problem created by this reference to the 'Buddha's hand.' What did it mean? What could it mean? His mind churned away at this until it eventually gave way (we are told that it took all of ten years to accomplish), that is, it abandoned the unequal struggle to solve the question by intellectual means. It arrived, thereby, at the unutterable, unutterable not because of any divine mystery but because, as we have seen, as soon as one begins to talk about subjectivity, it becomes objectivity and, therefore, something other than itself. Perhaps it is for this reason that we know so little about Watt's employer, Mr. Knott. We have only intimations about him and never a clear description.

The reason that Beckett confronts us with insoluble problems, believes Steven Rosen (and I agree with him), is possibly to make us 'experience the indeterminability of such issues and thus become aware of our ignorance.'[66] This ignorance is an ignorance of basic issues such as a knowledge of ourselves (our minds), of a reason for living, of death, of the existence of a higher order of mind than our own (God), of suffering and desire.

DEMONSTRATING THE CHAOS

Several examples of form serve as a vehicle to transmit Beckett's metaphysical import.[67] By 'form' I mean simply the techniques that Beckett uses in his novels and plays. There is the discourse on the dog's food in the house of Mr. Knott in the novel *Watt*[68] continuing, unabated in scrupulous detail and, as Doherty puts it, 'shining, brightly lunatic' for five pages, to end finally, with four, numbered and lengthy alternatives, topped with a table of possibilities. There is the pedantic punctuation – or none at all – the acrostics and genealogies, the inane speculations on number and permutation (in *Watt* and *Murphy*), the careful tedium of much of *The Unnamable*. There is the ferocious rigour of *Endgame*, the dark interaction of the characters Moran and Molloy, the enormous energy devoted to the inconsequential, sometimes for dozens of pages and occasionally even longer, the absence of what we are accustomed to recognize as 'progression' in both the novels and the plays, the innovative 'shape' of *Waiting for Godot*, which has been described as a play in which 'nothing happens — twice.'[69] The audience is kept waiting for a denouement, which never comes.

To add to the confusion, Beckett occasionally indulges in the 'straight' narrative (*Moran*) and dramatic piece (*Play*). Beckett's energy, his flow, the concinnity and succinctness of his expression, which has been called his 'classical' restraint, all leave the reader baffled as to the objective of such a display. It can be understood only if the techniques are regarded not as narrations but as states of mind. They are intended not to baffle, not to 'obfuscate the critics,' but to demonstrate a state of dilemma. This is why they do not 'progress.' It is not the resolution of situations that Beckett wishes to convey but the nature of what he described to Driver[70] as the 'chaos.' In this way, it is the *course* of the novel or play that is of primary importance in Beckett, not the individual action or actions, which combine to 'lead somewhere.' To present us with the omnipresence of dilemma, a state of the unresolvable, Beckett keeps the reader and spectator on tenterhooks. This is the purpose of his 'imitative form.'

Again, how often in Beckett's work are there examples similar to this, taken from *Endgame*:[71]

Will it not soon end?

or from *Waiting for Godot*:

Estragon: I can't go on like this.
Vladimir: That's what you think.[72]

or from *How It Is*:

...can't go, we're talking of me not Pim...[73]

These examples indicate both the continuum of the

dilemma and the frustration at the failure to resolve the causes. Beckett's entire *œuvre* is concerned with impotence in the face of those dilemmas that we have so far alluded to. Beckett has said as much. He rejects all action that 'develops' as we normally use the word in its application to narrative and dramatic structure. He considers such action as 'puny exploits' on a 'dreary road' as we shall see later.[74] That which resolves is a descent into what he calls, derisively, 'literature.'[75] The attempted answers to the dilemmas he projects in his work, philosophy and religion, he can only describe sardonically as the 'old answers.'

> I love the old questions (With fervour) Ah the old questions, the old answers, there's nothing like them! (Pause.)[76]

Beckett is someone who has given the most serious reflection to the essential nature of being and the problem of mind. Even if all proof to support this statement that his writing provides is dismissed, we could still say as much by reference to his occasional observations:

> Because the self is unknowable, when man faces himself, he is looking into the abyss.[77]

Anyone who can make such a remark has not only travelled far on the road to self-knowledge (from the Buddhist point of view) but has also given considerable thought to the nature of the mind. 'Beckettian man's concern is primarily metaphysical' writes Eugene Webb[78]...'Even his earliest writings reveal preoccupations with the same problems that he examines in his later works. Beckett's basic subject has been, from the very beginning, the difficulties of twentieth-century man in his efforts to understand his place in the universe...He (Beckett) is disillusioned with the hopes that previous generations have had for ameliorating their lives by making changes in the world around them, and he is also disillusioned with all the religious systems or metaphysical theories that previous generations have used to enable themselves to feel more or less at home in the universe. Beckett's career began with an examination of some of these previous systems and theories, and his writings as a whole can be read as...an extended commentary on the inadequacies of these systems of thought.'[79] Webb, I feel, has the matter well within his sights.

Part Two
The Human Condition

2   *What the Critics Say*

While Beckett's work often represents a fusion of what is known as form and content, it nevertheless embodies certain central themes, which can conveniently be called 'content.' Without knowledge of what this content is, the form presumably can have no meaning. What then is the content?

By considering the greater part of criticism of Beckett's work and listing the principal themes that run through it, we find that the subject that receives most attention is the one that is usually referred to as the 'human condition' or 'human predicament.'[80] Acknowledgement of this concept, whether tacitly or directly expressed, accounts for approximately seventy percent of the critical analyses on Beckett. Unfortunately, however, the expression 'human condition' is only rarely treated in any depth by the critics. Moreover, it is clear that no common denominator has been found that could justify such a global term of reference. For the most part, the term 'human condition' is allowed to stand as if it were generally understood. This is doubtful.

It is also interesting to note at this point that critical opinion of Beckett has undergone a change in order to accommodate itself to what Robin Lee[81] calls Beckett's 'fictional topography,' his 'map of mind.' The criticism has, so to speak, followed Beckett into the domain of mind. Some twenty years ago, for example, the phrase 'human condition' was not so commonly used.

THE EARLY CRITICS

The following example, written in 1964, suggests that Beckett can be regarded as a 'philosophical fantasist.' In leading up to this remark, Frank Kermode touches upon the essential problem of subject-object discussed earlier. He comes close to the core of the problem only to leave it again by passing on to another aspect of Beckett's writing:

> The fundamental absurdity of the subject-object situation is for him figured in clowns and clochards; and so is our imperfect control over space, time and death...Beckett can thus be read as a philosophical fantasist: His bicycles are Cartesian symbols, his submen Prousts who have *really* contracted out and so forth...To emphasize the formal interest can be a fashionable way of concealing the true nature of our curiosity. Beckett is a puzzlemaker, quaint and learned. We look for clues, guess at meanings. His former sophistication may be the meat the modern burglar brings along to quiet the *avant garde* house dog. Under it all, he (Beckett) is rather an old-fashioned writer, a metaphysical allegorist.[82]

Kermode goes on to support his view by a short discussion of *Watt*. He reiterates the assertion that Beckett is the reinventor of a philosophical and theological allegory. Thus Beckett is dismissed as Vladimir Nabokov once dismissed him, as an 'old-fashioned' writer. Such views on Beckett's work can be regarded as outdated. By this I mean not simply no longer in fashion but obsolete and irrelevant.

A more serious view of Beckett's work was provided in 1965 by Edith Kern. In describing *Waiting for Godot* in an article entitled 'Drama Stripped for Inaction,' she said:

> It is Beckett's genius to have found the simple word, the absurdly comical situation to express his thoughts on a man's place in the universe.[83]

It seemed that now a more thoughtful light had been shed on the work. But what did Professor Kern mean by 'universe'? There is no doubt that the universe is rather large and, according to astronomers and scientists, expanding every day. It is extremely doubtful, moreover, that Beckett wishes to indicate in any way that man has a 'place' anywhere, as is suggested here. On the contrary, the fact that modern man especially ('modern man' having been referred to by Beckett in the interview with Driver) has *no* place in the scheme of things in the sense envisaged and spoken of by Dante and Shakespeare is one of Beckett's most insistent themes. Does he not speak of the 'mess' and the 'chaos'? Where can there be a place in a chaos? And how can we account for the dislocation and alienation that characterizes Beckett's work, including *Waiting for Godot*, if we do not recognize that, for Beckett, there is no Ulyssean world of 'degree,' certainly not here on earth and perhaps not anywhere else either? The quest for identity in the novels among 'nameless things' and 'thingless names'[84] is page for page testimony that there is no place anywhere. There is only a search, a search that ends in failure. What Kern no doubt means is that Beckett, in *Waiting for Godot*, has given dramatic form to his conception of human beings as unaccommodated, lonely, waiting and yearning for the salvation that never comes. She suggests that this is how Beckett visualizes the predicament of humans. Kern's article was a step in a direction that was more likely to lead to a better understanding of the forms that Beckett adopts to transmit his feelings.

Other Beckett critics writing at this time, however, showed no interest in the questions of identity, suffering, Time, dilemma or the ego. One of these was Hugh Kenner, who over the years has become an icon of Beckett criticism. His work is frequently spoken of as 'brilliant' and everywhere acknowledged as that of an extremely perceptive critic. One cannot deny that Kenner has something of interest to say about Beckett. In addition to his own erudition, he has had the privilege of speaking at length with Beckett himself. He should, therefore, be better informed with regard to

Beckett's motivation. This does not appear to be the case, however. An example of his evasion of central issues can be found in the 1976 publication, *A Reader's Guide to Samuel Beckett*.[85] Intended as an introduction to Beckett's works, it contains no reference whatsoever to the topics outlined in this essay or considered germane to any earnest reflection on Beckett by most other serious commentators. Furthermore, Kenner evades what he himself designates as the 'human condition' in his *Samuel Beckett, A Critical Study*. In the chapter 'The Rational Domain,' he says:

> In this other domain which we can think about but not enter with our minds the irrational numbers exist more numerous even than the infinitely numerous rationals. And it is this analogy between these interpenetrating but commensurable domains that Beckett discerns his central analogy for the artists's work and the human condition.[86]

No more is said about the 'human condition' except in terms that are borrowed and mathematical:

> The very shape of the Beckett plots, as Vivian Mercier has brilliantly noted, can be prescribed by equations, Cartesian Man's inflexible oracles: Watt's career the curve of a function that approaches and turns round zero (Knott) before disappearing irretrievably off the paper.[87]

And so sophistry continues. Clearly, the more one reads, the stronger is the impression that Kenner is interested more in form, its deviations, colours and possibilities than in content. Kenner is also responsible for the perpetration of the myth of Beckett's commitment to an impossible task. He likens him to the clown, Emmett Kelly, who attempts to sweep a circle of light into a dustpan. The image is seductive and other critics have eagerly taken it up. For example, F.J. Hoffmann in *The Language of Self*, says:

> For Beckett the clown's gestures are a way of appealing, solemnly but also wrily to metaphysical

certainties that in their very nature are guaranteed
not to exist; or, assuming their non-existence at the
start, they are comic forms of intellectual concentration. Hugh Kenner likens them to Emmett
Kelly's 'solemn determination to sweep a circle of
light into a dustpan: a haunted man whose fidelity
to an impossible task — quite as if someone he
desires to oblige had exacted it of him — illumin-
ates the dynamics of a tragic sense of duty.'[88]

Hoffmann speaks of this gesture as both 'comic and dignified because it points to an unachievable universal power,'
and of a 'man striving to be more than an existent being.'
This is all very vague. What 'metaphysical certainties' is
Hoffmann thinking of? He makes no mention of them; their
existence is simply assumed. If something is a 'certainty,'
how can it be 'guaranteed not to exist'?

Both Kenner and Hoffmann concur that Beckett is attempting the impossible and that, in doing so, he presents his
characters as comically dignified in their persistence. This
may apply to the tenacity of the clochards' waiting in *Godot*
but does it apply anywhere else? Would it, for example,
apply to *Endgame*, where, admittedly, there are passages that
are comic and where a certain dignity can be detected in the
relationship between Hamm and Clov? But where is the
impossibility of endeavour? Is not the tone more one of
savage abandon? Beckett himself described the play as:
'Rather difficult and elliptic mostly depending on the text to
claw, more inhuman than *Godot*.'[89] 'To claw,' we note; no
comic toying with dustbins here, but a savage commentary
on a situation of dilemma, whether it is better to die or to
continue to exist, opting finally for the former. There is the
search, the quest in *Molloy* and the terrible disintegration of
mind and spirit, the lacerations of disappointment, of frustration. There is the savagery, the clawing and scrambling
for a vestige that will give meaning to existence in *Malone
Dies* and *The Unnamable*. All of it is a testament of failure but
not one trivial enough for a brush and pan. The image
cheapens and reduces the work of an artist aiming to expose

the lack of satisfaction in life and the apparent impossibility of resolving the situation.[90]

Let us consider Hoffmann's criticism on its own merits. Like others,[91] Hoffmann has sought to place Beckett within a western tradition. He compares his work with delineations of the self as they have been drawn in the twentieth century, especially with those occurring in Russian literature. He compares Beckett with Dostoyevsky. There is little doubt that the Russian writer had deeply considered the problems that Beckett studied. In speaking of 'The Underground Man,' Hoffmann cites Dostoyevsky's dilemma, which is his doubt about the historicity of Christ:

> The gamble his heroes take in their actions is a risk that Christ may not have existed — or, rather, that He too had been deceived and had suffered His crucifixion and death in the service of the 'great lie.'[92]

For Beckett, the problem is whether God exists. This doubt, Szanto asserts, becomes a 'living force' for Beckett. We can see it in *Godot*, *Endgame*, and *All That Fall* as well as *Happy Days*. Like Dostoyevsky, Beckett has serious doubts about the vaunted rationality of human beings. Indeed, as far as Beckett is concerned, one could say that all his work throws suspicion on the idea that humans are rational creatures. Much of his work is satirical of the rational philosophers, especially Descartes, Berkeley and Hume, steadfastly turning away from any rational explanation of existence. All his work is informed by great intensity of feeling. Beckett once described himself as 'all feeling.' None of Beckett's plays or novels has what perhaps can be described as a 'rational framework,' the accepted tradition of progression from one rationally acceptable situation to another until a resolution is reached. Alec Reid described the play *Waiting for Godot* as one that 'is striving all the time to avoid definition.'[93] Irrationality is also seen in the attitudes of Beckett's characters, in their 'pernicious and incurable optimism' spoken of in Beckett's *Proust*. Two outstanding examples occur in *Waiting for Godot* and *Happy Days*.

But Hoffmann never attempts a definition of self. Its nature is implied by what he says of its connection with the development of the selves in certain areas of literature. He ably demonstrates the activity of what he calls the 'self,' and relates it in a tenable way to a background. 'The history of literature,' he says, 'as it affects or is related to a study of Samuel Beckett, is a history of the effort to define self in space and to speculate about its power of initiating and maintaining identity.'[94] Instead of continuing in the manner in which he had started the chapter, that is, by a consideration of the relationship of the 'self' and 'things' (the ego and the environment, or, as I have termed the latter, phenomena), he immediately refers to Kenner's 'brilliant essay "The Cartesian Centaur" as an indispensable beginning,' losing his way in an unnecessary consideration of Cartesian concepts.[95]

Hoffmann later[96] returns to the themes that 'plague the Beckettian *res cogitans*' and asks: 'May we say that to know God is to assume a God who is capable of creating a thing which knows God? If so, what is the responsible relationship of the God who creates and the creature who knows Him?'[97] This relationship in particular is of considerable importance as far as a study of Beckett is concerned. Again, however, the author is clearly more interested in the technique of posing such a question than in discovering how Beckett answers it. Nevertheless, Hoffmann places essential questions to the fore.

> The basic materials of Beckett's work are selves as inquiring beings, selves as objects, other objects and the degrees and forms of distance between one of these and another.[98]

> The matter of dying in Beckett's work is basically a question of self-inventory; who is it that is dying? How may he identify himself if he is to die? How may he die 'significantly'?[99]

These observations deal with themes at the centre of Beckett's art. Consideration of them is thoughtful and sensitive but lacking in psychological depth.

There were perceptive critics even as early as 1956 who discerned that there was more to Beckett than merely a theatrical innovator. Patrick Bowles was probably the first to coin the phrase 'human condition' when he commented in *The Listener*[100] on *Molloy* four years after the production of *Waiting for Godot* in 1952 and at a time when the play had not received the universal acclaim that it enjoys today. Bowles also says in *The Listener*:

> Already, behind the grotesquerie and sardonically balanced phrasing, the anguish of the later books begins...[101]

> Just as Beckett seems to have set the 'I am' of identity afloat, so the emotional content of experience seems insecure. What we perceive does not come to us cold, but is momentarily joined to us, object and subject in an unbreakable relationship. The 'I' feels helpless. What is usually known as an independent self seems lodged in the world, among the other objects of perception, among the tables and chairs of English philosophy and the paradigm of the universe Plato liked to imagine.[102]

Here for the first time, we encounter the idea of a relationship between the journeys of Molloy and Moran and the quest for identity.

One of the first full-length books to deal with what may loosely be called for the moment the 'human condition' was Nathan Scott's *Beckett*, which was published in London in 1955. Here Time and Being are mentioned (p.89 and p.93) but, like Edith Kern's references to man's place in the universe, many of his terms lack definition and dilation. For example, he speaks of the French theatre of Ionesco (p.22) and the avant-gardists as a theatre that is in fact an 'anti-theatre.' One:

> deliberately disdaining subject-matter and 'anthropomorphism' and intent on exposing the veritable nothingness that is at the centre of human life.[103]

We may agree with this but would like to know at the same time what Scott means by a 'veritable nothingness at the centre of human life.' Furthermore, Scott shows that he is an early critic of Beckett by referring to the concept of nihilism. 'In him,' he says, 'the dark, seedy, claustral universe of the new nihilism has its most ingenious and resourceful cartographer.'[104] He later speaks of what he calls '*le néant*,' once more in a discussion of the French post-war theatre:

> ...Man is nothing, and that Man is nothing because there is Nothing either in or beyond existence that sanctions or gives any kind of warrant or dignity to the human enterprise. Indeed, the nihilism of this writer is not only present in the images and situations which he selects as vehicles for this meaning, but is even operative in the nervous rhythms of his sentences...[105]

We are left to guess what this 'Nothing' is. Nevertheless, the beginnings, imprecise as they are, can be seen. It is difficult to understand how 'nihilism' can be reflected in rhythm; the whole is sententious.

Scott's treatment of Time, with reference to Beckett's *Proust*, is perceptive but short. He speaks with insight when he announces that the two tramps of *Waiting for Godot* are two unhappy martyrs 'fated irremediably to suspire under the absolute dominion of *chronos*.' He poses this against the Greek term '*kairos*,' which he describes as the 'right time,' or the 'fulfilled moment.'[106] A little later, he describes the human condition, as he feels Beckett envisages it, as a condition of poverty and denudation:

> The tramp...in his poverty, in his denudation, in his clumsiness, in his vulnerability, mirrors for Beckett the general human condition: he stands for solitariness and the dereliction that are most essentially constitutive of what it means to be a man.[107]

Once more, a step has been taken in what we might call the 'psychological direction.' Scott hangs on to the idea, however, that Beckett is a nihilist. Quoting Dietrich Bonhoeffer's *Letters and Papers from Prison*, Scott says that now the world has come of age and also more godless, it is perhaps for that very reason nearer to God than ever before. He then goes on to compare Beckett with Camus, who in his opinion, reveals much more of what he calls 'hopeful godlessness' than Beckett does: 'that of Beckett is soured and bitter and utterly hopeless.'

In the last pages of *Beckett*, Scott succeeds in coming to grips with what I suggest is the essence of Beckett's writing and with what I have chosen to consider here as 'content' or 'content-in-form.' He declares that:

> Man...as he reasons, does not stand outside Being, and he cannot as it were, approach it head-on, in the manner he approaches various other less universal objects of thought. The enquiry into the nature of Being has always to be conducted in relation to special types of existents...and in relation to the nature of human existence itself, since at this point we bear the privilege of a uniquely intimate kind of insight...;[108]

He then proceeds to cite Heidegger's metaphysics (the constitutive principles of whose study of human existence is that of the concept of freedom), 'the power to actualize possibilities in-the-world: this is indeed what he declares human being to be — a being in the world in a way that is never completed, since, up to the moment of death itself, man is confronted by an enormous range of possibilities clamouring for choice. Man in fact *is* possibility: the human condition, in other words, is always that of becoming....'[109] This, too, is the Buddhist standpoint.

Commentary on form alone leaves too much unsaid and the school of 'It means what it says' is abandoned for what might be a more fruitful investigation. For example, Ross Chambers is one of the first critics to draw attention to the reiterative element in Beckett's work. In the opening words of his essay *Samuel Beckett and the Padded Cell*, 1962, he cites

Proust as having once observed that writers spend their lives writing the same work. He states that this fact is 'strikingly borne out by the example of Samuel Beckett.'[110] He sees Beckett's inspiration both before and after the war as a 'compulsion to write endlessly, turning constantly about the same questions — Who? Why? Where? When? working and re-working the same motifs and themes...in a hopeless effort to free himself from them.'

SPACE AND TIME

Taking Beckett's description of Murphy's mind as a starting point (*Murphy*, pp.112—113 of the edition used in this essay), Chambers draws a parallel between this and the quests of Molloy and Moran, the experience of *Malone Dies* and the stasis of *The Unnamable*. In short, he sees the trilogy in particular as a spiritual journey through layers of mind towards an ineffable freedom, a release from which he calls 'the temporal dimension.'[111] In doing so, he uses Beckett's own phrase in this connection to describe a condition that is 'improved out of all knowledge,' a state that also proves itself 'unattainable.' He says:

> This state (i.e. that of the Unnamable), however, proves unattainable, so that in his final novel life appears as an exile from the paradise where the spatial and the temporal would be abolished and the self attain its true existence.[112]

Here, at a very early date in Beckett criticism, Chambers has seen the connection relative to Beckett's work between Space and Time as experienced by the individual mind and what he describes as the 'self.' He sees the progress of the trilogy in the same way that Alvarez does, as a progress of withdrawal. However, Alvarez[113] conceives this as a retrogressive step away from the explicitness of the traditional novel, in which the world has 'always been reflected.' Chambers, on the other hand, sees it as an attempt to escape from the 'hell' of spatial existence and the 'purgatory' of temporal existence. He demonstrates this further by quoting the final lines of *Malone Dies*:

> never anything
>
> there (i.e. in space)
>
> any more (i.e. in time)[114]

'In this way,' Chambers continues, 'the escape from space and time has been effected but at the cost of annihilation,' (p.458). Thus, like the candle in giving light, it has expended itself. At the same time, Chambers discerns the dilemma inherent in the situation.

> In the annihilation of the where and when, a who has survived to ask questions about itself (i.e. the Unnamable): there is then some consciousness existing outside space and time. But as soon as it asks questions about itself, it restores the where and when: it cannot conceive itself except in space and time. The latent conflict in Murphy's concept of the self at last explodes: the abolition of time and space results in nothing, yet if the self exists at all it is as a timeless, spaceless *something*. It does exist: here it is, the Unnamable having survived the abolition of time and space and saying 'I'. But − and here is the anguish − what else can it do?[115]

This is the very nub of the situation, the essence of the Beckett dilemma and the Beckettian impasse. It is also the beginnings of Buddhism in asking: What then is this 'I'? Beckett himself speaks of the impasse, into which he had written himself when he completed *The Unnamable*.[116]

THE ESSENTIAL NATURE

Chambers takes up the point discussed earlier in this essay, that is, the relationship between the subject and its object:

> No description will ever allow the 'I' to utter, for whatever the self may describe will be the *object* of

its consciousness not the subject. As soon as subject and object become one, they can no longer be
described or thought about.[117]

and concludes:

> Only by discharging this absurd imposition (i.e.
> the 'pensum' of having to write to atone for the 'sin
> of having been born') can it (the self) become free
> and not have to speak any more, but in order to
> discharge it, it must...find itself and that is pre-
> cisely what language cannot help it to do.[118]

From here it is but a step to the generality of 'the human
condition.' This subject became the theme of a whole chapter
in Jacobsen and Mueller's *The Testament of Samuel Beckett*,
published in New York in 1964. On the first page of this
chapter, they make the following remark:

> The whole of Beckett's work moves relentlessly
> towards the answering of one question: What is
> existence? or, What is man?

The emphasis, however, is on the expiation of sin and guilt
and the causes for the 'absurd pensum' alluded to by
Chambers above. Jacobsen and Mueller quote Beckett
appositely in support of this assertion, in *Proust* (p.49),
where 'the tragic figure represents the expiation of original
sin...the sin of having been born,' and again in *Malone
Dies* (p.67) where Malone reflects on Macmann. This,
Jacobsen and Mueller say, is 'the perplexity of man's theological position, of his relationship to sin and guilt, to
atonement and punishment.'[119] They pursue this line of
argument with:

> Beckett's theologically framed reflections on man's
> condition are thorough even if ambiguous.
> His most extended meditation on man's ultimate
> destiny is found in *The Unnamable* in a passage
> abundant in oblique references to the 25th Chapter
> of the Gospel according to St. Matthew.[120]

A few pages later,[121] in considering another aspect of the condition of man, Jacobsen and Mueller announce that 'Beckett's main concern, like that of any great writer, is to define man.'

While it is true that Beckett does refer to this sin of expiation both in *Proust* and indirectly in his other works, this does not, in my opinion, constitute the essential nature of man's condition, nor, it should be added, the essential feature of Beckett's quest and subsequent dilemma. Care should be taken, too, in aligning this with any interpretation that involves Christian principles. In speaking of what he calls the 'myth' of Christianity,[122] Beckett makes clear that while he does not subscribe to the Church's interpretation of Christ's teaching, he does use the material of its history and dogma in his art. There is no doubt that these authors are well aware of this fact.[123] But is Beckett trying to 'define man' in the way that the two authors assert? The term is too large and its edges too hazy. It stands here in relation to Beckett's alleged reaction to the 'prevailing literary and philosophic views of a recent generation' and, again, is well justified. However, whether the intense, all-reducing, all-consuming quest of the self is what either of the two authors mean is left in some doubt. In short, is their attempt to relate 'man' in the nature of the scrutiny that Chambers undertakes or is it something shallower? Certainly the question of identity, when it is raised,[124] is treated only superficially.

Jacobsen and Mueller's book is informative (especially so at this period) on the methods that Beckett employs to project what the authors call his 'vision.' It is also an unpretentious attempt to grapple with the content of Beckett's principal themes. However, the writers' analyses fall well short of Chambers' insights. Moreover, the discussion of what I consider the essentials in their chapter on 'The Human Condition' fails to grasp the point.

AFFINITY WITH BUDDHISM

R. N. Coe produced the first book to mention an affinity between the Beckettian dilemma and Buddhism, also in

1964. Coe is the first to contest the term 'absurd,' one that had for a long time been applied to Beckett's work, especially his dramatic writing. At the same time, Coe condemns the label 'despair,' which at that time — and even now occasionally — was supposed to characterize Beckett's authorship.

> 'Despair', with all its inherent overtones, is a term which is wholly inadequate to describe Beckett's attitude towards the human condition; nor is this condition, in the most current sense of the definition, 'absurd'.[125]

Coe clears up common misinterpretations about the 'Void' as the word occurs in the *Three Dialogues with Duthuit*:

> The Void is not simply negative; it is not 'the obliteration of an unbearable presence', nor is it defined by simply being indefinable; 'the impossibility of statement' and the 'anguish of helplessness' are assertions about the mentality of the artist — they tell us nothing about the Void as such. No statement tells us anything about the Void.[126]

Professor Coe's Buddhism is clear and authentic. Although the terms he uses are essentially Christian, as here, they allow a better understanding of the Buddhist concept of Self.

Having now cleared the ground for an explanation of Beckett's work, Coe declares:

> In terms of a different symbolism altogether, the condition of man is a kind of Purgatory, but of a very much more complex nature than that imagined by Dante. Man has a vision of Paradise — the ultimate realisation of the Self in a *néant* beyond space and time, a void united with a void; yet to desire such a Paradise is to be aware of a Self desiring, and a Self desiring is not a void, and therefore cannot enter. The existence of man, then, is not Paradise, but neither is it hell, for a sort of hope remains, the hope, not of achieving the impossible, but perhaps of discovering, in the very

act of grappling with impossibilities, some new
synthesis of the Self...[127]

He continues with examples of Beckett's work, which come
close to what Hell and Purgatory could mean in this context.
At the same time, he reaches the heart of the problem of
Beckett's technique of reduction: 'by the progressive elimination of that which precisely *is* is there a remote chance for
the human mind to divine the ultimate reality which *is not.*'
(i.e. in the sense of being an object, concept or otherwise.) In
concluding the first chapter of his book, Coe asks:

> How am 'I', an a-temporal being, imprisoned in
> time and space, to escape from my imprisonment,
> when I *know* that outside space and time lies
> Nothing, and that 'I' in the ultimate depths of my
> reality am Nothing also?[128]

This is the substance of *Proust* as interpreted by Beckett.
   Coe refers explicitly to Buddhism and Buddhist practice in several places in his book and, on occasion, also to
Taoism, the influences of which can be detected in Ch'an
Buddhism.[129] Furthermore, his work is imbued with a
thorough knowledge of the meaning of such terms as *samsara*
and *nirvana*, the nature of the 'I' and, consequently, that of
the subject-object relationship. He even goes as far as to
state that it is Beckett's conviction that the Self is infinite
and void and that, in accordance with Chambers' view, in
'grasping' the void — an impossible task — the Self would
be annihilated (Chapter V). In doing so, Coe also demonstrates the essential dilemma of *The Unnamable*, which he
describes as 'one of the profoundest explorations of the
problem of self-knowledge ever attempted;...'
   In the same year that Coe's critical appraisal of Beckett
was published, 1964, Colin Duckworth brought out his *En
Attendant Godot, Pièce en Deux Actes*. It is primarily a scholarly analysis of the play. It is introduced[130] by an eminently
lucid account of *Godot*. He says:

> The true subject-object of Beckett's writing is his
> Self which is not the same thing as *himself*. He is

engaged in a perpetual search for the nature of his
personal identity. It is...a ruthless desire to expose the bottom-most layer of being in the full
knowledge or belief — that there may in fact be
nothing there.[131]

Duckworth is aware of the kernel of the Beckettian quest:
'What do I mean when I say "I"?' On the subject of the
human condition, so-called, he makes the interesting observation that Beckett's attenuation of his characters' individuality supports the intention that they 'represent and
express our common condition.'[132] Duckworth draws the
reader's attention to Beckett's art as part of a twentieth-century
phenomenon, that is, the anguish associated with what
Eva Metman called the 'unbearable contrast between conscious aims and unconscious needs.'[133] Although Duckworth
does not analyze the condition of dilemma as such, the
inner dilemma or spiritual dilemma facing the clowns in the
play is, nevertheless, implied throughout his work.

From 1969 on, Buddhism is referred to more frequently in
connection with Beckett's plays and novels. There is a
greater awareness that Buddhism or the way of liberation
deals directly with both elucidation and the resolution of the
problems that Beckett exposes in his work.

It is interesting to note that although the critics consider
the dilemmas of mind that appear in Beckett's writing in an
informed and competent manner, none of them prepares the
way for a thorough analysis from first principles of what
might conveniently be called the 'mechanism of mind.' Such
an analysis is necessary to an understanding of the nature of
the particular dilemma we speak of here, of how such a
dilemma arises and of how this in turn relates to what has
been called the 'human condition.' Moreover, none of the
critics suggests, even by implication, how these dilemmas
could be overcome. It will be argued that this is not the
province of literary criticism but that of Buddhism. I hasten
to agree. On the other hand, since the relevance of Buddhism
to the situations Beckett represents to us has been mentioned, an indication of a solution in terms of 'the mechanics

of mind' should follow.[134] In addition, practically every critic has assumed that the dilemmas so far alluded to are in fact insoluble. In most cases, it is not clear whether the problem is considered not resolvable because of the direction that Beckett's work has taken or whether the problem is *per se* incapable of resolution.[135] The establishment of dilemma automatically implies the question of a solution. For this reason, one should at least be suggested.

SEARCH FOR THE SELF

Michael Robinson's *The Long Sonata of the Dead* is a keen appraisal of the essential features of Beckett's art. Although the author does not attempt a strict, sequential analysis of Beckett's material in terms of search, dilemma and impasse, he, nevertheless, discusses these with considerable discernment. The discussion reveals that he is well acquainted with Buddhist thought. In 'An Introduction,' he speaks of 'the shifting layers of identity within a single novel,' of Beckett's characters' search for Self.

> Through the stories the narrator creates a series of vice-existers...in the hope that one day he will accidentally describe the vice-exister, a version of himself that will be his true Self. What he forgets — or tries to ignore — is that to define this Self in words would be to place it in the world and therefore to destroy it.[136]

Robinson is sufficiently aware of the nature of what he calls the Self (subjectivity) to see that what the Unnamable does in continuing to speak (in order to maintain his identity) is, as he says, 'like the struggle with time' and 'leads straight into an impasse.' In speaking, we use concepts, stories in the case of the voice in *The Unnamable*. Where there are concepts, there also are the 'ten thousand things' of Chinese Buddhism, in other words, phenomena. This then is the 'shore of *samsara*,' as the Buddhist would say, not the 'hither' shore of *nirvana*, the noumenonal bank as it were.[137] He continues:

> The location of the Self is like the location of irrational numbers or the centre of a circle. The rational mind knows it is there, either through intimation or understanding, but is incapable of actually arriving at it.[138]

It should be noted that Robinson here is speaking of the 'rational mind.' It is the 'rational mind' that cannot 'arrive.'

There remains an aspect of the mind that receives little or no attention in the West except as an adjunct to the appreciation of art that is 'irrational.' That is to say, the mind is non-conceptual. Because it is non-conceptual, the Self (which it is) cannot be 'located' in it. It (the Self) can be realized only by 'throwing oneself off a hundred-foot pole' as Zen puts it, the nonsensical leap into the void that is not a void. The Unnamable declined to make this leap and must not make it while the voice remains embodied in a novel because the 'leap' would simultaneously be one into silence.

Robinson maintains that the search 'for a dimension of the Self outside both time and words is the main preoccupation of the Beckett hero.'[139] He goes on to say that, among a variety of influences lying below the surface of consciousness, there begins somewhere and sometime the need to search. This search is a search for God. For our purposes, I would say that God is Certainty, That which is unchanging, which gives us identity and meaning and without which, as the author asserts, existence is '*angoisse*.' This search, he maintains, is even more important in an age of absence of God than it would be in another. At the same time, the search raises the question of how to carry on a meaningful existence where God is not.

> The discovery of the Self therefore, of the irreducible element that exists somewhere in man and which is opposed to the nothingness in the void about him is more crucial now than in the past precisely because of this awareness of an 'empty hole' in the sky.[140]

Buddhism would hold that the 'discovery of the Self' is and always has been the most 'crucial' aspect of life. This is why the ancient Buddhists used every occasion in life to 'wake up' the aspirants with whom they came in contact. To 'wake up' meant and means to become aware of the mind-built dream, which in our ignorance we believe is real; to see, suddenly, that this is not the case is to be at once enlightened. To deepen this enlightenment (for it can be either shallow or profound) is the Buddhist life. This, one is told in the monastery, is where the true religious life begins. For, with the deepening of Enlightenment comes understanding, and with understanding comes compassion.

Void is not a nothingness in the sense that we normally conceive as void. Although it is unlikely that Robinson himself errs in this regard since his concern is to propound a viewpoint, void is often taken for mere nothingness when placed next to descriptions of existence with reference to Beckett. It is neither 'somewhere' in humans nor opposed to anything except in the sense of being the reverse of what we have designated as 'phenomena.' It *is*.

Alan Watts helps to resolve the difficulty that such a statement presents to some people. He asks us to imagine a coin's thickness as 'is-ness' or quiddity running through it at all points and in all directions. The Euclidean surfaces that represent its 'head' and 'tail' are merely 'unreal' abstractions. Thus it is with Mind. This is what the Zen masters wish us to understand. There is no dichotomy but only an imagined one. There is essentially only what the masters call 'One Mind.' Like the dual faces on the coin, we are inseparably and wholly united with the 'Suchness' or 'Thatness' that is in fact All. There is, therefore, no 'hole in the sky,' for how could there be in such a situation? All that is required of us by those who are enlightened to this fact is that we see with an inward eye what this means for ourselves.

But Beckett's heroes have no such inkling; they struggle on, not in Professor Coe's Purgatory but in a veritable hell of not knowing:

> The hero therefore moves forward perpetually
> but with an extremely hesitant motion, frantically

desiring to cease yet determined to arrive. His
dilemma is heightened by the existence at moments
when he almost believes he has reached the end of
a voice bidding him to continue. The voice he
christens the 'hypothetical imperative'.[141]

Robinson sees Beckett as a 'mystic without a centre,' his
gallery of moribund beings as just so many ciphers embarking on a hopeless quest.

Where Beckett differs from the early mystics, however, is that even before he commences to search
he knows that what he is looking for does not
exist.[142]

A truer assessment of the situation can be found in the
Buddhist dictum that there is nothing to be grasped, attained
or proceeded towards. All such notions arise from egocentricity. Without taking the risk of carrying our analogy too
far, we can say that any perceiving mind imagined within
the material of our coin could not possibly learn of its own
substance by acquiring a view to the outside. Only by
looking inwards would such a possibility arise. So it is with
the human mind. A simple Zen aphorism sums up the
situation:

The eye sees but cannot see itself
The sword cuts but cannot cut itself.

This means that in looking out towards the world, the eye
sees all there is, that is, phenomena. If it were able, figurat-
ively speaking, to look at itself, it would see only void, that
is, the noumenon, the complement of the phenomenal aspect
of existence.

Robinson has also examined *Proust* in order to trace its
relationship with Beckett's later *œuvre*. In this analysis, he
makes the following observation:

Both Beckett and Proust attempt to reach this final,
real Self, whose essence would be reached in
instantaneous moment, in a leap beyond the immediate fetters of time. But whereas Proust felt
he had reached a solution through his idea of

'involuntary memory' Beckett cannot entirely concur.[143]

This appears to be indicated by Beckett's work. It would be an assumption perhaps to say the same for Beckett himself.

THE PERCEIVING MIND

Steven Rosen, for his part, is principally concerned with demonstrating Beckett's place in what he calls 'the pessimistic tradition.' Beckett is an author who shuns consolation. Rosen is of independent mind, not taken in by current enthusiasm for Beckett. He says:

> For Beckett's art is nothing if not a repository of unconventional attitudes: infantile, narcissistic, non-productive, spiteful, futile, dangerous unhappiness. Still more remarkable than these attitudes, however, is the reader's provisional acceptance of them — a bemused acceptance of feelings he would normally dismiss as outrageous and absurd.[144]

Rosen turns to the question of 'Which traditional meanings, being judged inappropriate or unpleasant, motivate Beckett's scepticism?' He acknowledges that it is the element of dilemma. He remarks that (p.29) 'as man withdraws from the world and approaches the self, Beckett's trilogy suggests, the self becomes successively emptier, even finally without distinct identity at all. Furthermore, as vacant and uninteresting as this self is, it still resists real possession. In *Film*, for example, Beckett's theme is the mind's bifurcation into perceiving subject and perceived object; subject and object can never be united, and thus the heroes' self-consciousness effects an anxious and perpetual self-entanglement.'

The author may be speaking for the artist or he may be expressing his own convictions. As we have seen from the illustrations above, neither I-supposed-subject nor I-supposed-object are 'real' in the primary sense, being figments or projections of subjectivity, that is, 'One Mind.'

They are manifestations of that subjectivity. At the moment of Buddhistic perception, both manifestations disappear with the result that subject and object become one. Zen masters talk, therefore, of 'transmitting the teaching of "One Mind".' At the moment of that perception, there is no more 'bifurcation' but one-ness or totality. Buddhists talk too, therefore, of 'whole mind' as opposed to 'split mind' or 'everyday mind.'

In a chapter on 'Relativism,' Rosen lists the philosophical implications of the Buddhist point of view (p.154). In speaking of what the Buddhist calls 'existence in *samsara*,' that is, seeing the world in the 'split-mind' state of consciousness, the following problems arise:

(1) . . . there are no absolutes or privileged points of reference, including God . . .

(2) . . . that all thought is contradictory; thus the curse of consciousness separates the subject from his own experience and even denies the experience at the moment he becomes aware of it;

(3) all experience, but especially the most authentic, is atomized; and

(4) no self-integration, sincerity or real responsibility is possible. In consequence of these realizations of failure, it follows that meaning, satisfaction and consistent systems of value are all, strictly speaking, impossibilities too. Of somewhat greater interest, perhaps, in the works of creative artists, are the emotional pathologies often concomitant with these reflections: (1) an exasperated and resentful sense of having always to react instead of act or a consciously futile desire, as Satre puts it, to be one's 'own basis'; (2) the suspicion that life is a dream − being the object of some other subject − with attendant feelings of alienation, paranoia and apathy; and (3) the

fear of being stuck in the moment, unable to
progress in one's being.[145]

Such reflections as these, at once profound and disturbing,
are to be found at the centre of Buddhist teaching. It is
for this reason that Buddhism has often been referred to
through time as 'nihilistic.' The logical extension of such
ideas and their practical application in society would very
soon lead to anarchy, chaos and bestiality. It was for this
reason that since the beginnings of Buddhism such primary
tenets of the teaching were reserved for the few who were
morally mature enough to receive them. This, too, is why
Buddhism, among other teachings, places emphasis on the
highest moral standards in thought and conduct (Sanskrit,
sila), and, moreover, why students of the higher teaching are
chosen with the greatest care. It should also be added that
the intention is not to create an elite. Those who apply
themselves to the practical injunctions of the teaching will
come to see, sooner or later, that all things are relative in the
sense abbreviated above. As the student progresses, he or
she will, as a matter of course, improve in character as the
knowledge becomes more profound. Compassion for all
sentient beings, human and animal, is the fruit of such
knowledge, compassion and non-injury (Sanskrit, *karuna*,
ahimsa) even unto death.

We can see immediately that if, after the most searching
rational self-analysis, the propositions of Relativism are
accepted, we then stand on the brink of an abyss. We are
faced with the agonizing dilemma of going forward into the
void of unknowing (if we can) or going back to what is
recognized as a shadow-world. Beckett has reached this
brink of the abyss. Rosen, for his part, sees two possible
ways of resolving such a dilemma:

> Basically, there are two ways of dealing with an
> irresolvable dilemma. One, without denying the
> conditions that constitute the problem, is to deny
> them their problematical interpretation, either by
> finding some associated benefits, or else by exag-
> gerating the problem to the point where one

simply must become resigned to it. The other basic
alternative is to transcend the dilemma by a simple
assertion of faith, claiming that in some other
realm or by some means not immediately apparent,
the problem is actually solved. The different variations upon these strategies philosophers develop
often become the means used to distinguish
them.[146]

Rosen proceeds to show how Hinduism, Greek philosophy and the Christian doctrine of the Trinity as well as
Proust's 'leap' were and are solutions to the basic dilemma
described above. He contends, however, that this is not
Beckett's 'way' and suggests that 'his tactics are paralleled
. . . in Buddhist thought, particularly in the *Madhyamika*
school.' Rosen then describes how Proust's thought was
concerned with the problems of suffering, mutability and
death. He points out that Nagarjuna,[147] 'like the author of
Proust,' also 'finds that craving underlies the whole conceptual framework (Beckett uses Schopenhauer's term
"Will").' Rosen sees the solution to the Beckettian dilemma
in Buddhist terms by amplifying his use of the word 'exaggeration'; he says, 'not only are other relations possible, but
all relations are equally possible, and what results is:

> Nirvana, the quiescence or equalization of all plur-
> ality, because when it is critically realized there is
> for the philosopher absolutely no differentiation of
> existence. Thought and feeling do not arise in this
> *undifferentiated whole, there is no subject and no
> object of knowledge*, there is consequently no
> turmoil like birth, old age and death, there is
> eternal bliss. . . [148]

Later in his analysis, Rosen calls this state of consciousness 'quietism,' a term that is misleading. It is not at all an
objective to which the true Buddhist subscribes. Buddhism
has little to do with 'sitting quietly, doing nothing.' A
technique used in Buddhist practice is, admittedly, one
whereby the mind is stilled, all thought being brought to a

temporary cessation. The achievement of this brings about the condition known in Sanskrit as *samadhi*, or deep, thoughtless contemplation. But this state is lit by awareness in the true meditator and is under no circumstances to be thought of as an end in itself. On the contrary, it is a beginning. It is what the Buddha described as a 'fruitful' state of mind, a soil in which the seed of Enlightenment may germinate and finally come to flower. Under other circumstances, he observes, the conditions of germination, although possible, are not so favourable.

In the Zen tradition, meditators are warned not to take such a blissful state for final realization. This is a rock upon which many a well-intentioned Buddhist has foundered. For meditation to be effective, there must be what is called 'one-pointedness' or intense concentration, often resulting in the state of *samadhi*, together with a spirit of enquiry. This, after all, according to the Zen Buddhists, was the way that Buddha himself reached Enlightenment. As an illustration, there is the Zen anecdote of the monk Ma'tsu (d.788), who used to sit cross-legged all day in meditation. His master, Nan-yuh (677–744), found him one day in this position and asked him what he hoped to gain thereby. The young man replied that he hoped in this way to reach Buddhahood (i.e. Enlightenment), whereupon the master stooped and picked up an old tile that was lying in the grass and began to polish it vigorously, ignoring the seated monk.

> 'What are you doing with that stone, O Master?' enquired the young man, now overpowered by curiosity. 'I am intent on making a mirror,' replied the master. This puzzled the monk and he ventured: 'But no amount of polishing like that will ever produce a mirror, Your Reverence,' the meditator protested. 'Quite so,' answered the old one, 'and no amount of sitting cross-legged like that will ever bring you to Enlightenment.'

Rosen compares the apparent indifference occasioned by *samadhi* with what he calls the 'extreme indifference exemplified in Molloy and Malone' and with the indifference that is most characteristic of Beckett's later writings. He traces how this is developed in *Murphy* and how it reached its zenith in *The Unnamable*. Although this may be an interesting speculation, I do not hold it to be the case at all. I agree with Rosen, however, when he maintains that 'What Beckett cannot accept in Buddhism is its assurance that Enlightenment will bring liberation' (p.159). Rosen adds:

> But note, it (suffering) all depends on ignorance; wisdom annuls the whole process of suffering. And this hope is what Beckett's *Watt* explicitly denies:[149]

> And if I could begin all over again, knowing what I know now, the result would always be the same.[150]

This comment may be acknowledged for the moment with 'Perhaps.' We can draw our own conclusions within the context of *Watt* later in this discussion.

The critic, Ronald Hayman, has also recognized the subject object relationship and the part that the perceiving mind plays in Beckett's work. He maintains that 'Beckett's rejection of naturalism in art follows logically from his scepticism about the perceiving mind. He sees it as an instrument incapable of registering accurately the reality that confronts it' and adds:

> There is no direct and purely experimental contact possible between subject and object, because they are automatically separated by the subject's consciousness of perception and the object loses its purity and becomes a mere intellectual pretext or motive.[151]

Hayman speaks of the censoring mechanism of the mind, which sifts experience in the manner described above. The reality we see around us, he asserts is 'just a projection of our consciousness.' He proceeds to draw the conclusion that with regard to writing...

> If you genuinely believe that what normally passes for reality is actually so much fiction, the most

real element in the fiction you write will be uncertainty...[152]

He illustrates this point by referring to the visit of the piano
tuners, Gall and son, in *Watt*. He accounts for what I have
called 'reduction' in Beckett's work as a focusing of the
hero's mind 'away from the frustrations of external circumstances on to the mind itself. The more the body is pared
down and immobilized, the less there is left to get in the
way of our seeing just a mind working,' (p.54). I am completely at one with him on this. Hayman does not go into
any depth, however.

On the other hand, David Hesla[153] touches the quick of
the matter in asking what is absurd in human existence. The
word ' absurd' is a general epithet that is applied to existentialist theatre, including Beckettian drama. 'Why is human
existence absurd?' Hesla asks. He answers his own question
by saying that being *human* and *existing* are mutually
contradictory.

> One could be a human being if one did not have to
> exist, and one could exist though not as a human
> being. But one cannot exist and be a human being,
> in the same place, at the same time.
>
> There are a number of reasons for this: To be a
> human being is to be body and mind; but what
> one needs and wants as body is what, as mind,
> one neither needs nor wants; and vice versa.
>
> To be a human being is to want to know and love
> — that is to say, to become one with — the Other,
> but the Other is precisely that with which one
> cannot become one. To be a human being is to
> want to say who one is, but who one is, precisely,
> is what one cannot say.
>
> To be a human being is to want to be self-
> grounded, but self-grounded is precisely what a
> human being is not and cannot be. In other words,
> man is not congruous with the conditions — the
> only conditions — provided for his existence. He
> and his world do not suit each other, do not make a
> fit.[154]

Here is the dilemma we have discussed so far stated unambiguously. This is the origin of *dukkha*. The restless ego searches thirstily for a means to solve the dilemma, a way out of the impasse. For the most part, it is content with fallible substitutes. This is the meaning of the parable of the Prodigal Son, which, incidentally, occurs in many traditions other than the Hebrew from which it comes to us via Christianity. Although one may seek everywhere for satisfaction, 'the eye is not filled with seeing, nor the ear with hearing.' In time, perhaps, we come to ourselves. This, according to the Buddhist view, may take many lives to achieve. Because of our stubbornness, we are forever turning to things outside the mind. Suffering will always be the result. How could it be otherwise among things of transience and decay?

I have examined in some detail that body of criticism that touches upon our theme of the problems of dilemma and the meaning of the term 'human condition.' Having done so, I am aware, nevertheless, that I have not referred to an enormous corpus; some of this will be alluded to as we go along. There are two reasons for not having cited all the criticism. The first is relevance. For example, although Ruby Cohn is among the foremost to be considered in any analysis of Beckett, she does not address herself to the principal issues that we are discussing. The second reason for apparently ignoring, for example, the work of such able critics as John Pilling and Eugene Webb is that what they say on dilemma and the human condition coincides with the observations of other critics. Hence, the work that seems to consider the problems of dilemma most narrowly was preferred to that which either mentions the matter in passing or considers it only in general terms.

Having discussed the problem of dilemma and its relation to what I have called, following the example of others, the 'human condition,' I should like now to consider how Beckett himself sees the problem. This can be done quite easily by taking a glance at *Proust*. In this work, we find the first formulations of what we have been at liberty to call the 'Beckettian dilemma,' a position that finds its crystallization in the *Three Dialogues* many years later.

3 *Time, Habit and Memory:* Proust

Samuel Beckett's critical essay on Marcel Proust's *A la recherche du temps perdu* was first published in March 1931. Producing the essay required the reading of Proust's novel, which, we will recall, embraces sixteen volumes (*Nouvelle Revue Francaise* edition). According to Raymond Federman, Beckett is reported to have remarked that the book was a 'hard job' and that writing it was not an enjoyable task.[155] We are also informed from the same source that a second reading of this monumental work was necessary before the essay could be finished. But, enjoyable or not, we may reasonably deduce that there must have been a fundamental interest to supply the energy to accomplish such a task.

At the same time, a book on Proust at this period of Beckett's life is a surprise if we look back over his entire work from this point in time. Aware as we are from this standpoint of all the allusion disseminated throughout his work, we might have expected an essay on, for example, Dante, St. Augustine or 'the beautiful Belgo-Latin' of Arnold Geulincx, on the philosophy of Malebranche perhaps or of Descartes.[156] Proust is never directly alluded to in Beckett's work whereas all those mentioned above can be quickly discovered: in the character of Belacqua, Dante's Florentine friend, the lazy lute-maker; in Act I of *Waiting for Godot*, St. Augustine's admonition of the thief saved and the thief damned in the clochards' exchange in the record of St. Luke; and in *Murphy*,[157] Beckett's quoting of Geulincx: '*Ubi nihil vales, ibi nihil velis,*' (where you have no say, you should have no wishes). Moreover, the influence of Descartes' thinking is to be seen everywhere in Beckett even if, as is generally the case, this is a 'rejection of Descartes' consolations. The Occasionalist, Malebranche, is similarly traceable in the method of locomotion of Watt, to refer to only one example.

Proust, on the other hand, is not so much recognizable through overt allusion as through an analysis of the assumptions on which Beckett's work is based. R.N. Coe makes the following observations on Beckett's *Proust*:

> Its style is jejune in the extreme, a tapestry of academic *bon mots* decorated with cornucopias of metaphors; however, discarding this tiresome verbiage and discounting the occasional platitude, *Proust* reveals itself not only as one of the first really serious analyses in depth of *A la recherche du temps perdu*, but as a sort of preview of almost all the main themes in Beckett's later work.
>
> Essentially, what Beckett discovered in Proust, and later developed in his own writing, was an attempt to resolve the conflict between 'awareness', which is instantaneous, and the linear extension of time of that same awareness when translated into language. Because words 'take time', they are fundamentally ill-adapted to the task of defining an aspect of absolute reality since all ' reality' — in any metaphysical sense — is in the present, that is, it is instantaneous. Proust believed that the human essence was endowed with an absolute reality outside time and space; whereas, in this life, it found itself imprisoned within time and space, denied even a full awareness of itself, since the 'Self' which it could conceive was compounded of memories accumulated by arbitrary selection from the past, and the 'past', being forever beyond its grasp and comprehension, has no reality of its own.[158]

It is true that Beckett's *Proust* is, so to speak, 'written from a great height,' that it has something of the style of *Dante. . Bruno. Vico. .Joyce*, the tortuous language and implicit condescension of which are certainly a shield for Beckett's youthful shyness. However, if considerations of style can be put aside for a moment, as Coe suggests, we can see that both Beckett and Proust are concerned with fundamental issues. These are the issues, I venture to suggest, that supplied the flame of interest, which enabled Beckett to reduce Proust's sixteen-volume compendium to its essentials. The essentials are: Time, Habit and Memory.

THE NULLITY OF TIME

It is very important to this argument to consider the three essentials (as Beckett and Proust considered them) as attributes of the perceiving ego (self). The strictures that apply to our argument above on perception in *Watt* are also relevant here. We are narrowly concerned only with (1) a perceiving subject (which in reality is an object of awareness or subjectivity) calling itself 'I' and (2) an object or objects. Into this bare minimum, Time, Habit and Memory fit as functions of what we call mind. Let us consider what this means by taking a look at Time from this point of view, applying Wei Wu Wei's formulation as we do so. What accounts for our concept of Time? How is the idea brought about?

Buddhism considers the phenomenon on the following principles: The self, here understood as a perceiving awareness, is also a function. It is a function because it is a manifestation of subjective awareness, the true subject postulated above. Now Function implies Movement, and Movement, Direction. Direction implies Space. Movement in Space gives rise to the concept of Time since Time is recognizable only by measuring Movement in Space. Time is a function of Movement in Space and this is the way that Time is apprehended by the mind.[158a] Time is said to 'move,' as we have just shown, linearly, from a concept of the future, through a theoretical present to a concept of past. As Time thus 'passes,' however, serial phenomena occur, or, as we may term them here, Events. We can say, therefore, that Events are a function of Time. Where Time is, there Events are also; where there is no time, there cannot be phenomena.

This idea has been summed up by the distinguished Zen master, Dogen (1200–1253), who was the founder of the Soto school of Zen in Japan.

> 'Being-time' means that time is being. Every exist-
> ent thing (phenomena) is time...in this world
> there are millions of objects and that each one is,
> respectively, the entire world...when one per-
> ceives that fact, (one perceives that) every object,
> every living thing is the whole, even though it
> itself does not realise it. As there is no other time
> than this, every being-time is the whole of time:
> one blade of grass, every single object is time (...)
> Do not regard time as merely flying away; do not
> think flying away is its sole function. For time to
> fly away there would have to be a separation
> (between it and things). Because you imagine that
> time only passes, you do not learn the truth of
> being-time.[159]

This is an interesting passage if only for the fact that it is comparatively recently that physicists have arrived at similar conclusions, which hold that time can exist only where there is a mind to perceive its apparent existence. For our present purposes, what is important to grasp is that behind phenomena there is an ultimate reality, which is misapprehended by what we may justifiably call a split in our mental attitude, our habitual way of looking at things. This dichotomy is caused by the mind (subjectivity) project-ing apparent objects by means of apparent subjects. In other words, subjective 'I' gives rise to objective 'I,' which per-ceives and interprets other objects. 'Objects' here also mean the objects of thought, that is, abstractions such as concepts, images, ideas, etc. Because these objects are a product of the mind's projection, they are no more real than the projected images on the cinema screen, with which we become so imaginatively and emotionally involved. 'Reality,' Buddhism maintains, is that which is 'before a thought arises' since thought is the precursor to misinterpretation of our real nature. Buddhism asks us to turn our looking 'inward' and thereby apprehend the pure subjectivity that we in fact are.

This issue can be approached from another angle. Let us consider again the matter of apprehended Time when it is conceived as a linear phenomenon. Let us assume that, as far as we are concerned, Time has the attribute of something that flows as described above. Let us look more closely at the idea of 'present.' For all practical purposes, we can talk of a 'now,' but once the 'now' is analyzed, it fails altogether to be a feasible phenomenon. The 'now' can be analyzed into ever-decreasing minuteness until, theoretically, it vanishes. From this we can see that 'now' exists only in terms of a past and a future. If, as we saw above, we can dismiss the past as memory and future as anticipation and, therefore, unreal, we have only what we call the 'present' left. It is not subject to any relation but the awareness of 'pure consciousness,' as Buddhists put it. This is the Eternal Now of the poets and thinkers of all ages. Its understanding is the goal of Zen training. We can see now why Buddhism, and especially Zen Buddhism,[160] stresses meditation. Meditation is an attempt to still the mind's associative processes and to exhaust it of its phenomenal contents by bringing the mind to rest in order that subjectivity might be apprehended.

This understanding was considered so important by the ancient masters that they occasionally resorted to physical violence in order to enlighten the monks. The following story is well known to Zen practitioners. It concerns the young Pai-chang Huai-hai (Japanese, *Hyakujo*, 724–814), who was attending his master Ma-tsu (Japanese, *Baso*), when a flock of geese passed overhead.

> 'What are they?' inquired the master.
> 'They are wild geese, sir,' replied the young man.
> 'Whither are they flying?'
> 'They have flown away, sir.'

At this point, the master took hold of Pai-chang's nose and abruptly gave it a twist, causing the lad to cry out in pain.

'How the devil could they fly away!' roared the master, whereupon the young man saw the point of Ma-tsu's remark.

We can see perhaps from this that Ma-tsu's aim was to get the monk out of his habitual, dualistic way of thinking, out of an outward to an inward perception.

Beckett says the following in *Proust*:

> There is no escape from the hours and days. Neither from tomorrow nor from yesterday, because yesterday has deformed us or been deformed by us...We are not merely more weary because of yesterday, we are other, no longer what we were before the calamity of yesterday. A calamitous day, but calamitous not necessarily in content. The good or evil disposition of the object has neither reality nor significance. The immediate joys and sorrows of the body and the intelligence are so many superfoetations. Such as it was, it has been assimilated to the only world that has reality and significance, the world of our own latent consciousness and its cosmography has suffered dislocation.[161]

Beckett is speaking of the usual experience of human life, the *samsaric* existence as we have chosen to term it. Time is felt to be a burden. We speak of the 'weight of the years' and the 'ravages of time.' Matthew Arnold, for example, says in one of his letters to his friend Clough: 'I am past thirty and half iced over,' while W.B. Yeats some years later expressed a similar sentiment:

> The years like great black oxen tread the world
> And God the Herdsman goads them on behind
> And I am broken by their passing feet.[162]

There is a feeling that Time will neither release us from the bondage of change, which requires our constant adaptation, nor deliver us by death. Time is felt to be burdensome particularly when we have to suffer or when we are bored. We have no choice but to live through the hours and days. On the other hand, when we are enjoying ourselves, Time passes quickly, unnoticed by the experiencing ego. This is undoubtedly the reason for Beckett's qualification when he says, 'yesterday has deformed us, or been deformed by us.' It is not Time, as such, that is responsible for our happiness or unhappiness but the self as it experiences Time's apparent passing. Here, too, the insubstantiality of Time is suggested.

Beckett says in the above quotation that we are not merely 'more weary...we are other.' This refers to change occurring with Time. In his poem, *Four Quartets*, T.S. Eliot refers in similar terms to the same phenomenon.

> When the train starts, and the passengers are settled
> To fruit, periodicals and business letters...
>
> To the sleepy rhythm of a hundred hours.
> Fare forward, travellers! not escaping from the past
> Into different lives, or into any future;
> You are not the same people who left that station
> Or will arrive at any terminus,
> While the narrowing rails slide together behind
>   you;[163]

Why, in Beckett's words, is yesterday 'calamitous'? I suggest that it is so because yesterday can be seen to have changed us but not delivered us. We change but we do not 'arrive'; we do not drink of fulfilment. The yesterday of disappointment was once the promise of tomorrow, to put it in somewhat oracular terms. As Beckett adds, the day itself need not have been of calamitous content in order to engender the feeling of disappointment. This, in substance, is the theme of *Waiting for Godot*. Waiting for what? we ask, to which the answer is: fulfilment, the resolution of all our yesterdays and tomorrows in the present, the Now of reality. The fact that Beckett knew, even at this time, that such a reality underlies our conceptual projection of existence is shown in the final sentence of the above quotation from *Proust*.

The nullity of Time has, as we have already seen, been thrown into suggestive prominence. So too has the idea of a self because if yesterday has changed us or, as Beckett suggests, 'deformed' us and if, like Eliot's railway passengers, we are not the same people arriving at our destination as those that left the station, that is, if we are not the same from one day to another, what are we? These ideas are incorporated in Beckett's *Waiting for Godot* at numerous places. Two examples may suffice here to demonstrate the point. In the opening exchange of Act I, we have the following exchange:

> Vladimir: So there you are again.
> Estragon: Am I?[164]

and in Act II Vladimir tries to draw Pozzo's recollection to their previous encounter but Pozzo cannot remember. Here, both the idea of a personal identity (self) and the idea of Time 'passing' into yesterday are questioned:

> Vladimir: Are you Pozzo?
> Pozzo: Certainly I am Pozzo.
> Vladimir: The same as yesterday?
> Pozzo: Yesterday?
> Vladimir: We met yesterday. (Silence.) Do you not
>   remember?[165]

Again at the end of the play, the theme occurs in the only soliloquy given to the tramps, to Vladimir, who muses:

> Tomorrow, when I awake, or think I do, what shall
> I say of today? That with Estragon my friend...
> I waited for Godot? That Pozzo passed with his
> carrier and that he spoke to us? Probably. But in all
> that what truth will there be?[166]

HABIT, A GREAT DEADENER

Speaking for Proust, Beckett says that 'Memory and Habit are attributes of the Time cancer.'[167] A little further on he dilates on the point:

> Habit is the ballast that chains the dog to its vomit.
> Breathing is a habit. Or rather life is a succession of
> habits, since the individual is a succession of
> individuals; the world being a projection of the

individual's consciousness (an objectivation of the
individual's will as Schopenhauer would say), the
pact must be continually renewed, the letter of
safe-conduct brought up to date. The creation of
the world did not take place once and for all, but
takes place every day.[168]

This is an unambiguous confirmation of the propositions
set out so far in this chapter, that is, that the 'world' as Beckett
calls it (our 'phenomena') is a construction of the mind. The
above also adds another aspect to a point that is made in the
Buddhist canon. In his reflections just quoted, Vladimir
says: 'Tomorrow, when I wake, or think I do...' This means
here that he wakes physically from sleep but not to what
Buddhism would call his 'true nature'; hence, the 'think I
do.' When Vladimir wakes, he re-asserts himself or re-estab-
lishes his view of the world, that is, his conception of
the world, which we have seen above to be unreal and,
therefore, false. For most of us, the 'creation of the world,'
that is, our mind-projected conception of it, is reconstructed
each time we wake from sleep. As the years pass, the
habitual orientation we gradually acquire as children fixates,
making it difficult for us to 'wake up to our true selves'
(subjectivity) as Buddhists term it.

Habit, or the false personality, enchains us. Beckett's
unpleasant simile in connection with the word 'chain' is
almost certainly an indication of his understanding of —
and his contempt for — the automatism in us. What Beckett
(and Proust) call Habit, Buddhism would call Ignorance.
Habit, for the Buddhist, is merely a function of Ignorance,
an ignorance of the fact that, fundamentally, we are not what
we think we are; Ignorance could be described as the
fundamental ignorance while Habit is the machinery that
confirms and re-confirms this basic ignorance. Essential
ignorance of our real nature, of ourselves, leads to suffering.
This is a generalized condition among humans, accounting
for what Aldous Huxley called, in speaking of human
history, 'a record of crime and folly.'

But despite the fact that our political history portrays, among other things, the clash of habits of thought over several centuries with all their shameful consequences, not all habits of mind are necessarily bad. They are not bad, but binding and delusive. Habit engenders the feeling of security and roots in us an identification with the things that we do. Most people, for example, go to work regularly through most of their adult lives, identifying themselves with what is done at work, with colleagues, with the firm and its affairs and their relation to these. They associate with those sharing similar interests, marry, raise children, carve a career, draw a pension and die. Usually, this leaves little room for self-reflection even if it were desired. Self-reflection is generally not felt to be desirable because it may undermine what we have taken so much time to build up for ourselves, the image of our false personality. Any attrition here is considered a loss both to ourselves and our security. Consequently, both must be defended at all costs. In this way, we can see that where the ego is very strong, there is little likelihood of the penetration of an idea which seeks to demonstrate that the ego does not exist. In Buddhism, we may say that subjectivity is revealed in proportion to the erosion of the ego, the ego being considered as the prime obstacle to understanding and enlightenment.

Christ may also have had this in mind when he referred to the rich man and the eye of a needle. Riches although not invariably, are frequently an extension of the ego, and for that reason are a hindrance in the quest for understanding. Zen Buddhism sees the matter as follows: if you are rich, do not be attached to your riches; if you are poor, do not complain of (be attached to) your poverty.

Attachment then is the real bugbear in the human drama. By offering us a substitute for fulfilment, it is in reality deluding us. The tragedy is that the delusion may last a lifetime. It presents us with the dilemma: How can the chain of attachment be broken once it is recognized as a bondage? Beckett, via *Proust*, says that this is only possible during moments of suffering, at which time we may be deflected from our usual attitudes of mind to issues that we may have never considered before. He puts it in the following way:

> Habit then is the generic term for the countless treaties concluded between the countless subjects that constitute the individual and their countless correlative objects. The periods of transition that separate consecutive adaptations...represent the perilous zones in the life of the individual, dangerous, precarious, painful, mysterious and fertile, when for a moment the boredom of living is replaced by the suffering of being.[169]

Suffering here creates an opportunity for self-reflection and inasmuch as it does this it may initiate a change of habit or even a change of heart. Buddhism, for its part, would require us to change completely and look into our real nature. The old Zen masters were well aware of the truth of Vladimir's observation that 'habit is a great deadener.' For this reason, they were not squeamish about breaking through habit in any way they could. This attitude often occasioned a few moments of suffering for those who crossed their path, either mental suffering in the form of acute embarrassment or confusion or, sometimes, downright physical pain. It was, so to speak, a rap over the knuckles, a sharp call to order. It was not a question of inflicting punishment as some ill-informed critics of Zen have supposed. Habit is fixed; the ignorance that underlies it may last a lifetime unless some agent intervenes to destroy it.

A famous Zen anecdote in this regard concerns the so-called Boat Monk, Teh Ch'eng. This man was probably one of a body of wayfaring sages that were to be found in China in the ninth century. This particular monk had adopted a livelihood by ferrying people across a river. Since it is the duty of every enlightened master (*Bodhisattva*) to enlighten others, the monk took every opportunity to do this wherever and whenever he could in the manner of a true Zen master.

One day, he was sitting idle in his boat when a customer appeared. This occasioned the following interesting exchange:

Seeing the traveller to be a monk, Teh Ch'eng asked:

'O Virtuous One! At what temple do you stay?'

(Here we can reasonably assume that the Boat Monk's overture contained some irony.) The young monk, Chia Shan, not to be outdone by a boatman, sought to put him off by resorting to Zen parlance. He announced:

'That which is like it does not stay and that which stays is not like it.'

This means that that which is the truth of Buddhism is not confined to one geographical spot such as a temple and, on the other hand, that 'which stays' cannot be the truth either since the Truth referred to here is everywhere. This was all very clever but the Boat Monk, being a shrewd old fellow, felt that there was a bit too much book-learning in the remark and probed further.

'I see. Well, if there's no likeness, what can it be?'

This was a reasonable counter but at the same time took the matter to a deeper stage. If the young fellow can answer this correctly, (i.e. reveal the depth of his spiritual understanding), he may satisfy the questioner. Chia answered:

'It isn't anything you can see.'

In saying this, Chia betrayed his immaturity. Although his answer is technically correct, it smacks too much of superficial understanding. It does not indicate that the speaker has really felt the truth of his remark in his bones. The master, therefore, replied:

'Where have you learned all this?' to which the young monk answered:

'Neither the eye nor the ear can reach it.'

But the old one is still not sure of the monk's real understanding. He feels that the pat answers are just too clever, almost, one might say, a matter of Lao Tzu's 'Too much cleverness is as bad as stupidity.' Ch'eng already has enough evidence by now to confirm his suspicions. He remarks:

> 'A good sentence is a stake to which a donkey can be tied for ten thousand aeons.'

This means that such a fine sentence (as that of Chia's) could provide one with a comfortable habit pattern for many a lifetime (symbolized by the donkey tied to the stake.) The clinch question is already at hand:

> 'When I let my line down for a thousand feet, the fish is three inches (i.e. the length of the tongue) away from the hook...Speak! Speak!

(The fish here is the truth of Buddhism or the apprehension of subjectivity not yet on the 'hook' for the monk, or three 'inches of talk' away.) The boatman seizes a paddle and wallops the lad on the side of the head and into the river. The young man tries to scramble back into the boat but receives another sound thwack while the Boat monk roars 'Speak! Speak!' (Show your understanding.) This was the moment of Chia's Enlightenment. On coming to the boat the next time he nodded three times in approval and gratitude.[170]

There are many instances of this kind of treatment in the annals of Zen. We can see how important it is for breaking the cage of *samsaric* thinking. Beckett, for his part, reserves his most scathing language for the habits of mind that are both hermetic in the sense of the above example and unfeeling.

> Morning is the time to hide. They wake up, hale and hearty, their tongues hanging out for order, beauty and justice, baying for their due...Day is the time for lynching, for sleep is sacred, and especially the morning between breakfast and lunch.[171]

The figure of Pozzo in *Waiting for Godot* is a personification of the same idea while in *How It Is*, Pim's manipulations of

Bom are not mere endeavours at communication as most critics believe but a violent attempt to force him to tell the truth of 'how things are' above and simultaneously to confirm the narrator's existence.

> but he can't affirm anything no deny anything no things may have been different yes his life here pause YOUR LIFE HERE good and deep in the furrows howls thump face in the mud nose mouth howls good he wins he can't ABOVE the light goes on little scenes in the mud or memories of scenes past he finds the words for the sake of peace HERE howls this life he can't. . .[172]

'The old ego dies hard,' Beckett proclaims, 'such as it was, a minister of dullness, it was also an agent of security. When it ceases to perform that second function, when it is opposed by a phenomenon that it cannot reduce to a comfortable concept, when, in a word, it betrays its trust as a screen to spare its victim the spectacle of reality, it disappears, and the victim, now an ex-victim, for a moment free, is exposed to that reality − an exposure that has its advantages and disadvantages. It disappears − with wailing and gnashing of teeth.'[173]

This corresponds exactly with the Buddhist point of view. When the ego and its machinery of conceptualization are halted for a moment, there, for immediate perception, is our true nature or 'reality' as Beckett calls it. Buddhism also holds that if apprehension in such a case is shallow, the memory of its recognition does in fact quickly disappear. On the other hand, if perception is keen and if the student has earnestly sought the experience of 'in-looking' for some time, months, years or even decades, the perception will be such that it will not easily fade. On the contrary, the experience is similar to that of emergence from an egg; we can never return. From that moment on we are truly free.

> Virtuous man, you should know that body and mind are illusory impurities and when these illusory impurities vanish for ever (i.e. in the

moment of true perception) there will remain only purity and cleanness (freedom) in the ten directions of space. (i.e. when the mind is properly orientated, everything everywhere is acceptable — mountains are mountains and rivers are rivers again).[174]

Thus the Buddha himself.

Another Chinese Zen master of the ninth century, Huang Po, said in answer to a monk's question:

Ordinary people indulge in conceptual thought based on environmental phenomena, hence they feel desire and hatred. To eliminate environmental phenomena, just put an end to your conceptual thinking. When this ceases, environmental phenomena are void: when these are void, thought ceases.[175]

To conclude, Beckett puts the matter in his own way:

Unfortunately, Habit has laid its veto on this form of perception, its action being precisely to hide the essence — the Idea — ... in the haze of conception.[176]

Buddhism, as we noted earlier, is nothing mysterious. It is even irreligious in the affective sense. Zen Buddhism is nothing less than a tool for bringing the mind of the individual to an abrupt awakening of his or her original One Mind, (i.e. subjectivity). This done, there is no more to be said. In the West, however, one is left to one's own devices more or less to discover this, the Original Nature of human beings. Suffering may indeed be a mind-opener. There is another way of discovering reality, however. I would like to suggest that Beckett himself is among those who have taken this way. They are the seekers of truth, those who see through the crystallized concepts that humans have erected for themselves, those who, like Beckett, have abandoned all concepts and burrowed into their minds for an answer.

Memory is the third culprit in the conspiracy of delusion. It is the last accomplice, according to Beckett, in the crime of keeping us in ignorance. Beckett refers to Proust's memory as 'an instrument of reference instead of an instrument of discovery.'[177] 'Memory,' he continues, 'is obviously conditioned by perception. Curiosity is a non-conditioned reflex...' He then proceeds to compare memory and curiosity, arriving finally at a distinction between what he describes as 'voluntary' and 'involuntary' memory. He says — and here we will recall Vladimir again — that 'When the sleeper awakes, this emissary (memory) of his habit assures him that his 'personality' (false personality) has not disappeared with his fatigue.'[178] 'Voluntary memory,' aided by Habit, daily resurrects the concept of I-as-object. Reminiscence, sweet as it may be, is only a conscious re-confirmation of the ego 'as it was then,' unassailable behind the locked doors of past time.

This may seem hard but the objective of Beckett's scorn in saying '...if habit is the Goddess of Dullness, voluntary memory is Shadwell...' is to draw our attention to the possibility of what he calls 'involuntary memory,' 'an immediate, total and delicious deflagration...in its flame it has consumed Habit and all its works and in its brightness revealed what the mock reality of experience never can and never will reveal — the real.'[179] The experience corresponds to what the Buddhist Calls Enlightenment (Chinese, *Wu hsien*; Japanese, *satori, kensho*).

Krapp's Last Tape is the fruit of Beckett's reflections on these matters in *Proust*:

> Tape: Spiritually, a year of profound gloom and indigence until that memorable night in March, at the end of the jetty in the howling wind, never to be forgotten, when suddenly I saw the whole thing. The vision at last.[180]

'Involuntary memory' seizes him. This is most important.

Voluntary memory is mere 'crap' by comparison. He continues:

> This I fancy is what I have chiefly to record this evening against the day when my work will be done and perhaps no place left in my memory, warm or cold, for the miracle that...(hesitates)... for the fire that set it alight. What I saw then was this, that the belief I had been going on all my life, namely...[181]

Krapp impatiently switches off the machine. He has forgotten and does not want to be reminded because this will shatter his comfortable reminiscence, 'crap' though it may be...

> Krapp: Just been listening to that stupid bastard I took myself for thirty years ago, hard to believe...[182]

it confirms him in his conception of himself. His last words are:

> Perhaps my best years are gone. When there was a chance of happiness. But I wouldn't want them back. Not with the fire in me now. No, I wouldn't want them back.[183]

Or alternatively and more significantly, these closing words may mean that because he can see that the past is an illusion, he would not want to re-live it. This would explain the phrase, 'Not with the fire in me now,' which would refer to an association of 'fire' as used in connection with 'understanding' (in *Krapp's Last Tape*) and 'deflagration' with 'reality' in *Proust*.

'This accidental and fugitive salvation in the midst of life may supervene when the action of involuntary memory is stimulated by the negligence or agony of habit, and under no other circumstances,'[184] Beckett asserts a little later. Whether he is speaking of his own conviction or that of Proust is difficult to know here. However it is, it is quite untrue. There are in fact many ways to reach the condition of realization, as described above.

Alan Watts isolates the component parts of this machinery of deception when he puts the spirit of the Buddhist *sutras* (the recorded teaching) into modern example. He shows how Time, Habit and Memory work together to dislocate a true relationship with ourselves.

> It is not that *satori* (i.e. the understanding insti-
> gated by what Beckett calls 'involuntary memory')
> comes quickly or unexpectedly, all of a sudden, for
> mere speed has nothing to do with it. The reason is
> that Zen is a liberation from Time. For if we open
> our eyes and see clearly, it becomes obvious that
> there is no other time than this instant, and that
> the past and the future are abstractions without
> any concrete reality.
>
> Until that has become clear, it seems that our life is
> all past and future, and that the present is nothing
> more than the infinitesimal hairline which divides
> them. From this comes the sensation of 'having no
> time,' of a world which hurries by so rapidly that
> it is gone before we can enjoy it. But through
> 'awakening to the instant' (a Zen term) one sees
> that this is the reverse of the truth: it is rather the
> past and future which are the fleeting illusions,
> and the succession of time is a convention of our
> single-track verbal thinking, of a consciousness
> which interprets the world by grasping little pieces
> of it, calling them things and events. But every
> such grasp of the mind excludes the rest of the
> world, so that this type of consciousness can get an
> approximate vision of the whole through a series
> of grasps, one after the other. Yet the superficiality
> of this consciousness is seen from the fact that it
> cannot and does not regulate even the human
> organism. For if it had control of the heartbeat,
> the breath, the operation of the nerves, glands,

muscles, and sense organs, it would be rushing wildly around the body, taking care of one thing after another, with no time to do anything else. Happily it is not in charge, and the organism is regulated by the timeless 'original mind' (Zen term) which deals with life in its totality and so can do ever so many 'things' at once.[185]

Beckett also suggests this when he says, 'But our vulgar perception is not concerned with other vulgar phenomena...At best, all that is realized in time (all Time-produce) whether in Art or Life, can only be possessed successively, by a series of partial annexations and never integrally and at once.'[186]

THE LEAP INTO THE VOID

Although the above may be apprehended in sincerity, there may still be a dilemma. Most students of Zen hesitate in effecting the 'great leap into the void' (Zen term). If this seems too florid an expression, we can say with equal truth that it means the abandonment of the phenomenal world — an abandonment which of course includes oneself. The student hesitates, therefore; his 'best' instincts are against such a risk. There is the promise of total freedom if he jumps, but he dare not. On the other hand, there is the perilous 'security' of *samsaric* life, the snares of which have been demonstrated. He must leap, therefore. But he dare not. Perhaps, he thinks, it will mean 'death' or 'oblivion,' a 'cold obstruction' and imprisonment in the 'viewless winds.' Here, the assistance of a master is invaluable in pushing the seeker into a new dimension.

In Beckett's works, this alternative to *samsaric* existence is always implied but never expressly alluded to. His characters' dilemma is that, even though they have abandoned everything, they are unsure of what to do next.

But I am human, I fancy, and my progress suffered...from the slow and painful progress it

had always been...a veritable calvary with no
limit to its stations and no hope of crucifixion...[187]

The following example from *Happy Days* shows Winnie on
the edge of her predicament, so to speak. Like the student
above, she is considering whether it is really worth the leap.
But she, too, declines:

> Winnie: ...If the mind were to go. (Pause.) It
> won't of course. (Pause.) Not quite.
> not mine. (Smile.) Not now. (Smile
> broader.) No, no. (Smile off. Long
> pause.) It might be the eternal cold.
> (Pause.) Everlasting, perishing cold.
> (Pause.) Just chance I take it, happy
> chance. (Pause.) Oh yes, great mercies,
> great mercies. (Pause.) And now?[188]

In *Endgame,* the matter is shelved hastily:

> Hamm: We're not beginning to...to...mean
> something?
> Clov: Mean something! You and I, mean some-
> thing? (Brief laugh.) Ah, that's a good one.
> Hamm: I wonder. (Pause.) Imagine if a rational
> being came back to earth, wouldn't he be
> liable to get ideas into his head if he
> observed us long enough. (Voice of ration-
> al being) Ah, good, now I see what it is,
> yes, now I understand what they're at!
> (...Normal voice) And without going so
> far as that, we ourselves...(with emotion)
> ...we ourselves...at certain moments...
> (Vehemently) To think perhaps it won't all
> have been for nothing.[189]

The next example is from *Waiting for Godot.* The tramps have
waited. Pozzo has come and gone. The messenger has
confused them. There seems no hope. They are on the brink
of being 'saved,' of getting to know Godot. Now they don't
know what to do. They choose death.

Vladimir: We'll hang ourselves tomorrow.
          Unless Godot comes.
Estragon: And if he comes?
Vladimir: We'll be saved.[190]

In the novel *Malone Dies*, the narrator has denied himself the pleasures of the world, has discovered the vacuity of the world of phenomena and of his own personality (ego) but finds no answer. He changes the subject and so the tedious 'seascape' of *Malone Dies* continues:

> ...no, not happy, I was never that, but wishing night would never end and morning never come when men wake and say, Come on, we'll soon be dead, let's make the most of it. But what matter whether I was born or not, have lived or not, am dead or merely dying, I shall go on doing as I have always done, not knowing what it is I do, nor who I am, nor where I am nor if I am.[191]

This is a recognizable stage that is reached by those who study Zen seriously. It is the end of the phenomenal world. The mind is at zero but the final explosion, the 'deflagration' of *Proust* has not yet occurred, the final step has not been risked. This is sometimes alluded to in Zen terms as a 'stone girl' (signifying form but no life) or finding oneself before an 'iron hill.' The mind is virtually 'dead to this world' but not yet alive to any other. Here, the master must quickly assess the situation and, as in the example of the Boat Monk, catapult the meditator out of complacent torpor. If not, the student may succumb to physical illness, or loss of will or, in the worst case, to insanity. This is rare, however. Usually something intervenes as a natural occurrence, often a sound, or perhaps a remark or physical contact with something. This has the effect of tipping the balance and propelling the student's mind into the state of *satori*. The seeker's mind is propelled forward into understanding the meaning of the 'Who am I' above.

According to Beckett, Proust apparently experienced this on at least eleven occasions. Beckett lists them with references.[192] In one case, the banging of a spoon precipitated his mind into this new dimension. The records of Zen over some two thousand years give a variety of causal incidents[193] such as the sound of a frog plopping into a pond, or a glowing piece of charcoal at night or, as in the case of Gautama Buddha himself, the sight of the morning star after a night of meditation.

The state known in Buddhism as 'awakening' is usually preceded by a state of intense spiritual inquiry so that:

> Not a thought, not an emotion is stirred in the mind which is now entirely and exclusively occupied with the *koan*.[194] At this moment, they (the meditators) are asked not to cherish any feeling of fear, to hold no idea of discrimination (i.e. distinction between this and that as the rational mind is all too prone to make), but to go resolutely ahead with the *koan* (i.e. to contemplate it) when all of a sudden, they experience something akin to an explosion (Beckett also uses the word in the same connection) as if an ice-basin were shattered to pieces, or as if a tower of jade had crumbled, and the event is accompanied with a feeling of immense joy...[195]

Such is the nature of the 'great leap' that we have referred to. Beckett's men and women never make it. They are similar to reconnaissance scouts, who have approached the borders of no-man's land, made a guess at its geographical features but have not yet entered. They have recognized the duality inherent in living. Because of this, they suspect the substantiality of life. This in turn causes the suffering that accompanies the state of dilemma. They can go neither forward nor backward, forward into the 'abyss' that Beckett has spoken of, nor backward into the 'shadow-world' of relative values. Instead of taking the Empedoclean leap, the Beckettian characters grow weary of this life and long for death, a physical death, which indeed may not solve the dilemma. This suspicion only increases the intensity of the dilemma. When they reach the stage of the 'stone girl,' they hesitate and thereby recognize themselves as 'impotent.' This, I suggest, is the meaning of the word 'impotent' as Beckett uses it. We can now see the reasons for Beckett's reticence in public.

4 The Obligation to Express: Three Dialogues

'When the subject is exempt from will, the object is exempt from causality (Time and Space taken together). And this human vegetation is purified in the transcendental apperception that can capture the Model, the Idea, the Thing itself.' Beckett announces this towards the end of *Proust*,[196] speaking as Proust's interpreter. In the *Three Dialogues*, he speaks in similar terms for himself.

The conversations with Georges Duthuit on the subject of pictorial representation contain, by inference, many of the convictions that inform Beckett's art. It is surprising, therefore, that critics have not yet analyzed this work thoroughly. Perhaps the reason is that, without knowledge of the subject-object relationship outlined above, connection with the rest of Beckett's writing is missed and the task of elucidating these recondite discourses becomes almost impossible.

Eighteen years have elapsed (1931−1949) since Beckett wrote his criticism on Proust. Duthuit, editor of the literary publication, *Transition*, is talking with Beckett on Tal Coat's painting (Conversation I).

> Beckett: What we have to consider in the case of
> Italian painters is not that they surveyed
> the world with the eyes of building con-
> tractors, a mere means like any other, but
> that they never stirred from the field of
> the possible, however much they may
> have enlarged it. The only thing disturbed

by the revolutionaries Matisse and Tal
Coat is a certain order on the plane of the
feasible.

To this Duthuit, probably incredulous, replies:

Duthuit: What other plane can there be for the
maker?

Beckett: Logically, none. Yet I speak of art turning
from it in disgust, weary of puny exploits,
weary of pretending to be able, of being able,
of doing a little better the same old thing, of
going a little further along a dreary road.

Duthuit: And preferring what?

Beckett: The expression that there is nothing to express, nothing with which to express, nothing
from which to express, no power to express,
no desire to express, together with the obligation to express.

Duthuit: But that is a violently extreme and personal
point of view, of no help to us in the matter of
Tal Coat.

Beckett: —

Duthuit: Perhaps that is enough for today.[197]

I have quoted this excerpt at length because it indicates
the relationship between the two men on this occasion. It is
clear that Duthuit is irritated by Beckett's pronouncement
that, among other things, there is 'nothing to express.' This
to him does not seem to be any kind of an answer but the
expression perhaps of an odd, self-centered point of view,
which cannot be evaluated objectively. Beckett is clearly
obsessed on some point and it is useless to waste time on
such aberrations. Beckett remonstrates but is bidden Good-
day.

Duthuit is evidently a practical man, that is to say he is
concerned with the efficient management of situations that

arise in the phenomenal world. For this he should not be criticized. What Beckett wishes to point out with dismissive terseness is that art is preferred if it does not deal with objects, does not continue to do what it has done over the centuries — representing what he calls 'the field of the possible,' 'the plane of the feasible.' Instead, art should say something of subjectivity. This is logically impossible, however, as we have observed. Subjectivity cannot be seen as an object is seen. Whenever thought (conception) or language (articulation of conception) is used, subjectivity is lost. Tsung Kao (1089–1163)[198] says that the moment we want to grasp what we are (subjectivity) 'it runs away from us (because only objects are graspable), but if we cast it away (forget to form concepts) it continues to be there all the time.' Huang Po likens subjectivity to sunshine, which is there but cannot be grasped.[199] Westerners, however, require help that is of sterner stuff than the gentle 'pointing the way' that Huang Po offers. This is given by a modern Ch'an master, whose syllogistic reckoning sums up the situation.

> Manifestation (form) is a manifestation of non-manifestation, and non-manifestation is non-manifestation of manifestation: there cannot be manifestation dualistically, and for that reason in reality there cannot be manifestation. The world is my concept, built of sense-perceptions: I cannot be real...Conceptually I must be, and via me the world must be. But beyond conceptualism nothing is, and that is void. The void is also a non-void, or a plenum, in so far as it is a concept. There is just absolutely nothing that can be said about this. But it can be cognised, by cognition that is definitely beyond thought. Trying to say it, trying to make it a concept is futile.[200]

From this point of view, there is clearly nothing to express and the painter's canvas remains blank. This, at least, is the logical standpoint. There is still, however, the 'obligation to express.' We will consider this in a moment.

The next conversation in the *Three Dialogues* concerns the painter Masson, (II). If we recall the arguments made above, Beckett could well be describing his own position in answer to Duthuit's question of how Masson could be expected to paint the void.

> Beckett: He is not (...) Here is an artist who seems literally skewered on the ferocious dilemma of expression. Yet he continues to wriggle. The void he speaks of is perhaps simply the obliteration of an unbearable presence, unbearable because neither to be wooed nor to be stormed. If this anguish of helplessness is never stated as such, on its own merits and for its own sake...the reason is doubtless, among others, that it seems to contain in itself the impossibility of statement...[201]

This, surely, is the kernel of the dilemma that I have taken pains to present in the material above. How else, for example, could *The Unnamable* be described than as something 'skewered on the ferocious dilemma of expression' and yet continuing to 'wriggle'? In the cognizance of the Void, 'mountains and rivers' have become something other than what they were; to paint them is to paint the shadows of reality, the very suspicion of which is of immense significance. With this realization, the world is suddenly dwarfed; every creative undertaking, which does not include the great Significance, is of necessity a 'puny exploit,' one more step along a dreary road where everything has already been attempted.

The dilemma lies in the question: Knowing this, what is to be done? How can one state the 'unstatable'? Clearly, one cannot. One can intimate its presence, however. This is what the artists of ancient China and Japan in fact did. They did this by innuendo, by leaving most of the canvas quite blank. Into this blankness they introduced their subject. In this way, the 'All' as they have described it through the centuries was always implied. Mountains and rivers once again assumed their place in the cosmos.[202] By this simple means, the eastern artists overcame what for Beckett, and perhaps Masson, is the problem of impotence.

Notwithstanding this, we should remember that the ancient masters of the brush lived in a cultural environment, in which the acknowledgement of subjectivity was taken for granted. This is especially true of Japan where Zen has influenced practically every aspect of cultural and social life since the eighth century. Another consideration is that many of the artists were themselves enlightened individuals, who had not simply come to acknowledge the presence of the Void intellectually but had accomplished that revolution of mind needed to fully apprehend the Void.[203]

At the close of the second interview between Beckett and Duthuit (Caldar and Boyar's edition), Duthuit questions the position that there 'is nothing to express' etc. He describes this as painting 'authentically fruitless, incapable of any image whatsoever to which you (i.e. Beckett) aspire and towards which... perhaps Masson tends. But must we really deplore the painting that admits the things and creatures of spring, resplendent with desire and affirmation, ephemeral no doubt, but immortally reiterant, not in order to benefit by them, not in order to enjoy them, but in order that what is tolerable and radiant in the world may continue? Are we really to deplore the painting that is rallying, among the things of time that pass and hurry away, towards a time that endures and gives increase?'[204] Beckett's answer is signified by

Beckett: − (Exit weeping)

This may again be confirmation that the final leap has not been made.

What does Beckett mean by 'obligation' when he says 'obligation to express'? He reiterates his standpoint in the third conversation, this time turning upon the painter Bram van Velde. Again, Duthuit is courteous but sceptical. He asks Beckett to clarify his position:

> Duthuit: Would it be too much to ask you to state again, as simply as possible, the situation and the act you conceive to be his?
>
> Beckett: The situation is that of him who is helpless, cannot act, in the event cannot paint, since he is obliged to paint...
>
> Duthuit: Why is he obliged to paint?
>
> Beckett: I don't know.[205]

This is Beckett's 'hypothetical imperative' again. Buddhism would simply call it 'craving.' Buddhism holds that desire (craving, or *tanha*), as we noted earlier, is the prime mover in all our affairs, the thirst for satisfaction, the common denominator of all action. Experience teaches that there is noble and ignoble action, the latter increasing distress and suffering and the former striving towards a union with subjectivity. In the example of van Velde, the painter attempts to portray the subjectivity that he feels is at the root of phenomenal existence and experience. He finds himself in a dilemma for the reasons set out above.

> Duthuit: Why is he helpless to paint?
>
> Beckett: Because there is nothing to paint and nothing to paint with.
>
> Duthuit: And the result, you say, is art of a new order?

This exchange must have been amusing; Duthuit's guarded, cultured scepticism on the one side and Beckett's 'absurd' insistence on the other.

> Duthuit: One moment. Are you suggesting that the painting of van Velde is inexpressive?
>
> Beckett: (A fortnight later) Yes.
>
> Duthuit: You realize the absurdity of what you advance?

Beckett: I hope I do.[206]

Our intention so far is to prove that Beckett does in fact realize the full significance of the dilemma he reiterates in his novels and plays, that this dilemma — broadly speaking — is a metaphysical one. We have also seen that Beckett is concerned essentially with the nature of what we call the 'self.' We have noted how the experience of his characters and his own private observations parallel the tenets of Buddhist thinking. In addition, we have shown that, in his quest for self-identity, Beckett has abandoned philosophy as well as every other system of thought. The ideas that he interprets on behalf of Proust are later made his own. These ideas are remarkably consistent over a long period and, carried to a logical conclusion, have led to a spiritual and literary impasse.

Having said this, I feel that it is now incumbent on me to investigate what could be meant by the general term 'the human condition' with reference to what has already been outlined. We shall then be in a position to move on to consider how the human dilemma finds expression in Beckett's work.

5   *The Source of Suffering*

Karl Menninger once remarked, observing the human animal from the vantage point of his position as Head of the Menninger Foundation, the largest psychiatric unit in the United States:

> Try as we may, it is difficult to conceive of our universe in terms of concord; instead we are faced everywhere with the evidence of conflict. Love and hate, production and consumption, creation and destruction — the constant war of opposing tendencies would appear to be the dynamic heart of the world. Man runs the eager gamut of his life through hazards of sickness and accident, beasts and the vengeful hands of his fellow men...While these spectacular rages of Nature (speaking of a Mississippi flood catastrophe) were wreaking destruction on defenseless millions, millions more lay in hospitals slowly or swiftly succumbing to the destructive inroads of bacteria, toxins and cancer. And sprinkled here and there throughout these miseries were the daily occurring accidents in the ordinary pursuits of life bringing death and destruction in sharp, unexpected flashes. One would expect in the face of these overwhelming blows at the hands of Nature, man would oppose himself steadfastly to death and destruction in a universal brotherhood of beleaguered humanity. But this is not the case. Whoever studies the be-

havior of human beings cannot escape the conclusion that we must reckon with an enemy within
the lines.[207]

Menninger wrote this in 1938. A year later, the world was
embroiled in a struggle which involved untold suffering.
Today, roughly seven billion dollars a day are spent by
humanity to, as Menninger puts it, 'manufacture instru-
ments designed for the tearing and ripping and mangling of
human beings similar to ourselves, possessed of the same
instincts, the same sensations, the same little pleasures and
the same realization that death comes to end things all too
soon.'[208] Because of an economic imbalance, an estimated
fifteen million children alone die each year either directly or
indirectly from starvation. Add to this the tyranny and
exploitation, the destruction of the environment, the con-
temptible squabbling over territory, conflicting national
interests, hate, self-interest and injustice and one wonders if
the world in which we live is not indeed a kind of hell.

Beckett appears to share this sentiment. He is quoted by
Tom Driver in the interview mentioned earlier as follows:

> Some people object to this (distress) in my writing.
> At a party an English intellectual — so-called —
> asked me why I write always about distress. As if it
> were perverse to do so! He wanted to know if my
> father had beaten me or my mother had run away
> from home to give me an unhappy childhood. I
> told him no, that I had had a very happy child-
> hood. Then he thought me more perverse than
> ever. I left the party as soon as possible and got
> into a taxi. On the glass partition between me and
> the driver were three signs: one asked for help for
> the blind, another help for orphans, and the third
> for relief for war refugees. One does not have to
> look for distress. It is screaming at you even in the
> taxis of London.[209]

Hell would be, conceivably, a place of no escape, a misery
sustained under duress with no hope of redemption.

Although there are aspects of worldly existence that can be hellish, the character of our world according to Buddhism is not like this. It is mutable, like the character of human beings on which it depends. It can be Heaven or Hell. The decision as to which it is to be lies with humans themselves.

If Buddhism emphasizes the sourness rather than the sweetness of life, this does not make it a fundamentally pessimistic religion as Schopenhauer and other have misinterpreted it to the West. Buddhism simply says that existence is not as good as the mind would conceive it to be. It does not deny joy and pleasure, remarking upon these matters only when they are put forward as objections to Buddhism's primary dictum: Ah yes, but how quickly these things pass and how durable suffering is! The Buddhist conception of suffering is more complex than this superficial comparison suggests. It divides suffering into three categories, viz: (1) the clearly recognizable, intrinsic suffering of mind and body, (Sanskrit, *dukkha-dukkhata*), (2) the suffering of the Aggregates (Sanskrit, *sankhara-dukkhata*) and (3) the suffering of transience (Sanskrit, *viparinama-dukkhata*).

For our purposes, the Aggregates can be thought of as components of the body-mind unit, including consciousness, although they are further divided into specific functions (the Sanskrit *skandhas*). Since the Aggregates are constantly changing as sensation, thought and mood arise and pass away and as the organ of sensation or faculty itself concurrently arises and passes, there is an ever-present awareness of uneasiness and instability. This awareness is generally below the level of consciousness and is disguised by our volitional activity. It can be described as a flux wherein there is no permanence. There is only a coming to be and a passing away. Because there is nothing permanent in the process, one feels ill at ease. This in turn denies fulfilment to whomever, waking or sleeping, seeks it. There is, therefore, suffering. This feeling of uneasiness is often brought to consciousness in the case of those who have been isolated from all human contact for a considerable period and then return to find themselves, their friends and all that they once knew changed almost beyond recognition, a fact referred to as the 'ravages of time.'

The third kind of suffering, the suffering of transience, arises from the perception of impermanence. Since everything is in a state of flux, happiness, by definition, cannot last. We are forced to abandon our memories, which perpetuate happiness, and to turn to the exactions that life imposes upon us. Lost happiness and departed joy are themes that fill our anthologies. Literature alone, if we can view it as a repository of recorded human feeling, could testify to the sadness occasioned by transience.

Buddhism often refers in its literature (the *sutras*) to life's 'deathly ocean.' The metaphor is a good one insofar as it suggests a permanent flux without issue but full of danger. With this in mind, the Buddha declared: 'Birth is suffering, decay is suffering and death is suffering. All the aggregates are transient, and therefore subject to suffering; all things are devoid of entity that is permanent. Body is transient; sensation is transient; perception is transient; consciousness is transient. That which is transient is involved in suffering. Mind itself is transient (i.e. mental functions, the intellect, memory etc.).'

The Buddha is referring here to the *skandhas* or components that make up what we apprehend as the individual. Personality is the coming together of these components and nothing more. There is no 'soul' or permanent quality to be observed. There is only an 'aggregation,' which is dependent on conditioned causes. This has already been understood from our discussion of Time and from the subsequent treatment of the nature of the self or ego. We spoke there of 'bifurcation' and 'dichotomy' and of 'split mind,' preferring neutral, scientific terms to others which could be misinterpreted. Transience is the root of our suffering.

In his book *The Perennial Philosophy*,[210] Aldous Huxley considers all the 'higher religions,' as they are referred to, as linked by what he calls the 'unitive knowledge of God.' He points out that it is the absence of God and the assertion of the ego, which creates the suffering that is common to all humanity. In making this point, he cites many sources, including Catherine of Siena, Meister Eckhart and St. Philip Neri. His own incisive analysis is equally revealing. He describes suffering as the result of 'the urge-to-separateness,

or craving for independent and individual existence.'[211]
He then says that this craving for an individualized existence can manifest itself on all levels, from the 'merely
cellular' to the 'fully conscious.'

> It can be the craving of a whole organism for an
> intensification of its separateness from the envir-
> onment and divine Ground. Or it can be the urge
> of a part within an organism for an intensification
> of its own partial life as distinct from (and con-
> sequently at the expense of) the life of the organism
> as a whole. In the first case we speak of impulse,
> passion, desire, self-will, sin; in the second, we
> describe what is happening as illness, injury, func-
> tional and organic disorder. In both cases, the
> craving for separateness results in suffering, not
> only for the craver, but also for the craver's sentient
> environment − other organisms in the external
> world, or other organs within the same organism.[212]

Christianity has produced the Devil to account for this
seduction; Buddhism, as we have seen, says that it is
simply deluded desire rooted in ignorance.

The Buddhist conception of craving and the results of
craving are not confined to a world where goodness on the
one side is opposed to evil on the other. Valuable as such a
split would be, it is, nevertheless, like the imaginary lines of
latitude and longitude on a globe, − useful in the matter of
orientation but with no real existence. Buddhism sees the
world and the cosmos to which the world belongs as phenomena sustained by craving, by the urge to protect its infinite
variety of expression. This view is suggested by recent
scientific endeavour.

Beckett refers to this urge as a 'hypothetical imperative,'
as we have seen at various points in the discussion. It is
'hypothetical' because we need not respond to its demands;
the human mind, unlike that of an animal, can become
aware of its exigences and waive them. The character of

Belacqua, for example, attempts at least for the period determined as the length of his life to suspend the demands of an
imperious God by sitting under the rock and practising the
wisdom contained in the axiom: *sedendo et quiescendo et
anima efficitur prudens*, (sitting quietly and doing nothing
one acquires wisdom).

The same idea is at work in *Murphy*. Strapped in his chair
and so restricting all physical movement, alone in his room,
eschewing Celia and all other exactions upon his time such
as others who seek him and the need to earn a living,
Murphy devotes himself to the discovery of his mind. While
he does this, the 'imperative' is removed — at least for a
time. For this reason, some critics have scented a connection
between his behaviour and 'esoteric Buddhism.' There is a
small grain of truth in this. In the practice of Buddhism,
'looking inward' is carried out in a sitting position, whenever possible, free from disturbance and where the distrac-
tions of everyday life are reduced as much as possible. It
should be noted, however, that at the same time meditation
in this form is not an absolute prerequisite for the breakthrough known as Enlightenment. The essential detection of
the delusion under which we live does not necessarily have
to be the result of formal meditation although this is generally the case.

Beckett, for his part, has seen straight to the centre of the
problem in his recognition of craving as both 'imperative'
and 'hypothetical.' We can see from what has been said
above that the Buddhist interpretation of the 'imperative' as
'desire' is the prime mover in all activity. It is not the Devil
'who goeth about seeking whom he may devour,' but the
imperative to move towards self-fulfilment. Suffering is the
failure to find that fulfilment among the seductions of the
world. This much, too, Beckett has discerned. He can see
that literature for the most part has been and remains
the 'reflection' that Alvarez speaks of, that is, as a whole, the
embodiment of all the thoughts, feelings and actions of an
imagined as well as historical humanity.[213] At the lowest
level, it can be described as 'telling stories about ourselves,'

a kind of incestuous, never-ending round of titillation. Television, for example, comes very near to this. For Beckett, it is at best the representation of *samsara*, the subject-induced twilight-world of objectivity, which most people take at face value as being real, the mechanics of which we have isolated above. For Beckett, this is Plato's cave; this is 'puny exploits along a dreary road.' Because Beckett sees this so clearly, he turns to other possibilities. Since one world is so vigorously characterized by action and movement towards something else, 'this having ended, this now begins,' the 'one-damn-thing-after-another' of temporal and spatial existence, he turns deliberately (some have said 'wilfully') to another world that is devoid of will (and therefore desire) to impotence. He speaks in this connection of an 'exploration' of a zone hitherto unexplored in literature, which could possibly yield fruit of a different kind. This repudiation of the external world also explains, in my opinion, his emphasis on reduction wherever it can be applied. Such deliberation implies that Beckett sees the human situation as an inner phenomenon.[214] The journey that his characters make or the stasis in which they find themselves, is a mental situation and, as we have seen, more frequently than not, one of dilemma.

The intractable dilemma at the root of human existence, which forms the basis of Beckett's art, has been summed up by Richard De Martino. As well as being a graduate in philosophy, De Martino has also had the opportunity to study Zen under the late Dr. D.T. Suzuki. Since the study of Zen involves applying oneself practically to its understanding rather than just acquiring intellectual knowledge of the subject, he is in a position to speak with some authority. He gets to grips here with the fundamentals of Huxley's term 'separation.'

> It is precisely this — the dichotomy of its subject — object structure — which constitutes the inherent existential ambiguity, conflict, and, indeed, contradiction of the ego in ego-consciousness. Bifurcated and disjoined in its unity, it is delimited by, but

cannot be sustained or fulfilled in, itself. Isolated and excluded in its relatedness, it is restricted to, yet shut off from, a world in which and to which it belongs. Having and not having, at once bound to and conditioned by, and at the same time separated and cut off from, itself and its world, the ego is rent by a double cleavage, split within as well as without. Never pure subject in its subjectivity, never absolutely free in its freedom, it is neither the ground nor the source of itself or its world, both of which it has, but neither of which it ever completely has. This is the predicament of the ego in ego-consciousness. This is the misery of man in human existence.[215]

This, too, is the Beckettian impasse because the situation is never transcended. There is only a 'going on' under the coercion of a desire to know and a desire to find. As De Martino rightly observes, the ego is 'object-obstructed.'[216]

Available to itself — even as it contemplates its own subjectivity — only in terms of some object cast of itself, the ego naturally comes to confuse being fulfilled with 'being something.'[217]

Whether the object-image envisioned becomes actual or remains fanciful and idealized, the basic deception involved is the same. The ego in its totality is never merely any object-feature of itself or its actualized subjectivity — its body, mind, talents, position, 'personality', goodness, profession or vocation, social or biological function, class culture, nation or race...

and what has issued from such conceptions in terms of the history of mankind can now easily be deduced. De Martino continues:

However truly great the husband, wife, parent, ruler, scientist, thinker, artist, professional or business man or woman, however much richer such an ego is, however much more it has itself, it does not have itself fully as ego, nor has it realized itself as human.[218]

This observation on being 'human' is interesting. It corresponds to the Buddhist use of the word 'awakening.' When one has apprehended the fact that there is no 'I,' the sensation is very similar to awaking from a dream, or suddenly receiving the answer to a question, which has haunted one for years. When this happens, the mind is integrated for the first time. With further, deepening experiences of the kind, the mind can be fully and permanently integrated. From this time onward, St. Paul's 'new man' is born and literally a new dimension of life is opened.

A great Sufi poet and mystic[219] was once asked how old he was. At that time being a man well advanced in years, he replied: 'Four years!' His astonished hearers were struck dumb with embarrassment because of what seemed either an insult to their senses or an attempt to belittle them. Seeing their doubt, the old man went on: 'It is four years since I have been enlightened upon the matter of God and Myself. Four whole years have I been human and lived with God; the rest of the time I was dead.' He meant by this that the 'old man' (St. Paul's significance) the ego, is dead; while he lived thus under its delusion, the other life, the life of conscious subjectivity, was 'dead' or, as the Buddhist would put it, 'not realized.' The ego, therefore, stands in the way of enlightenment or freedom (Beckett's 'eleuthéria').

But these are highly-coloured references, in themselves concept-laden. Buddhism, and especially Zen Buddhism, eschews all artifice. Doing away with scripture[220] and all the appurtenances of organized religion, it 'points directly to the heart of man' in an attempt to liberate him from his cherished delusions and desires. We have seen in one or two instances above how this 'pointing' was accomplished with regard to those whose minds were 'ripe' for the experience.

We are concerned here, however, with the state of mind prior to that inner cataclysm. De Martino again:

> Unable to sustain itself (i.e. the ego) within itself and perhaps tormented by feelings of its un-deservedness, guilt or sin, it comes to know melancholy and despondent moments of loneliness, frustration and despair. Inwardly plagued by restlessness, insecurity or contempt and even hatred of itself, outwardly it possibly manifests any number of psychosomatic disturbances.
>
> Yet often the ego manages to contain these pangs of disquietude and to finish out its life in just this condition. But even as it does so, it is under the continual threat that the smouldering deep-seated uneasiness may erupt and surge forth in an anguish and dread which is uncontainable. This could occur should the ego no longer be able to rationalize away its sense of unworthiness or its sense of guilt, should it become morbidly uncertain of the divine forgiveness of its sin, or should the components necessary to maintain its object-image otherwise come to be lost, destroyed or unavailable, or, while remaining, prove disillusioning, grow empty, or simply cease to be engaging. Finally, some ordinary occurrence in daily life can bring the abrupt traumatic realization that not only is every possible content transitory and ephemeral, but so, too, is the ego itself. Ever vulnerable, in youth as well as in age, to illness and infirmity in body and mind, it must die.
>
> Intellectually, the inevitability of its death is, of course, known to the ego all along. Actually experiencing, however, the prospect of its own non-being as a shattering existential shock in effect destroys the illusion as to the possibility of its consummation in terms of any object-image... Caught fully and apprehensively in the double

anxiety of having to live and having to die, the ego undergoes the excruciating torment of the most piercing indecision of all: to be or not to be.[221]

This, essentially, is the anatomy of the human dilemma. The fact that it reads like a psychological summary of Beckett's work will not escape notice. The observations of *Proust*, too, are in the background. For half the time or more, humanity is not aware of its condition. What Beckett calls Habit and what we have called Ignorance 'sicklies o'er' the reality of the situation, drugging us to the urgent need to resolve the dilemma.

Both Beckett and De Martino are in accord with one another on the point that suffering or shock may be instrumental in deflecting us from the 'metalled ways' of our 'appetency' and by doing so bring us face to face with our primary 'dis-ease.' But the dreadful fact is that while suffering may force us to an awareness of our fundamental problem, even to an exposure of the ego and all its works, it may not be efficacious in laying the problem low. Beckett's *'Je souffre donc je suis'* is not enough; what is needed is a leap into Pascal's *'Qu'est-ce que le moi qui souffre?'* This is the heart of the matter. Something more is generally needed to answer this question. Because it involves a 'death,' very few individuals are able at one stroke to annihilate their egos and their suffering into a condition of *'je ne suis pas.'* Here is where the guiding hand of a qualified person is necessary to throw us into the Void.[222] If this does not occur, we shall 'dwell in the world of hungry ghosts' as Buddhism puts it. This means that we neither enjoy the sensual world of *samsara* nor that of *nirvana* — an unenviable position and one which constitutes the Beckettian impasse in all its desperation.

Part Three
The World of Hungry Ghosts

6   *Quest for Inner Peace:* Murphy

Beckett's first novel, *Murphy*, should be briefly discussed because it contains elements which are elaborated in Beckett's later work. *Murphy* is also interesting as a point of reference in showing how different the later work is from Beckett's earlier writings. In any discussion of Beckett, this metamorphosis, approximating to the interval occupied by the Second World War, is abrupt and spectacular. The pre-war novel, with its linguistic furbelows, arcane references and scholastic flourish together with its effervescent academic banter and its amused, aloof, third-person story-teller...

> This view of the matter will not seem strange to anyone familiar with the class of pentameter that Ticklepenny felt it his duty to Erin to compose, as free as a canary in the fifth foot (a crucial sacrifice, for Ticklepenny hiccupped in end rimes) and at the caesura as hard and fast as his own divine flatus and otherwise bulging with as many minor beauties from the gaelic prosodoturfy as could be sucked out of a mug of Beamish's porter.[223]

never found expression again after 1938. Perhaps Beckett felt that Joyce's manner was a borrowed mantle, a most sincere compliment no doubt to his friend and countryman but not true to himself. After many years, he was able to comment on this:

> I'm no intellectual. All I am is feeling. *Molloy* and the others came to me the day I became aware of

my own folly. Only then did I begin to write the things I feel.[224]

Murphy, then, and to some extent all the work that preceded *Watt* (itself a transition piece) can be regarded in the main as experimental, the expression of a Beckett who has not yet found his true *métier*. On the other hand, this early work is sufficiently different from Joyce to merit our attention even if only by way of comparison. Beckett's work lacks the Joycean all-inclusive grandeur, the sweep and scope, the gusto and the sunny, Jovinian humour of the elder man. The primary difference between the two, however, is that Joyce's writing is 'universal' in character whereas Beckett's is concerned to analyze and exhaust one particular area of experience.

Beckett himself outlined the situation to Israel Schenker in 1956.

> The more Joyce knew the more he could. He's tending toward omniscience and omnipotence as an artist. I'm working with impotence, ignorance ...There seems to be a kind of esthetic axiom that expression is achievement — must be achievement ...[225]

and in another place and at a later date he confessed:

> ...optimism is not my way. I shall always be depressed, but what comforts me is the realization that I can now accept this dark side of my personality. In accepting it I will make it work for me.[226]

Murphy is already concerned with impotence of a kind, or at least with worldly disinclination. The main character, with his laziness and shiftlessness, is reminiscent of the earlier Belacqua. The novel could be seen as representing two camps, that of worldliness, the 'big, blooming, buzzing confusion'[227] portrayed by the interaction of Wylie, Neary, Cooper, Miss Counihan and the rest, and the other of Murphy himself, withdrawn and unworldly, while Celia acts as a neutral between the two. All the characters of the first camp, including Celia, desire a closer communion with

Murphy, but Murphy himself wishes to be free of them all. Finally, he does manage to escape by taking employment in a mental hospital. Even here he shuts himself off from the company of his fellow-warders by arranging for an attic to be at his disposal and reached only by a ladder, which he is able to draw up after him.

The novel already has the form of a quest, that of those seeking Murphy and that of Murphy seeking inner peace. Already, too, we can see Beckett's preoccupation with mental processes in his description of Murphy's mind, for example, and in his interest in the insane. We can recognize the re-appearance of the 'hypothetical imperative,' which had occasionally afflicted Belacqua. In *Murphy*, Beckett's 'imperative' is that which succeeds always in deflecting Murphy away from attaining bliss in a semi-permanent state of deep introspection.

The problem of Time is also posed in this way. Murphy desires to be rid of its demands by retreating into himself but is always brought back to the world of time (and therefore change) by the interruptions of others. Time, described in *Murphy* as an 'old fornicator,' is ridiculed in its remorseless re-enactment of celestial movements: 'The encounter, on which so much hinges, took place on Friday, October 11th... the moon being full again, but not nearly so near the earth as when last in opposition.'[228] There are similar references throughout the book to the 'sun in the Virgin' and 'The sun shone, having no alternative, on the nothing new.' This is the opening sentence of the novel. Such references and those dealing with Murphy's concern with astrology are scattered throughout the book. They form a subsidiary theme closely interwoven with Murphy's convictions. Indirectly implied is the implacability of Time, its role in the world — as Beckett sees it — which cannot be transcended.

The hopelessness of the sentient, thinking being, trapped in *samsara*, is already foreshadowed in the much-quoted observation

> So all things hobble together for the only possible.[229]

In connection with this and because of this, there is the suggestion of the theme to be developed later, that it is better not to have been born:

> 'Never fear, sergeant,' he said, urging Neary towards the exit, 'back to the cell, blood heat, next best thing to never being born...'[230]

Transcendence of life's predicament, which is unsuccessfully attempted by Murphy, is asserted as impossible by Neary. (The name Neary, as David Hesla notes,[231] is a scrambling of the word 'yearn.') He says:

> The syndrome known as life is too diffuse to admit of palliation. For every symptom that is eased, another is made worse. The horse leech's daughter is a closed system. Her quantum of wantum cannot vary.[232]

The point made by Eugene Webb in his chapter on *Murphy* that 'Neary is the most prominent example in the book of a person enslaved by attachments' suggests that the book could have been written from a 'Buddhist's point of view,' since it is 'attachment that imprisons one in the temporal world and binds one to constant activity.'[233] If this is the case, then Murphy's conduct is the foil to Neary's yearning and constitutes the 'ablation of desire' suggested in Beckett's *Proust*.[234] Similarly, it is of interest perhaps that his state of 'ablation' was not to be discovered among the mentally deranged.

In that strange, almost frightening scene where the intrigued Murphy bends over the comatized Mr. Endon (note: Greek *'endon'* = 'within') and looks into the schizophrenic's eyes, he sees nothing but a reflection of himself.

> The relation between Mr Murphy and Mr Endon could not have been better summed up by the former's sorrow at seeing himself in the latter's immunity from seeing anything but himself... Mr Murphy is a speck in Mr Endon's unseen. That was the whole extent of the little afflatulence.[235]

Apart from the fact that Murphy's death is adumbrated in this short scene, what was it that Murphy wanted to see in the patient's doll-like eyes? Was it that he wanted to find confirmation of himself by seeing himself, perhaps hinted at in the use of the Latin *percipere* and *percipi* a page before this incident? The matter is difficult to determine since Beckett uses the word 'sorrow' in the quotation just alluded to and yet, a moment later, describes Murphy as 'incandescent' compared with the cold, grey winter's morning. In making his way to the male nurses' home, he casts off his clothes, lies in the grass a moment trying to recollect himself, gives up, and hastens to his garret where he ties himself to the chair. He then enters into his customary meditation, his object being to attain freedom. But he dies in the attempt by inadvertently gassing himself.

Beckett does not dwell on the subject of Murphy's quest, which is in fact the core of the work. In view of his later work, however, and in retrospect, we know that *Murphy* is concerned with the nature of the real 'I.' In looking into Mr. Endon's eyes, Murphy naively believes that he will discover that Nothing alluded to a page or so earlier, the Abderite's Nothing,[236] forgetting of course that this can never be apprehended as a relationship of two objects, (i.e. Mr. Murphy and Mr. Endon). Suddenly realizing this, he pauses three times to convince himself of the truth of the matter, indicated by Beckett in punctuating his sentences: 'A rest./ A rest./ A long rest.'

Finally, Murphy replaces Mr. Endon's head on the pillow and leaves the building, we are told, 'without reluctance and without relief.'[237] It is without reluctance because now half his problem is solved; he knows that there can be no objective answer to his problem, the problem of Who am I? He knows that it must be solved 'within,' and 'endon/Endon' is his clue. Surmising in this way, he hurries away to put his newly won knowledge to practical test. In his enthusiasm, an oversight leads to his demise. The 'death by misadventure' is essential since if Murphy were successful in realizing the truth about his real nature, this could not be communicated in a way that would be congruent with the terms of the novel.

7   The Thirst for Knowledge: Watt

The cataclysm of the Second World War began one year after the publication of *Murphy*. Beckett was thirty-three years of age. He was still in the possession of a passport issued by the Irish Free State and eked out a meagre living in France, the country of his adoption. He was caught now between neutrality and commitment. He intended at first to remain a neutral alien, but Hitler's insanity did not enable him to remain one for long. 'I was so outraged by the Nazis, particularly by their treatment of the Jews, that I could not remain inactive.'[238] Perhaps what finally drove him to commitment was the internment and subsequent death in 1942 of his Jewish friend, Paul Leon.

In late 1940, Beckett began working for the French Resistance. His job was to collate photographs and despatch them to British intelligence organizations. The group to which he belonged was discovered. He narrowly escaped from the interest of the Gestapo, fleeing from Paris by train and on foot. He first went south-west to Arcachon, the geographical features of which are mentioned in *Watt* as 'a great alp of sand, one hundred metres high, between the pines and the ocean.'[239] The reference is to Pilat, which is not far from the city and is just as Beckett describes it. He then proceeded south to the unoccupied zone, which included the Vaucluse. It is often said that Beckett lived as a peasant during this time. This is not quite true. It is correct that he did occasional work for payment in kind, for vegetables, eggs and the like. In doing so, he may have donned the attributes of a French farm worker. For the most part, according to his biographer, Deidre Bair, he stayed in a dilapidated hotel with other refugees from Nazi persecution, living a life of boredom alternating with anxiety.[240]

What Bair has to say about Beckett's state of mind at this time is important to fuller understanding of the novel *Watt*, which he now began to write. Apart from the fact that *Watt* contains a great deal of autobiographical detail, which is itself interesting, it also reflects a state of mind. The geographical and psychological isolation, the absence of his friends together with the uncertainty of their whereabouts or even existence, the uncertain outcome of the war and its abrupt termination of his career as a writer all combined to produce feelings of acute frustration and desperation. Bair describes his mental condition at this time as one in need of a psychiatrist and as a 'raging battleground.'

> He discovered that the most effective way to bring himself under control was to channel all his confusion into his writing. . . He (Beckett) set up a smoke-screen of obscurity and complexity behind which he carefully hid tantalizing clues for his readers. . .
> He made his aloneness into a sanctified obsession which he protected behind impenetrable labyrinthine defenses. He would not permit himself to reveal himself. For Beckett, sanity became analogous with secrecy and cunning. He had to work to stay sane; thus *Watt* became his daily therapy, the means with which he clung to the vestiges of his idea of sanity.[241]

There is undeniably an element of madness in *Watt*. This can be seen in the seemingly senseless tendency the novel has for permutative speculation, in its apparent lunatic intensity, especially where trivia are concerned, and in its defiance of logic. Moreover, the novel has neither a clear-cut development nor, on the face of it, any articulate statement about life outside a mental hospital. Add to this the vagueness of Watt's character and that of the other persons in the novel and the ostensible absence of motive for any of their actions and one has not only a novel reflecting insanity, a cracked vessel, but also a bad novel.

> *Watt* is often cited as one of Beckett's most obscure
> and puzzling books, deliberately secret, tantalizing,
> revealing only to withdraw into qualification and
> denial...it is the first of those maddening fictions
> where Beckett deliberately steps in to undercut and
> belie any meaning of appreciation...He has no
> system, no easy answer for anything, and he won't
> allow the reader to find one either.[242]

While this may be true from one point of view and while
Watt may be a 'bad novel' if we assess it by the standards of
literary excellence before Beckett's time, there are, nevertheless, aspects in it of unconscious experience and ontological
questions of first importance. Autobiography there is too, as
Deidre Bair insistently points out.

There is also an autobiographical feature in this book that
goes deeper than the recall of past experience or the record
of a state of mind. In one sense, it is the autobiography of
every human being because it deals primarily with the
problem of whether human beings can ever know anything,
either themselves or the objects in the world they see about
them. Never questioning the matter, most people assume
that they can know both. Should the question be raised, it is
a matter for the philosopher to answer if he can. There the
issue is conveniently shelved. For most people, the problem
never obtrudes into the daily practicalities of living. After
all, who could seriously doubt that stone is stone and iron is
iron? *Cogito ergo sum*. But it is this that Beckett throws into
question; for him, the reverse is more likely to be true, viz:
Sum ergo cogito. Consider, for example, Watt's walk:

> Watt's way of advancing due east for example was
> to turn his bust as far as possible towards the north
> and at the same time fling out his right leg as far as
> possible towards the south, and then turn his bust
> as far as possible towards the south and at the
> same time to fling his left leg as far as possible
> towards the north and then again to turn his bust
> as far as possible towards the north and to fling
> out his right leg as far as possible towards the
> south...[243]

This is Cartesian man's method of locomotion. He is 'think-ing' his walking instead of leaving it to the other, uncon-scious mind of which we spoke above. Alan Watts described the unconscious as being able to do 'ever so many things at once,' a mind that is a precursor to the lauded thinking mind. I may 'will' myself to walk, for example, inasmuch as I decide to walk. It is to that extent described as a 'voluntary action,' as distinguished from the activity of the heart and kidneys by comparison. However, as Aldous Huxley points out in his essay on the nature of the ego: 'I will all right, but I haven't the faintest idea how the act is performed,' and goes on to add, 'We have discovered, as a result of very long and arduous research, that the processes involved in lifting my hand are incredibly complex, but I have, as a self-conscious being, absolutely no idea what they are. I merely give a command and leave it to "somebody else" to carry it out.' Huxley explores the nature of this 'deeper self' which, he says, works in an infallible way on the psychological level. He is quite right. Indeed, if we attempt to interfere with the 'deeper self's infallible activities, the result is nearly always a catastrophe for the individual.'[244] Watt's walk, we may add, is a ludicrous example of such interference on the part of the Cartesian 'I.'

Let us now look at the structure of the novel, *Watt*. The first trap that is set for us lies in our conception of the term 'novel.' We can disabuse ourselves immediately of the notion that we are about to receive a 'story' in the sense that there will be an interaction of character towards the solution of a situation, which mirrors our actual or imaginable ex-perience. Beckett's works are not novels in that sense. They are, rather, what we might call figurative statements or statements about the metaphysical basis of existence as in the case of *Watt*, which uses as illustration the material common to everyday experience. There may or may not be movement but this is rarely of any consequence as far as the narration goes; the movement is all within, represented by the various turns of mind as it concerns itself with one line of thought after another.

Watt is the story of someone who goes to work for another, whose identity is unclear and whose habits are mysterious. He is not the first to have worked as a servant to the enigmatic Mr. Knott. Watt leaves Knott's service in disappointment but not before having met a friend, Sam, who later becomes the narrator and reports Watt's thoughts. Both end up in what is probably a mental hospital where the narration continues. The title, *Watt*, is indicative, as is frequently the case in Beckett's work. It asks: What? What is the nature of existence? It is a desperate question and we should bear this in mind during the analysis that follows.

The novel begins with an unusual prologue before embarking on the details of Watt's quest for knowledge. It appears to have nothing to do with the subsequent events and soliloquies. It involves one, Hackett, a hunchback, in a dilemma. When he is out for a walk, someone occupies his favourite seat. He does not know whether to return or stay. He looks at the occupants and finds that they are lovers. This gives Beckett opportunity to dilate briefly on the 'delights' of physical love, or, as here, the prelude to it. The tone is caustically satirical:

> Mr Hackett decided that if they were waiting for the tram they had been doing so for some time. For the lady held the gentleman by the ears and the gentleman's hand was on the lady's thigh, and the lady's tongue was in the gentleman's mouth.[245]

In the midst of this description there is a footnote announcing the author's abandonment of the 'plethoric reflexive pronoun after *say.*'

After calling a policeman and complaining of the couple's indecent behaviour, Hackett claims his seat and settles to look at the last trams of the evening. After a time, he is joined by a man and a woman, who talk in a manner reminiscent of well-bred English people in the latter half of the nineteenth century.

> Oh, my dear, he said, there is Hackett.
> Hackett, said the lady. What Hackett? Where?

You know Hackett, said the gentleman. You must have often heard me speak of Hackett. Hunchy Hackett. On the seat.
The lady looked attentively at Mr Hackett.
So that is Hackett, she said.
Yes, said the gentleman.
Poor fellow, she said.
Oh, said the gentleman, let us now stop, do you mind, and wish him the time of the evening. He advanced, exclaiming, My dear fellow, my dear fellow, how are you?[246]

These inane exchanges ripen to conversation:

You remember Grehan? said Mr Hackett.
The poisoner, said the gentleman.
The solicitor, said Mr Hackett.[247]

Sandwiched between these interlocutions is a brilliantly impudent parody, *To Nelly*, at once incisive and suggestive.

Into this uncompromising caricature of literary urbanity, the figure of Watt appears, ejected from the tram after an altercation with the conductor − ostensibly for not paying his fare. The trio find him before them on the opposite side of the street. The receding light of the tram throws the figure into the semi-darkness 'until it was scarcely distinguished from the dim wall behind it.' Mr. and Mrs. Nixon, the lady and the gentleman referred to above, are about to take their leave. On seeing Watt, Mrs. Nixon remarks that she cannot tell whether the figure is that of a man or of a woman. Hackett thinks it might be a parcel, a roll of carpet, for example.

From this point onwards, the novel changes its course. Although the conversation continues for a while longer, the element of satire recedes and concentration is on Watt. Mr. Nixon crosses the street and argues with the figure over a small sum of money that is owed to him. To the observers on the other side, Watt remains unperturbed as if 'he had been of stone and if he spoke he spoke so low that they did not hear him.' Meanwhile, the other two watch intently. Hackett is intrigued by the scene:

> Mr Hackett did not know when he had been more intrigued, nay, he did not know when he had been so intrigued. He did not know either what it was that so intrigued him. What is it that so intrigues me, he said, whom even the extraordinary, even the supernatural, intrigue so seldom, and so little. Here there is nothing in the least unusual, that I can see, and yet I burn with curiosity, and with wonder.[248]

Here we have one of those ambivalent situations, for which Beckett is notorious and to which Mrs. Bair referred above as a 'smoke-screen of obscurity.' We can, if we like, accept Hackett's strange excitement just as part of the bland exchanges and reflections of the preceding pages. This view would seem to be supported by the inclusion of the stylized 'nay' with its pompous overtones, perhaps illustrative of the character of Hackett, and also by the use of the words 'burn' and 'wonder,' which we shall immediately take for satire, particularly if we are on the lookout for ironic innuendo. On the other hand, however, Hackett's sensations of curiosity and wonder could be interpreted as subconscious recognition. He feels that he has some kinship with the shadowed figure opposite. Because he knows that he has never met Watt formally and does not even know his name, he is filled with curiosity on the one hand and with astonishment on the other.

When Nixon returns, Mr. Hackett enquires twice after Watt's name. Neither Hackett nor Mrs. Nixon has heard of Watt. The following conversation ensues:

> Known him long? said Mr Hackett.
> I cannot really say I know him, said Mr Nixon.
>
> Since when can't you really say you know him? said Mr Hackett.
> My dear fellow, said Mr Nixon, why this sudden interest?

Do not answer if you prefer not to, said Mr Hackett.
It is difficult to answer, said Mr Nixon. I seem to
have known him all my life...[249]

Hackett asks why Nixon had never mentioned him. He
rejoins that a person like Watt does not invite mention —
'there are people like that,' to which Hackett says: 'Not like
me.'

Is that so, said Mr Nixon. The curious thing is, my
dear fellow, I tell you quite frankly, that when I see
him, or think of him, I think of you, and that when
I see you, or think of you, I think of him. I have no
idea why this is so.[250]

We may ask ourselves what relationship there could be
between Beckett's anthropomorph, Watt, and these two,
Hackett and Nixon. In the story itself, there is no structural
relationship since the last two do not appear again. Why
should Nixon say that he 'seems' to have known Watt all his
life? It is difficult to conjecture. On the other hand, the
matter is tantalizing because it is plain that this moment in
the book is one of transition from whatever it is that Beckett
wishes to introduce into his story of Watt's journey at the
beginning and the actual commencement of that story.

What, in short, is the meaning of this prologue? That it
is satirical in nature has already been suggested. Could it
also be some form of comparison? We can recognize the
humanity of the three characters of this introductory quartet,
viz. Mr. and Mrs. Nixon and Hackett. Their corporeality
and, therefore, their credibility is further strengthened by
the fact that the incidents take place on a certain evening in
a town, where there are such substantial entities as a court-
ing couple, a park bench, a tram, the dying rays of the sun
and an irate policeman and conductor. Despite the banality
of the discourse, which takes place amid this concreteness,
we feel we are in a 'real' situation. The figure of Watt,
however, is little more than a strange presence. What
human form could resemble a roll of carpet? He is...

Like a sewer-pipe, said Mrs Nixon. Where are his
arms?[251]

As so often with this author, one is tempted to capitulate before what appears to be either fortuitous perhaps — and, therefore, probably insignificant — or, alternatively, allegorical, which may lead us to Swift's labours of self-deception. Or, again, we can assume, as some critics do, that it is Beckett's wont simply to reveal and then to revoke. It is a deliberate game to circumvent the 'spread nets of habitual meaning.' If this is the case, what could be the motivation for such puerilities?

I think we may say two things: The first is that all Beckett's work has the character of a psychological investigation. This investigation is also metaphysical inasmuch as it deals mainly with man's relationship with God. The second is that much of this examination is based on autobiographical detail. What this amounts to is that when we come to consider any of Beckett's work, we are also likely to encounter Beckett the man. Such a situation is not unusual. However, this particular author finds any intrusion into his private life offensive, to say nothing of the world's intrusion into his inmost thoughts. Hence, we have the track-covering technique, which Bair and others find so exasperating.

The kernel of the issue under consideration is whether *Watt* is human. Certainly he is not quite as human as the characters that first appear in the novel. This is borne out not only in the circumstances of the prologue but also later in the book. Beckett makes this clear. In addition, the author shows that by virtue of the difference between Watt and the other characters, the attitude to the writing of a novel is to be completely different. The old style, like the characters of Hackett and Nixon, is to be abandoned forever. Old Hackett is left on his bench to contemplate the last of the evening and at the same moment Watt introduces the beginning of the novel proper.

To all appearances, Watt is a human being. We are told that he uses a train, that he has a large red nose, a skin that does not heal well, that he possesses bags and wears a hat. Most of what we are told about him as a human being in the first twelve pages, from his arrival at the station to his entry into Mr. Knott's house, is reasonably plausible although strange. Thereafter, he suffers attrition, and we know him in mind only. He becomes less a man in the usual sense than an enquiring spirit, mulling over the problems presented to it. There is a high degree of concentration on this process of grappling with such problems, exterior circumstance being of small importance. Watt, it would seem, is the unaccommodated person in us all, as much to Nixon who, we are told, seems to have known him all his life (but who apparently never recognized him as such) and to Hackett (Beckett), from whose quiescent mind, where the 'western sky was as the eastern, which was as the southern, which was as the northern,'[252] Watt seems to issue.

John Fletcher, in *The Novels of Samuel Beckett*,[253] observes that 'the really burning question (in *Watt*) concerns the difficulty, the impossibility in fact, of all knowledge, even of the simplest kind, such as the knowledge of physical things.' This, I feel, goes straight to the point. However, Watt's incapacity to understand things concrete and abstract is also a dilemma. He wants to know, feels that he ought to be able to know, but finds to his confusion that he cannot know. Finally, he breaks down, utterly defeated, and retires to a mental hospital. Beneath the circumstantial features of his story, there is this experience of disappointment which, in my opinion, is the story's true substance. It is the tale of an endeavour that discovers its own impotence. The impossibility of knowing, a term we shall examine more closely in a moment, is already heralded quite early in the novel as Watt lies in a ditch and listens to the 'voices, indifferent in quality, of a mixed choir,' descanting on the digits of pi.

> Fifty-one point one
> four two eight five seven one
> four two eight five seven one
> oh a bun a big fat bun
> a big fat yellow bun
> for Mr Man . . .[254]

This is not merely a mathematical or a philosophical 'dilemma.' It is linked with the idea of 'metaphysical' nescience alluded to above. It is supported by the fact that Beckett sets the tone of his novel by Watt's encounter with the editor of the Catholic monthly, *Crux*,[255] whose name is

Mr. Spiro. 'My friends call me Dum,' said Mr. Spiro, 'I am so bright and cheerful. D-U-M. Anagram for mud.' None of this needs comment. The encounter is an opportunity for mordant satire, the undertow of which is a comparison between Watt's fundamental dilemma − albeit here in anticipation − and Spiro's trivial conundrums.

> Sir,
> A rat, or other small animal, eats of a consecrated wafer.
> 1. Does he ingest the real Body, or does he not?
> 2. If he does not, what has become of it?
> 3. If he does, what is to be done with him?
>
> Yours faithfully,
>
> Martin Ignatius MacKenzie
> (Author of the Chartered Accountant's Saturday Night)[256]

Beckett keeps up his satirical attack to the very end, perhaps revealing thereby the intensity of feeling he entertains personally on the subject. It is also, by implication, an attack on the Church, and may indicate, for this reason, a profound dissatisfaction with the solutions provided by that body for the various dilemmas that gnaw the Beckettian character's vitals.

What should concern the open-minded critic at this juncture is that now, at the outset of Watt's journey, an incident should take place that has religious overtones. We can dismiss it, of course. We can say that it is merely an amusing incident; Watt meets a travelling companion, who happens to be the editor of a Catholic monthly. This does not give us *carte blanche* to assume that the rest of the book is of a religious nature. No, to be sure. There is, nevertheless, an interesting antithesis to Spiro's answer to MacKenzie's letter which runs as follows:

> Mr Spiro now replied to these questions, that is to say he replied to question one and he replied to question three. He did so at length, quoting from

St Bonaventura, Peter Lombard, Alexander of Hales, Sanchez, Suarez, Henno, Soto, Diana, Concina and Dens, for he was a man of leisure. But Watt heard nothing of this, because of other voices.[257]

These 'voices' sing and cry, state and murmur in Watt's ear, but not all at once. Beckett, typically, lists all the possible variations of these utterances, thus giving the reader the first taste of shock by permutation (p.27). We can deduce from this that these voices are insistent but we know nothing of the intelligence they convey. Watt's understanding of what is happening ranges, we are told, from total to zero comprehension, as now. We may be at liberty, therefore, to assume that the answers proposed by Mr. Spiro in this case do not satisfy him because they are not fully apprehended.

The word 'Spiro' itself is indicative of a mind that wishes to satirize and condemn. If we turn again to the dictionary,[258] we find that 'spiro' is one found in combination from the Latin and ultimately from the Greek in such words as *spirobacteria* (those having spirally twisted cells) and *spiro-chaete,* (bacteria having a highly twisted spiral form). We are satisfied that there cannot be any correspondence here and that, in this case, there is not the ambivalence that is so often contained in Beckett's proper names, until, that is, we discover the word 'twist' a moment later, after Mr. Spiro has introduced himself and is speaking of the character of his magazine. There, he says:

> Our prize competitions are very nice. Times are hard, water in every wine. Of a devout twist, they do more good than harm.[259]

The word 'twist' in everyday English vernacular means: 'to betray,' or to 'deliberately deceive.' Those who practise such deceptions are known at large to be 'twisters,' (cf. 'dodger' in the same connection). *The Concise Oxford Dictionary* (4th edition p.1384), under the word 'twist,' at meaning 14., reads: 'Wrench out of natural shape, distort...' Could it be then that Beckett feels that the tenets of the Church are a 'twist,' that is, a distortion, either deliberately or plainly mis-leading? I do not wish to enter into such trivia too deeply but simply to note the fact and pass on. In a similar way, we can acknowledge the autobiographical detail of the Leopardstown Racetrack and the station (Foxrock) where Watt alights.

Spiro's closing remarks on 'pontifical decrees' are lost 'in a great rush of air' as the train continues its journey and Watt finds himself alone 'flying through the night.' The moon is on the wane. He begins his 'funambulistic stagger' from the station and launches out on the first stage of a journey that is in fact an inward one.

After an attack from Lady McCann and a short rest in the grass of a wayside ditch, Watt continues his journey. He arrives at Mr. Knott's house where the chimneys had been visible from the road by the light of the moon. The door is locked, the house in darkness. He tries the door at the back of the house and finds this locked too. He returns to the front. It is still locked. He goes round to the back once again and finds it open, much to his surprise. There follows a short disquisition on the possibilities of this occurrence.

One asks oneself about these permutations. It is difficult to reconcile them with what we normally understand as a work of literary art. What is their function, apart from being an irritating interruption? We feel that it is an attempt to know. Watt gives all the possibilities of a given situation. When all the permutations are exhausted, the truth must lie in one of them. This is suggested by the deliberately pompous introduction to many of them, initiated generally by the phrase '...and the reason for such an occurrence was this...' or, in the case of the notoriously thorough permutation with the businesslike phrase: 'Twelve possibilities occurred to Watt in this connection:'[260] All the twelve possibilities are then explored, much to the reader's surprise and perhaps chagrin. Beckett wants the reader to experience directly the problem of knowledge and also the impotence experienced at not being able to choose the correct possibility.

In the pursuit of science, Watt's method often proves itself invaluable in discovering the truth of a situation. Much of the energy of, for example, physicists, chemists, biologists and medical research is devoted exclusively to isolating possibilities and then eliminating those that are not pertinent to the situation under analysis. Eliminative reasoning is not always such a lucrative method when applied to some of the problems associated with existence. For example, we might quite reasonably ask ourselves why we exist or why innocence is so often the object of suffering, or whether the heart of man is essentially evil or essentially good, and no amount of permutation and elimination would help us. In the first place, we are not able to assemble enough possibilities. In the second, even if we possessed such a list, we would not have the requisite knowledge to reach a conclusion and, therefore, make a decision. Beckett wants us to feel the puniness of our intellectual apparatus when faced with such questions. At the same time, his satirical talents are directed at Cartesianism, the ultimate in the rational approach to problems and a model of thinking for generations. However, Cartesian methodology cannot help very much in the situations Watt and others find themselves.

Implicit in *Watt*, as we have suggested earlier, is that there must be another kind of mind than that which the word normally encompasses. It is implicit in Arsene's 'short statement,' (pp.37–62), for example, that poetic utterance of twenty-five pages where Beckett relates what is, in fact, a poignant exposition to the rest of the novel.

> ...because what we know partakes in no small measure of the nature of what has so happily been called the unutterable or ineffable, so that any attempt to utter it or eff it is doomed to fail, doomed, doomed to fail.[261]

Although another kind of mind might be implied, it is always – as here – negated or we are simply diverted from its serious contemplation. Beckett's humour distracts us from Watt's agony of not being able to know. Even in this example, the poignancy is detectable. The need to 'eff' it, that is, vulgarly curse the 'unutterable,' is implied dilemma; it implies an inability to understand and a subsequent abandon. The tolling 'doom' expresses hopelessness. The last two pages of Arsene's soliloquy and his final departure are highly allusive. One detects references to *Everyman*, from the Acts of the Apostles, the epistles of St. Paul, the church hymnal and the Church of England litany, which confer on these closing words both dignity and pathos. Despite this, Arsene's valediction is not very helpful to the reader. His speech is full of sound and what Doherty[262] calls 'dexterous rhetoric.' It conveys little to anyone desirous to come to grips with the central issue of the story. Beckett burns his bridges as he proceeds, leaving the reader no point of connection and therefore no firm point of reference. The ground, like the great sand dune at Pilat referred to above, slips perceptibly from under one's feet.

Some critics, and in particular Mr. Doherty, have taken great pains to elucidate the first part of this novel and, with considerable intellectual skill, have managed to wrench the disparate, contradictory elements of the novel to a plausible meaning. Doherty concludes:

> Watt is a Beckettian cousin to Swift's man, who is not a rational animal, but an animal capable of reasoning, *capax rationis*, or close to Rochester's Man:
>
> > Huddled in dirt the reasoning engine lies
> > Who was so proud, so witty and so wise.
>
> We are here at some tether's end and Watt is the question man is reduced to asking, not the 'why of scientific rationalism, nor the 'how' of technocracy, but the primary and basic question about 'reality.' We have to return to the beginning which is the only direction you can move in if you have come to the end...[263]

To tackle *Watt* satisfactorily, one should not just go through the book chronologically and work towards some thesis from what is said but should take a consciously un-literary critical attitude, form a thesis, and see whether *Watt* is in any way an expression of that thesis. For this, we shall adopt as an exception the so-called philosophical method, not necessarily towards the formulation of an '...answer which often turns out to be platitudinous, but in making the way clear for its acceptance.'[264] Before embarking on such an exploration, we should review the points already alluded to. First, *Watt* is the account of a man on a spiritual quest. Second, this quest is concerned with a search for fundamentals as, for example, a clarification of the act of knowing. Third, for the author the knowledge so far available on these matters, i.e. Cartesianism and the dicta of traditional religion, are of no help in providing an acceptable solution — acceptable to the author, that is.

As a starting point, we can consider the first problem that presents itself to Watt. This is the visit of the piano-tuners, Gall and Son. The substance of the incident is summed up in a few lines. The narrator (Beckett) says this event 'in a sense...resembled all the incidents of note proposed to Watt during his stay in Mr. Knott's house,' and the 'principal incident' in the early days of his stay:

> The mice have returned, he said.
> The elder said nothing. Watt wondered if he heard.
> Nine dampers remain, said the younger, and an equal number of hammers.
> Not corresponding, I hope, said the elder.
> In one case, said the younger.
> The elder had nothing to say to this.
> The strings are in flitters, said the younger.
> The elder had nothing to say to this either.
> The piano is doomed, in my opinion, said the younger.
> The piano-tuner also, said the elder.
> The pianist also, said the younger.[265]

This is the substance of an enquiry, which occupies a subsequent eight pages. For this reason alone, it provides grounds for critical comment. Reading the eight pages, which revolve around Watt's reception of this scene, will

strike the average reader of normal intelligence and sensibility as something written by one sick in mind:

> Finally, to return to the incident of the Galls, father
> and son, as related by Watt, did it have that mean-
> ing for Watt at the time of its taking place, and then
> lose its meaning and then recover it?[266]

> One more word on this subject.
> Watt learned towards the end of his stay in Mr
> Knott's house to accept that nothing had happened,
> that a nothing had happened, learned to bear it
> even, in a shy way, to like it. But then it was too
> late.[267]

> So Watt did not know what had happened. He did
> not care, to do him justice, what had happened.
> But he felt the need to think that such a thing had
> happened then, the need to be able to say, when
> the scene began to unroll its sequences, Yes, I
> remember, that is what happened then.[268]

The literary critic faced with statements such as these not
only needs considerable literary ingenuity but also a great
measure of goodwill towards the author in order to bring
the statements within the bounds of reason. A common-
sense assay on these reflections must conclude that Watt is
mad. There is nothing within the eight pages that offers
sane relief. To spare themselves the embarrassment of pronouncement, many critics either ignore the incident and
Watt's comment on it or attempt to rationalize it away. Both
tactics avoid the stark, uncomfortable fact of unintelligibility.

Let us return to the original issue, from which the unintel-
ligible comment arises. Two men, father and son, the elder
blind, consider a dilapidated piano. The instrument is in a
very bad state. All but nine of its dampers and hammers
have been eaten by itinerant mice. The strings themselves
are frayed beyond use. The piano is quite useless as a
musical instrument. It is described as 'doomed.' The word
implies judgement. Perhaps it is doomed to the bonfire. In
any case the word suggests an agent. The process of its

being 'doomed' has been set in motion long before the arrival of the Galls. The mice have helped time to bring about the doom. There is no hope. The process will go on inexorably until the remaining nine dampers and hammers have been consumed and every string has snapped. So much we may reasonably assume from the text. We are informed, in short, of a process of progressive deterioration. Suddenly, the attention of the reader is shifted to the piano-tuner. He, too, is doomed. And not only he but also the pianist, who at the moment is an abstraction.

All four subjects, three animate and one inanimate, share the same fate; all of them are subjected to the implacable influences of Time. The force that is a function of Time is change (and therefore deterioration). In this case, it is ir-reversible disintegration. If this is true, then Watt, too, is affected. However, he does not turn the light of his sudden perception of this situation onto himself and ask: If this is the case, then I, too, am changing; what substance then have I? What am I? Instead, he turns his attention outward to a consideration of the scene being enacted before him. He sees this as change. All too seriously, he perceives that time is changing the Galls and their piano and that this must be a continuous change. He reasons that what he sees before him cannot have any substance in the general sense of that word. It is only continuity he sees, literally a process of decay. If this is so, then the event cannot be truly known. It can be only partially understood.

This might be one way of looking at the incident. Beckett, however, goes on to describe his subject's reaction to the scene observed. He tells us that '. . . it continued to unfold in Watt's head, from beginning to end, over and over again, the complex connections of its lights and shadows, the passing from silence to sound and from sound to silence, the stillness before the movement and the stillness after. . .'[269] so that

> the scene in the music room with the two Galls,
> ceased very soon to signify for Watt a piano tuned,
> an obscure family and professional relation, an
> exchange of judgements more or less intelligible

> ...and became a mere example of light comment-
> ing bodies and stillness motion and silence sound,
> and comment comment.[270]

This 'fragility of outer meaning,' the author informs us, had
a bad effect on Watt since he was looking 'for some meaning
of what had passed in the image of how it had passed.'[271]
From the above and what follows, it is clear that Watt has
undergone an experience where the substantiality of things
seen and heard has been eroded. This is supported by the
narrative that immediately follows the visit of the Galls. It is
an incident 'of great formal brilliance and indeterminable
purport,' as Beckett describes it. The incident itself has so
receded in reality in Watt's mind that, two pages later, it is
reported to have 'ceased so rapidly to have even the paltry
significance of two men, come to tune the piano...that it
seemed rather to belong to some story heard long before, an
instant in the life of another, ill-told, ill-heard, and more
than half forgotten.'[272] It is for this reason that Watt tries to
reassure himself that something has happened. He wants to
know 'what?' definitely and tangibly, what had happened.

We learn that time passes (p.72) and that Watt's recollections are now even less clear and at the same time complicated by his own idiosyncrasies. After a moment of casu-
istry, Beckett takes up the problem again:

> What distressed Watt in this incident of the Galls
> father and son...was not so much that he did not
> know what had happened, for he did not care what
> had happened, *as that nothing had happened, that a
> thing that was nothing had happened with the utmost
> formal distinctness.*[273]

This, apparently, is the crux of the matter. The problem for
us is: What does it mean? Rationally, it means nothing.
From the experiential, non-rational point of view, however,
it means a great deal. A clue to its meaning and a justification for our liberty in interpreting *Watt* in this way is given
in Beckett's *Proust*:

> 'Man', writes Proust, 'is not a building that can
> receive additions to its superfices, but a tree whose

stem and leafage are an expression of inward sap. We are alone. We cannot know and cannot be known. Man is a creature that cannot come forth from himself, who knows others only in himself, and who, if he asserts the contrary, lies.'[274]

'We cannot know and cannot be known,' is, from the rationalist point of view, untrue. Of course we can both know and be known. In the same way, speaking of the incident of the Galls in *Watt*, we cannot say that *a* nothing *had happened*. 'Nothing happened' is absence of incident and, similarly, when 'a nothing' (whatever this may mean) 'happens.' It is like the zero in any equation that cancels all the other terms, whatever their purport.

However, if we rehearse the principles outlined in the exposition to this essay, we are able to say that (1) we have a perceiving subject (Watt) and (2) an event (inevitably involving objects, here the Galls and the piano). For some reason, perhaps because of the 'philosophical' nature of the discourse between father and son, that is, that we must all come to dust, Watt apprehends the fact that he, too, is involved in the process. At this point, (3) he sees himself as object, both of the judgement pronounced by the Galls and also as the object of his own perception (apperception). If Watt continues to look for a subject here, he will find only an object and so involve himself in an infinite regression like an object between mirrors placed opposite one another. If then there is doubt about the subject, there must in this case also be doubt about the object. Therefore, we cannot know and cannot be known. Yet, however vague the object, together with its hypothetical subject, there remains the act of perceiving. The observation 'I perceive, therefore I am' can no longer be valid, however, since if 'I' does not obtain, who does the perceiving? All we can say about the matter is that there is a perceiving. This must be true because how else could it be known that things come into being and pass away, that events like this take place in the music room? To use another analogy, we can say the situation is like a man standing on the bank of a stream, uncertain of whether the water is flowing or not (here the water can approximate to the occurrence of phenomena). He can find out by putting one foot into the water while keeping the other on the bank.

Watt suspects the presence of the *nirvanic* aspect. This is the reason for his inability to describe what he has faintly understood; to do so, he uses such phrases as 'stillness motion,' and 'silence sound,'[275] which, by cancelling each other out, give a vague idea of his apprehension. However, the fact that he as subject (and therefore object) might not exist depresses him. He flays about in his mind for self-justification. He looks for meaning in: 'What had passed in the image of how it had passed,' and would be content for the most 'meagre symbol,' but finds none. Further, there is resistance to the idea of there being 'nothing.' Although unaccommodated in Lear's sense, he is still ego-centred and searches desperately for confirmation of himself: 'But he felt the need to think that such and such a thing had happened then, the need to be able to say, when the scene began to unroll its sequences (when memory operates or the machinery of association begins), Yes, I remember (self-confirmation), that is what happened then.'[276]

We can see that instead of facing up to the problem directly and inquiring (irrationally) further into the *What*, our Watt retreats again to the position of self-affirmation and takes his dilemma with him. He cannot live comfortably with his realization. He does not see that it is Mind giving rise to objects — including his idea of himself — because he cannot think Mind. He is ripe for the kick or the slap that the ancient Zen masters were so adept at administering. *Le néant* is unthinkable but Watt will not accept the fact.

Here, one is reminded of an interview with Huang-Po, in which a monk earnestly enquires about the means to attain understanding of that which cannot be named. Part of the interview is represented below:

Q. What is the Way and how must it be followed? (the 'Way' here meaning the means to En-lightenment)

A. What sort of THING do you suppose the Way to be, that you should wish to FOLLOW it?

Here the monk is a little put off but rallies to:

> Q. What instructions have the masters everywhere given for *dhyana*-practice (meditation techniques) and the study of the Dharma? (Buddhist canon).

> A. Words used to attract the dull of wit are not to be relied on.

> Q. If those teachings were meant for the dull-witted, I have yet to hear what Dharma has been taught to those of really high capacity.

> A. Do not look to what is called the Dharma by preachers, for what sort of Dharma could that be?

The master is attempting to get the monk off the hook of both attempting to seek for something and hoping to find something. Huang-Po wants the monk to dismiss all such concepts and their associated objects. At this point, there is clearly a deadlock. The monk counters, perhaps more out of despair at not finding satisfaction than from a need to justify himself:

> Q. If that is so, should we not seek for anything at all?

> A. By conceding this, you would save yourself a lot of mental effort.

For the first time in the interview, the monk has said the right thing, but he cannot acquiesce to it entirely. By simply 'doing nothing,' he feels that nothing can be 'attained.' In *samsaric* existence, such an attitude is valid; the monk forgets (or cannot yet realize) that the *nirvanic* view cannot be grasped; what he is dealing with here is not an object and does not belong to the world of objective values. Thus, he is using the wrong tool for the job, so to speak. Desperately, he proceeds:

> Q. But in this way everything would be eliminated. There cannot just be nothing.

> A. Who called it nothing? (i.e. the concept of no-
> thing, or vacuum) Who was this fellow? But
> you wanted to SEEK for something.[277]

> Yes, Watt could not accept...that nothing had
> happened with all the clarity and solidity of some-
> thing...If he had been able to accept it, it would
> not have revisited him, and this would have been a
> great saving of vexation, to put it mildly. But he
> could not accept it, could not bear it.[278]

I am not the first in the field to hazard such an interpretation with regard to Watt's conduct and utterance. A.J.
Leventhal, writing on 'The Beckett Hero' in Martin Esslin's
anthology, *A Collection of Critical Essays*, cites the sophist
Georgias of Lentini (483–375 BC) from the *Encyclopedia
Britannica*. According to this, Georgias' philosophy was as
follows:

1. There is nothing which has any real existence.

2. That even if anything did exist, it could not be
   known.

3. That supposing real existence to be knowable,
   the knowledge would be incommunicable.[279]

This is a philosophy that accords exactly with that of the
Buddhist. The difference between the two is that where the
one ends in brilliant but brick-wall theory, the other finds a
way over the wall in practice. Where the one, like Watt,
screams in an impasse of despair, the other initiates a
revolution of mind that transcends both self and impasse.

Watt's residence in the house of Mr. Knott results in his
being wiser than he was when he first entered the back
door. One is reminded of Omar Khayyam's quatrain:

> When I was young I did eagerly frequent
> Doctor and Saint and heard great Argument
> About it and about, but ever came I out
> By that same Door as in I went.[280]

Several critics have observed Mr. Knott as that 'which is
not.' Watt meets Mr. Knott once in the garden (p.144),

but he remains a mystery throughout the novel. Watt's sojourn in the Knott establishment and his subsequent disappointment, hinted at by Arsene on the eve of his attendance, is the kernel of the novel. Beckett is sceptical that God (Mr. Knott or the nirvanic side of existence) can ever be known. We cannot be known by God nor can we know Him.

> What had he learnt? Nothing
> What did he know of Mr Knott? Nothing.
> Of his anxiety to improve, of his anxiety to under-
> stand, of his anxiety to get well, what remained?
> Nothing. But was that not something?[281]

Here we see at work the ambiguity that invests the novel. It is indeed something, a 'something' if one looks at it in terms of loss, but that is all. This is Watt's clockwork logic. However, nothing can palliate this disappointment; the 'some-things' by their irrelevance only add to his pathetic situation.

> He saw himself then, so little, so poor. And now
> littler, poorer. Was not that something?
> So sick, so alone.
> And now.
> Sicker, aloner.[282]

He goes downstairs to find Erskine gone, 'when the yew was dark green, almost black,'[283] and another man, a stranger, in the kitchen. The yew certainly symbolizes death, here the death of hope, of belief. Knott's presence was to give life meaning in the sense of 'I am come that ye might have life and have it more abundantly,' but although God exists, like Mr. Knott he is aloof, incommunicative, odd, unknowable and Christ's promises are empty. The effect of this on Watt is shattering. He feels unloved and utterly alone. The superlatives are justified here, I feel, because firstly the style at this point indicates such a catas-trophe and is perfectly without ambiguity, and secondly, this is the crisis of the novel. Watt's simplicity and humility go unrewarded, his thirst for righteousness, unslaked.

Watt's disappointment does not pass without reaction, however. The sceptical notes of satire, which are detectable throughout the novel and which have been acknowledged here and there in passing, now become hard and cynical. One can already note an attack on God's ordered universe, where all things work together for the best. (This sentiment is paraphrased in *Murphy* on more than one occasion.) It is a sneer, in Beckett's view, at what is naively considered the best possible of worlds in his description of the Lynch family. Here, bodily affliction, congenital and acquired, is an integral part of life. Beneath, like a strong, unseen current, is death, implied by the recurring phrase 'aged sixty-four years' and the interpolation of the word 'widower.' This suggests loss through death and is reminiscent of the official proclamations of death.[284]

> There was Tom Lynch, widower, aged eighty-five years, confined to his bed with constant un-diagnosed pains in the caecum, and his three surviving boys, Joe, aged sixty-five years, a rheumatic cripple, and Jim, aged sixty-four years, a hunch-backed inebriate and Bill, widower, aged sixty-three years, greatly hampered in his movements by the loss of both legs...[285]

There is grim, repugnant humour in Watt's sexual encounters with Mrs. Gorman. Surely it is not meant simply to amuse but to draw our attention to aspects of existence, which we all too readily try to evade but which are as much a part of life as the health, youth and well-being that we so much insist upon. Poverty, hunger, disease and death are more typical of the world's features. The question naturally arising from these considerations is: Where is the God of Love in all this?

> Another said — Why, ne'er a peevish Boy
> Would break the Bowl from which he drank in Joy;
> Shall He that made the Vessel in pure Love
> And Fancy, in after Rage destroy?

One answered this: but after Silence
A Vessel of more ungainly make;
'They sneer at me for leaning all awry;
What! did the Hand of the Potter shake?'[286]

Nine centuries before Watt's appearance, Khayyam had also had the same thoughts and proffered the same question. The 'What!' is incredulous. What we see does not in any way accord with what we are told. There follows a denial of the whole canon. The scene in the garden in all its savagery is a furious expression of Beckett's antagonism to such an idea as a God of Love in the best possible of worlds. Watt's friend, Sam (Beckett), makes his appearance at this point. The manner of the ensuing pages is:

> 'See! We can do what we like to other sentient beings; this God will not stop us, nor even notice; "the bastard doesn't exist!" '[287]

Underlying these emotions, however, is the burning anger of disappointment in God for not existing, a feeling of 'Let Him wreak His will for all I care! To the Devil with Him!' The figure of Christ crucified comes to mind as one similarly betrayed. While in this Gethsemane to Knott's house, Sam sees Watt coming towards him:

> His face was bloody, his hand also and thorns were in his scalp. (His resemblance to Christ, at that moment, to the Christ believed to be by Bosch, then hanging in Trafalgar Square, was so striking that I remarked upon it). And at the same instant suddenly I felt as though I were standing before a great mirror in which my garden was reflected, and my fence, and I and the very birds tossing in the wind, so that I looked at my hands and felt my face, and glossy skull with an anxiety as real as unfounded.[288]

Watt finally descends to lunacy, his sadness at first released in sadistic protest (in destroying the animals and birds) in the garden and later becoming inarticulate. His words and later his syntax become inverted. Sam grows used to the sounds Watt emits but cannot understand them nor their import.

> Taw ot klat tonk? Skin (*nichts*), skin, skin...
> Tonk ot klat taw? On. Tonk ta kool taw? On.
> Taw ta kool tonk? Nilb, mun, mud...[289]

Watt's quest has been a failure. The centre of the circle (God), a meaning to life, like the dot at the centre of Erskine's picture, cannot be reached. Only death will bring relief at last for all that is left is life in *samsara*, a depiction of which is now given, almost in the language of the Buddhist *sutras*.

> ...the darkening ease, the brightening trouble; the pleasure because it was, the pain pain because it shall be; the glad acts grown proud, the proud acts growing stubborn; the panting, the trembling towards being gone...[290]

Death is the only advantage, the only solution. Watt arrives at the railway station. He is like the spurned figure of Christ, taunted by those waiting.

> Give me a ticket if you please.
> He wants a ticket, cried Mr Nolan.
> A ticket to where? said Mr Gorman.
> Where to? said Mr Nolan.
> To the end of the line, said Watt.
>
> He wants a ticket to the end of the line, cried Mr Nolan.
> Is he a white man? said Lady McCann.
> Which end? said Mr Gorman.
> What end? said Mr Nolan.
>
> Watt did not reply.
> The round end or the square end? said Mr Nolan.
> Watt reflected a little longer. Then he said:
>
> The nearer end.[291]

8 The Dilemma of Identity

Beckett began writing *Molloy* in September 1947 and finished it in the following January. To have written it so quickly suggests that the material had been well pondered over. In speaking about this creative feat to his friend Alec Reid, Beckett said:

> I realized that I knew nothing. I sat down in my mother's little house in Ireland and began to write *Molloy*.[292]

What does Beckett mean by 'knowing nothing'? Perhaps Ruby Cohn has the answer when, speaking of Beckett's pronouncement on his 'folly,' she says that the 'stupidity' he became aware of is to be taken literally. 'After absorbing much knowledge, Beckett became aware that one can know too much to know that one must return to the innocence of stupidity in order to feel.'[293] This would certainly seem to be supported by the phenomenon of progressive reduction that occurs in the trilogy, from Molloy's difficulty in walking to Malone's supine state and finally to the total immobilization of the Unnamable, who is stuck in his jar. We can regard it perhaps as a casting off of lendings, a stripping away of all that is adventitious to the man within.

In style, *Molloy/Moran* is altogether freer than that of the transition piece, *Watt*. It is written in the first person, without paragraphs, homogeneous in both its parts, free of intractable number − save for the short sucking-stone meditation − and of the constipating, self-communing cerebration of the earlier work. Moreover, all depiction of character, except for Molloy himself, Moran and his son, is either reduced to what we can infer (as in the case of the good Father Ambrose in *Moran*) or to a word or two or a line at the most. The work never lapses into what Beckett calls 'a wealth of filthy circumstance,' which we may take here to mean anything that is not conducive to the furtherance of the novel. And yet, paradoxically, there is no scheme or incident that can be said to support a movement in a particular direction towards a particular end. There is no 'development' in the usual sense that this word is applied to literary accomplishment, as we have pointed out earlier. There is, however, a circularity. It is this that supplies the 'form' of each section of the novel.

Both sections of *Molloy/Moran* involve a man on a quest. Both contain elements that are autobiographical. As in *Watt*, the landscape is that of Ireland. It is the area around Dublin, looking out to the sea in the east with the hills behind, the pastureland of the foothills with its eternal sheep, the Spenserian shepherds with their dogs. The air is filled with wind from the sea, the cries of the gulls and the bleating of the lambs. Here and there between the nestling villages and the small grey town, a man may be seen walking on the road 'hard and white,' rising and falling to the 'whim of hills and hollows.' Outwardly, the scene is one of utmost peace and natural beauty. Inwardly, there is the human heart to contend with: the village may contain a man like Moran, an agent who is paid to spy on other men, a brittle, lip-serving martinet and book-keeper; the sheep to a fleece are for slaughter and the man on the road may carry a club.

This inharmonious relationship between nature and the restless human heart must have often occurred to Beckett during the long walks he took with his father and brother when he was a boy. Now and again it finds expression as poetic utterance in *Molloy*. This is especially so when, for a moment, the narrative dwells on the purling flight of the buzzard, or the stirring night air, calling up the 'shy sabbath of leaves and petals,' or on the 'witless moon' scudding across the ragged night sky. The utterance is always brief, offering a moment's relief to the headlong rush of words in pursuit of self.

> But now he knows these hills, that is to say, he
> knows them better, and if ever again he sees them
> from afar, it will be to think with other eyes, and
> not only that but the within, all that inner space
> one never sees, the brain and heart and other
> caverns where thought and feeling dance their
> sabbath, all that too quite differently disposed.[294]

Beckett must have asked himself many times on these
occasions and certainly in retrospect why human beings are
quite differently disposed, why the operation of thought
and feeling in them should be a 'sabbath.' This is reminiscent more of the witches' sabbath, of something intense
and clandestine, than of a day of religious observance. This
play of thought and feeling, this inner activity, is the substance and expression of Beckett's writing, now brought to
full declaration in *Molloy* and the works that follow. Underlying the inner activity is a condition of restlessness, one
known to Buddhism as *uddhacca* in Sanskrit (from the
original texts). It precedes expression of any other kind. It is
allied to the thirst for satisfaction (*tanha*) referred to above.
In Beckett's work, the restlessness expresses itself in search,
which is not outwardly directed as is usually the case but
inwardly. An inward search is generally the mark of someone who is dissatisfied with the fruits of outward seeking.
This dissatisfaction is reflected in several places throughout
Molloy and also in subsequent works.

> For what possible end to these wastes where true
> light never was, nor any upright thing, nor any
> true foundation, but only these leaning things,
> forever lapsing and crumbling away beneath a sky
> without memory of morning nor hope of night.[295]

Intensification and concentration are achieved by eliminating everything that is not absolutely essential to a focus of
the reader's attention on the material of the meditations of
Molloy and Moran. Because of this sharp focus on the
associative processes of the mind and its allied judgements,

several critics have referred to Beckett's work as 'a map of mind' or a landscape of mind.

MOLLOY, THE SEEKER

Into this landscape, the outer and the inner, steps Molloy, the seeker. We meet him first in 'my mother's room,' to which he has returned after the adventures of succeeding pages. He is writing an account of these, his report. He is under some compunction, which is not made very clear, to have the pages ready each week for collection by a certain man, who is unknown by name. He arrives on Sundays and is always thirsty. After a little light banter, which sets the tone of the novel, its key so to speak, the narration passes insensibly into a scene of observation from afar of two persons, A and C, who are walking towards each other and are at some distance from one another.[296] After a little while they meet, exchange the time of day and pass on in opposite directions. The one, uncertain of the way perhaps, moves on hesitantly, accompanied by his Pomeranian dog. The observer, Molloy himself, hesitates to run after the walker and rehearses in his mind the possible disadvantage of such an attempt to introduce himself,

> I am not a pretty sight, I don't smell too good. What is it I want? Ah, that tone I know, compounded of pity, of fear, of disgust.

In this way the reader is introduced to Molloy, and immediately after, to Molloy's problem:

> There I am then he leaves me, he's in a hurry. He didn't seem to be in a hurry, he was loitering, I've already said so, but after three minutes of me he is in a hurry, he has to hurry. I believe him. And once again I am, I will not say alone, no, that's not like me, but, how shall I say, I don't know, restored to myself, no, I never left myself, free, yes, I don't know what that means, but it's the word I mean to use, free to do what, to do nothing, to know, but

what, the laws of the mind perhaps, of my mind, that for example water rises in proportion as it drowns you and that you would do better, at least no worse, to obliterate texts than blacken margins, to fill the holes of words till all is blank and flat and the whole ghastly business looks like what it is, senseless, speechless, issueless misery.[297]

The possibility of rebuttal invokes a mood of depression. There is doubt about the ego's relationship. The tacit rebuff of the other, which is revealed in his desire to get away as soon as possible, brings the ego of his counterpart into prominence. The ego cannot find confirmation of itself in the appraisal of another. Because there is lack of recognition, there is doubt about the ego's existence. To be lonely implies dependence: Molloy rejects this. Neither can one be restored to oneself, having never left oneself; this can only be a figure of speech to describe two different expressions of the same ego. He was beside himself with rage, we say, and was later 'restored to himself.' However, there are not two egos but only two different manifestations of the same thing or person. Molloy, therefore, chooses the word 'free,' probably having a positive connotation. There immediately follows the question harbouring a doubt: free to do what? *What* is free to do what? Again, the ego's existence is threatened. In every case where this happens, there is a desperate, furious attempt to re-establish itself. In anger here, Molloy throws the whole question overboard with a contemptuous self-justification based on disgust for life. The 'whole ghastly business' is existence seen from Molloy's point of view, senseless, incapable of communication and without means of relief or means of escape.

Molloy stays where he is but continues to reflect on the figure, asking himself whether he was taking the air in order to ensure a good night's sleep and a 'joyous awakening, an enchanted morrow. Was he carrying a scrip?' After a little more of such reflection, attention now centres on Molloy himself. He hints at his impending journey, which is to begin in the second or third week of June when 'over what is called our hemisphere the sun is at its pitilessmost and the arctic radiance comes pissing on our midnights.'[298] The journey to his mother, whom he now describes in revolting detail, is about to begin:

> I called her Mag, when I had to call her something. And I called her Mag because for me without knowing why, the letter g abolished the syllable 'ma' as it were spat on it, better than any other letter would have done.[299]

She is, he says, 'quite incontinent,' both of faeces and water, and the room smells of ammonia.

> She jabbered away with a rattle of dentures and most of the time didn't realise what she was saying. Anyone but myself would have been lost in the clattering gabble, which can only have stopped during her brief instants of unconsciousness. In any case I didn't come to listen to her. I got into communication with her by knocking her on the skull.[300]

The whole interview is hideous and pitiful, laced throughout with outrageous indifference, an indifference that is deliberate. If we were to say that it is Beckett's intention to awaken the reader to certain basic, animal performances, we would perhaps err slightly; what the reader thinks is almost certainly of no interest to Beckett. However, to say that Beckett's view is whole and not given to euphemism, that he acknowledges aspects of existence that are not normally spoken of in polite society or even among normal, civilized human beings, is undeniable. For surely these functions, too, are a part of our existence, a part of our daily routine of living, of experiencing. Because such subjects are usually alluded to only in medical circles, their reality is not diminished.

One fact of existence is aging. Old age and impending death, often entailing weakness and dysfunction, ugliness and mental disorientation, are matters that we instinctively put away from ourselves as though somehow we were immune to such changes. This relegation is also ego-confirmation. Buddhism draws our attention to the dangers inherent in such ostrich-like behaviour if we are serious about acquiring the liberating view of Enlightenment. It asks in its three Warnings:

> Did you ever see in the world a man or woman of eighty, ninety or a hundred years old, frail, crooked as a gable-roof, bent down, resting on crutches, with tottering steps, infirm, youth long since fled, with broken teeth, grey scanty hair or none, wrinkled with blotched limbs? And did the thought never come to you that you also are subject to decay, that you also cannot escape it?

> Did you never see in the world a man, or a woman who, being sick, afflicted and grievously ill, wallowing in his own filth, was lifted up by some and put to bed by others? And did the thought never come to you that you also are subject to disease, that you cannot escape it?

> Did you never see in the world the corpse of a man, or a woman one, two or three days after death, swollen up, blue-black in colour and full of corruption? And did the thought never come to you that you also are subject to death, that you also cannot escape it?[301]

Beckett does not shirk such considerations, finding perhaps that their evasion corresponds to lying to oneself just as our Victorian ancestors are said to have veiled the voluptuous legs of grand pianos in modest white linen in order not to outrage the prude daughters of good families. It is only a matter of degree from this ridiculous example to the hushing up of other matters vital to a full understanding of life.

Uninhibited literature, serious as well as popular, has been unable to draw, as Beckett does, the reader's attention to other matters that are also part of existence. One of these is the breeding and systematic killing of animals, which, in the Buddhist canon, is immoral. 'Thou shalt not kill' is to be applied literally to all creatures. It is the first of the *Five Precepts.*[302]

In both *Molloy* and *Moran* (as elsewhere in Beckett), the slaughter-house and butchery are mentioned without demur.

> ...for slaughter-houses are not confined to towns, no, they are everywhere, the country is full of them, every butcher has his slaughter-house and the right to slaughter according to his lights.

> ...left me with persisting doubts, as to the destination of those sheep, among which there were lambs, and I often wondered if they had reached some commonage or fallen, their skulls shattered, their thin legs crumpling, first to their knees, then over on their fleecy sides, under the poleaxe, though that is not the way they slaughter sheep, but with a knife, so that they bleed to death.[303]

We note that Beckett mentions both forms of killing, perhaps the more to implant in our minds the revulsion we should feel. Some critics have averred that these scenes are to remind one of ever-imminent death. This may to some extent be true although to demonstrate this Beckett could have used other material. It is not just death that he wishes to illustrate but also suffering and, moreover, the suffering of the innocent, which is part of the 'senseless, speechless, issueless misery' of existence. Of this apparently implacable suffering no sense can be made; in Beckett's view, one can know nothing of the causes of such brutishness or of the laws that govern its activity, if such exist.

The tendency then, as we have seen elsewhere in Beckett's work, is to call the name of God into disrepute. How could a loving Creator bring all this hateful mess together in the world? The Buddhist answer to this is that he who complains is looking in the wrong direction. The fault lies in the nature of humans not in the world of phenomena nor with God. A small adjustment in the way of looking at things, especially at oneself, or, as Huang-Po puts it, 'a hair's breadth and heaven and earth are set apart,' is sufficient to clear away the dilemma once and for all. For Beckett, the only solution is, as he related to Tom Driver, 'to let the mess in,' by which we assume he means to look at it fairly and squarely and not allow ourselves to be deceived. This, again, is a Buddhist attitude, at least a preliminary one to entering into the deeper aspects of its philosophy.

Molloy sets off on his journey, which is, he says, to find his mother. Rather, it is a psychological undertaking, a quest in search of his own identity. For when one has a mother, one has proof of one's identity. It is just this kind of proof that is required of him by an accosting policeman. He is discovered motionless on his bicycle, his legs a-straddle in order to support the machine, his arms on the handlebars and his head on his arms. The following 'music hall' dialogue ensues:

> What are you doing there?
> Resting, I said.
> Resting, he said.
> Resting, I said.
> Will you answer my question? he cried.

At this point, Molloy is reduced to what he calls 'confabulation,' his attitude being far from satisfactory in the eyes of the policeman.

> Your papers! he cried.
>
> Now the only papers I carry with me are bits of newspaper, to wipe myself, you understand, when I have a stool, no, but I like to be in a position to do so, if I have to. Nothing strange about that, it seems to me. In a panic I took this paper from my pocket and thrust it under his nose. The weather was fine. We took the little side streets, quiet, sunlit, I springing along between my crutches, he pushing my bicycle with the tips of his white-gloved fingers...I felt the faces turning to look

> after us, calm faces and joyful faces...I seemed to
> hear distant music. I stopped, the better to listen.
>
> Go on, he said.
> Listen, I said.
> Get on, he said.
> I wasn't allowed to listen to the music.[304]

Here we have an insight into the character of Molloy,
unresisting, ingenuous, like 'the wind which bloweth
where it listeth,' stopping to listen to music while under
official direction, truthful, uncomplicated.

Once at the police station, Molloy is further interrogated
as to his identity by a civil servant in shirt-sleeve order,
whose 'civility left increasingly to be desired.' Molloy is
threatened with a cylindrical ruler. It turns out that Molloy
has none of those external attributes that are the official seal
of identity; he has neither papers nor occupation nor domi-
cile. He cannot remember his mother's address, neither can
he remember his name. The former he can find — even in
the dark. Finally, it emerges that his mother lives near the
shambles. His mind turns a blank, closing his eyes, his face
proffered to 'that blandness of blue and gold,' which is the
hot summer day outside. Suddenly, he remembers his name.

> Molloy, I cried, my name is Molloy.
> Is that your mother's name? said the sergeant.
> What? I said.
> Your name is Molloy, said the sergeant. Yes, I said,
> now I remember.
> And your mother? said the sergeant.
> I didn't follow.
> Is your mother's name Molloy too, said the
> sergeant.
> I thought it over. Your mother, said the sergeant, is
> your mother's...
> — Let me think! I cried.[305]

This demonstrates that Molloy, although he exists, cannot
prove his identity officially. Officially, he does not exist.[306]
Molloy has travelled far along the road of ego attrition and

is long since rid of all the excrescences that we are wont to think needful for life. Even so, he is still not sure about his identity:

> And even my sense of identity was wrapped in a namelessness often hard to penetrate, as we have seen I think. And so on for all other things which made merry with my senses. Yes, even then, when already all was fading, waves and particles, there could be no things but nameless things, no names but thingless names.[307]

Looking at the matter a little more deeply, what does constitute personal identity? Like the word 'identity' in the dictionary, the concept is ambiguous. On the one hand it means: 'to be one and the same' as in *The Concise Oxford Dictionary's* term for its meaning (4th edition, p.589. co.ii) 'Absolute sameness;' and on the other: 'separate individuality' or reference to the same dictionary, 'individuality, personality.' Apparently it means both. It is the same with the verb 'to identify,' in the sense of to distinguish by the act of separation, and on the other, 'to merge, associate oneself inseparably with' etc.

The same incongruity exists with regard to personal identity on a superficial level. Every human being is identifiable with every other since they share the same characteristics. However, every individual, according to the findings of forensic medicine, is quite different from every other.[308] We have an identity in that our fingerprints, our dentition and the shape of our noses are unmistakably our own, just as, by scientific measurement, our manner of walking and talking[309] can similarly be established. Are we then these things? Yes, in a manner of speaking, we are. In a similarly related way, we are also the product of our upbringing and education; we are the resultant of all the pressures, forces and influences within and without, to which we have been subjected throughout our lives. By certain acts of volition, we are that which we want to be. This, in general terms, is what the psychologists speak of in using the word 'conditioning' and needs no amplification here.

The question the Buddhist now puts forward is: Is that all we are? There are some who maintain that this is indeed the case while others hotly contend such a conclusion. One means of dealing with the problem is that of systematic analysis. It is this that the Buddha himself adopted. However, we must not rely on his word as authoritative because this would embarrass our powers of reasoning. Instead, we should do as he urged and use our mental equipment in order to come to grips with the problem. The conclusions, the Buddha maintained, are verifiable, and each person should put them to the test for himself.

The systematic analysis undertaken by Buddhism is very thorough and cannot be quoted at length but must be simply outlined. Any responsible translation and commentary will suffice for those readers who are interested in pursuing the matter in exhaustive detail and from first principles.[310]

We can say, however, that it begins with the contemplation of the body. In its simplest terms, it asks: Is this body me? Analyzed, the body is then divided into its component parts (Sanskrit, *rupa-skandha*) and a demonstration follows that this body is not me. This should not delay us. There remains the fact of consciousness and the mental faculties allied to the body. After dealing with feeling (*vedana-skandha*), perception (*sanna-skandha*), and mental formations (volition; *sankhara-skandha*), consciousness itself (*vivana-skandha*) is considered.

> What now is consciousness? There are six classes of consciousness: consciousness of forms, sounds, colours, odours, tastes, bodily impressions and of mental objects (lit. eye-consciousness, ear-consciousness etc.)

Buddhism then goes on to consider these, one by one, in the following manner:

> Now, though one's eye be intact, yet if the external forms do not fall within the field of vision, and no corresponding conjunction (of eye and forms)

takes place, in that case there occurs no formation of the corresponding aspect of consciousness. Or, though one's eye be intact, and the external forms fall within the field of vision, yet if no corresponding conjunction takes place, in that case also there occurs no formation of the aspect of consciousness. If, however, one's eye is intact, and the external forms fall within the field of vision and the corresponding conjunction takes place, in that case there arises the corresponding aspect of consciousness.

Hence, I say: the arising of consciousness is dependent upon conditions and without these conditions, no consciousness arises. And upon whatever conditions the arising of consciousness is dependent, after these it is called.[311]

The same applies to the consciousness of smell, taste, touch and hearing. The whole is termed the Dependent Origination of Consciousness. The conclusion to its reasoning is that a self is not to be found in any of the individual aspects of consciousness. 'Sensation, perception, volitional activities and consciousness are all causally conditioned factors. Their "life" consists of thought-moments (*citta-skandha*), which arise and pass away with inconceivable rapidity. The real term of a being's conscious existence is no longer than the duration of one of these thought-moments of consciousness, which are strung, as it were, on the thread of cause and effect to give the illusory sense of self-identity.'[312] This leads to the conclusion that there is no substance to be discovered. Because of the transitoriness of the phenomena to which we have alluded, there is also suffering. The three features (Sanskrit, *tilakhana*), *transience* (*anicca*), suffering (*dukkha*), and absence of self (*anatta*), are the characteristics of existence.

We can look at the situation empirically for ourselves. If, for example, we were stripped of every title, deprived of all relationship, that is, with regard to occupation, abode, family and friends and all activity whatsoever (the condition of the

Unnamable), and if, in addition, all memory and all hope of the future were taken from one, what of the ego would be left? There would, presumably, be a sensing 'I,' which would still be sensible of heat and cold, lightness and dark etc., but, in watching their action (the action of the *skandhas*) on our body, we would be observing the reactions of a body, that is, an object and, from previous arguments, this cannot be us. Neither is a self to be located in the operation of the mind, for thoughts are also observable. We come then to a 'nameless thing,' the 'It,' of which all of this is a manifestation, a manifestation of 'thingless names' as we have already seen since, in the Buddhist view, it can have no substantiality, being mind-constructed.

This, however, raises a problem, no less for Molloy than for any thinking person. It must, despite the foregoing, be admitted that there is a perceiving; there is suffering; there is stimulation (in the scientific sense). What then is responsible for all this? This is the dilemma of identity. Molloy elaborates as he continues:

> I say that now, but after all what do I know about then, now when icy words hail down upon me, the icy meanings, and the world dies too, foully named. All I know is what the words know, and the dead things, and that makes a handsome little sum with a beginning, a middle and an end as in the well-built phrase and the long sonata of the dead. And truly it little matters what I say or any other thing. Saying is inventing. Wrong, very rightly wrong. You invent nothing, you think you are escaping, and all you do is stammer out your lesson, the remnants of a pensum one day got by heart and long forgotten, life without tears as it is wept.[313]

This statement could be recognized as resignation but for the irony and bitterness, which reveal it as dilemma.

However, Molloy comes near to self-realization in the Buddhist sense from time to time. For example in the following instance, Molloy is describing a garden. There occurs one of those short, poetic flights which here and there in Beckett's work come as a welcome relief to the intensity of his reflections.

> Yes, there were times when I forgot not only who I was but that I was, forgot to be. Then I was no longer that sealed jar to which I owed my being, well preserved, but a wall gave way...[314]

This, in fact, is the way to understanding of the *nirvanic* kind. We have seen above from the novice's interview with Huang-Po how important it is to give up everything, concepts, the idea of an 'I' — in short, everything one can possibly think of. However, the ego clings 'with its teeth clamped on a bramble over the edge of the abyss' according to the Chinese saying. It defends every ditch against its annulling and fights like a tiger for every vestige of confirmation left to it. In this way, it is rather like the inexperienced sailor in a storm who clings to every rag of sail he can find, hauling and fighting the wind for all he is worth whereas the only action he could effectively take in such a situation to save the boat and himself would be simply to let everything go and let the wind have its way. Yet this very resort seems at the time to be the last thing that should be done.

When Soen Roshi, one of the leading Zen masters in Japan today, was setting up a school of meditation in New York some years ago, a number of his young American students asked what the most appropriate reading material would be for meditators aspiring to Enlightenment. He gave as an answer *Alice Through the Looking Glass*. At the time, there were undoubtedly several people who thought this slightly absurd and others who would have liked to understand it but could not. Some, however, grasped the meaning that, as far as Zen is concerned, we must go back to go forward, like Alice. This means that, in the study of Zen, we must put away all noetic habits of thought, the 'way' forward which we have been accustomed to make use of since childhood. We must take what appears to be a step 'backward' (i.e. against all reason) by deliberately loosening our grasp on those things that we have hitherto thought so essential. This is done by 'non-thinking.' In other words, we do not think about anything but simply keep our minds on that which originates thoughts. For this there is no name.[315]

Han Shan (1546–1623) once said: 'Ch'an (Zen) training consists solely of concentration on that which is (self-existent) before your mind is disturbed by a thought, and if you exert yourself unremittingly, self-realization is bound to follow very quickly.' To this end, students of Zen are given what is called a *koan*, the nature of which we have explained earlier (see Note 194). One way of describing the object of the *koan* is to say that it is a means to bring about the stupe-faction of the intellect. To western ears, this is likely to sound undesirable. However, it will be seen at once from our arguments above that all intellectuality is concerned with objectivization (i.e. concepts), and that, further, the solution to the existential problem cannot possibly be solved via conceptualization. It is for this reason and in this way that conceptualizing is stopped and the student's mind brought to focus upon himself. He is supposed to 'look back' into himself and so discover what has been called the Undifferentiated. The *koan* is simply an effective block to the student doing anything else.

We can put the matter another way: anyone who has practised the technique of apperception even for a few minutes will know from experience that thoughts constantly arise in the mind. We call this activity 'thinking' although in fact it is purely mechanistic. It is an associative process and not thinking as in the sense of cerebration. However, for those meditating, it is important to recognize that this mechanism is such and that it is accompanied, more often than not, by feeling or emotion; we might even go so far as to say that each thought carries a 'charge' of emotion, one that varies according to the thought.

In Buddhist *vipassana* (insight meditation) technique, the student is asked to look into the nature of this thought-arising process. By coolly observing it, discharge it. With practice, it tends less and less to function until one comes close to Molloy's state of mind in forgetting who one is or where one is. Enlightenment, which is the release from this temporary suspension of spirit, is then very near.

For a fleeting moment in *Molloy*, the dilemma is removed. Molloy unconsciously stumbles upon the solution to his dilemma, even resorting to the language of the mystic as he does so:

> For to know nothing[316] is nothing, not to want to know anything but to be beyond knowing anything, that is when peace enters in, to the soul of the incurious seeker.[317]

To be 'beyond knowing anything' is to be in a preparatory state to truly knowing and constitutes having taken a step 'backwards' into Soen Roshi's conception of the 'Looking Glass' of Carrol's story. It is a step away from the snares and dilemmas of knowledge based on intellectual perception, the 'waves and particles' of the quotation above. It is a step toward a special kind of knowledge only accessible when the habit of seeking intellectual certainties is temporally and completely suspended. When this happens, we apprehend what the Hindus call 'the Ground of Being' and what the great Christian mystics, eminent among them, Meister Eckhart, personify as God.[318]

MORAN, THE EGOTIST

If Molloy is to a large extent a 'holy fool,' Moran is his worldly counterpart. To give an indication of his character, Beckett makes great use of the short sentence, a device that characterizes the entire section. The result is to convey the impression of general nervous irritability and uncertainty.

> It is midnight. The rain is beating on the windows.
> I am calm. All is sleeping. Nevertheless I get up and go to my desk. I can't sleep. My lamp sheds a soft and steady light. I have trimmed it.[319]

We learn that this man has a son whom he brings up with an iron hand. In this respect he is a veritable 'moron,' without the slightest understanding for the boy, a loveless figure-head and petty tyrant, whose small-minded repression earns him what he deserves — desertion in time of need.

We meet him first taking his ease in his garden on a peaceful Sunday in summer. 'The weather was fine,' the scene tranquil. On his knees a black book rests while in the nearby trees and bushes the songs of thrush and blackbird wilt in the heat. Into this state of delectable peace strides the figure of another man. We are to learn little of this man. His appearance, however, casts a long shadow over the rest of the novel because it is he who for some obscure reason initiated Moran's quest, his search for Molloy. His name is Gaber, which, if we choose to toy with names, could be associated with Gabriel, the messenger of God. He does in fact bring a message from his chief, Youdi. This name has been interpreted by many critics as the Hebrew Yahweh. It is perhaps a combination of this and the German '*Jude*' (Jew). However this may be, the instigation to track down Molloy has its origin in Youdi and is again a manifestation of the 'hypothetical imperative.' In *Moran*, it turns out to be purely and simply an imperative, which he obeys with a mixture of unwillingness and conceit in his ability as an agent.

It is notable that Gaber has a great thirst and is now provided with Moran's favourite beer. While he gives Moran his instructions, he now and then peers into his bowler hat 'as if in search of something,' reminding one immediately of the tramps in *Waiting for Godot*.[320]

When Gaber has gone, Moran prepares himself for a private communion with Father Ambrose. We have already briefly alluded to the substance of this. Apart from brilliantly conveying the relationship between priest and parishioner, Beckett very ably manages to project the embarrassed insecurity intrinsic to the character of Moran upon the reader. Prior to this inference, we are given other explicit information about Moran's personality:

> A neighbour passed. A free thinker. Well, well, he
> said, no worship today? He knew my habits, my

Sunday habits I mean. Everyone knew them and
the chief perhaps better than any, in spite of his
remoteness. You look as if you had seen a ghost,
said the neighbour. Worse than that, I said, you. I
went in, at my back the dutifully hideous smile. I
could see him running to his concubine with the
news. You know that poor bastard, Moran, you
should have heard me...[320a]

There is concern throughout the interview about the whereabouts of Moran's son, Jacques, who should be in church
but who may well be playing near the local slaughter-house.
This, too, adds to the discomfort of the scene in Father
Ambrose' parlour.

After Moran is 'despatched,' that is, has been given perfunctory communion from Father Ambrose' portable 'kit,' he
feels the urge to be off 'as quickly as possible and stuff
myself with stew.' However, he knows that he cannot just
leave after the offices have been said over him. He, therefore, resigns himself to giving his priest 'eight minutes'
since he is 'slightly in advance' of his 'schedule.' What
follows in this space of time is a piece of 'traditional writing'
of consummate artistry. Father Ambrose is evidently a
genial, eminently civilized man of kindly disposition. He
does not hesitate to be roused from his afternoon nap to
attend to Moran's spiritual needs. His conversation, moreover, is directed to ease Moran's obvious embarrassment
and turns upon the practical issues of the health of hens, on
the topic of which Father Ambrose reveals surprising erudition. Contrapuntal to this theme is that of laughter:

And I, not to be outdone, told him how worried I
was about my hens, particularly my grey hen,
which would neither brood nor lay and for the past
month had done nothing but sit on her arse in the
dust, from morning to night.
Like Job, haha, he said. I too said haha. What a joy
it is to laugh from time to time, he said. Is it not? I
said.
It is peculiar to man, he said.
So I have noticed, I said. A brief silence ensued.

What do you feed her on? he said. Corn, chiefly, I said.

Cooked or raw, he said. Both. I said. I added that she ate nothing any more. Nothing! he cried. Next to nothing, I said. Animals never laugh, he said. It takes us to find that funny, I said. What? he said. It takes us to find that funny, I said loudly. He mused. Christ never laughed either, he said, so far as I know. He looked at me. Can you wonder? I said.[321]

From the conclusion of this interview to the end of the novel, the narration is imbued with restless dissatisfaction. This is embodied in Moran's reflections after just leaving the presbytery.

> As I made my way home I felt like one who, having swallowed a pain-killer, is first astonished, then indignant, at obtaining no relief. And I was almost ready to suspect Father Ambrose, alive to my excesses of the forenoon, of having fobbed me off with unconsecrated bread. Or a mental reservation as he pronounced the magic words. And it was in a vile humour that I arrived home, in pelting rain.[322]

As the weather changes from dry heat to rain, the novel begins its preoccupation with Moran's quest to find Molloy.

One of Moran's principal characteristics is his suspicious nature. He suspects Father Ambrose, Martha, his cook and servant, and, above all, his son. Molloy, we will recall, is devoid of this characteristic. Moran wants to be sure of everything. By suspecting everything that comes within his purview, he can at least be sure of some things. He has his schedule, is a strict time-keeper, is a regular church-goer, carries a huge bunch of keys on a chain, and is punctilious in all things. As Molloy is unworldly and uncaring, Moran is narrow and discriminating. 'I don't like men and I don't like animals. As for God, he is beginning to disgust me'[323]

Moran takes pleasure in humiliating both his son and his cook not, perhaps, from motives of sheer sadistic pleasure but because it gives him temporary, pleasurable experience in projecting his ego, of confirming it, and, at the same time, his existence as a force in the world. The type is well known. It is the mark of the petty bureaucrat, insisting on the observance of clause and paragraph, the office tyrant and the minor official's contumely. Not, of course, that any of these traits, whether bureaucracy, church-going, time-keeping or even punctiliousness, are bad in themselves because there is a place in the world for them all. What is wrong is that 'thinking makes it so,' that the interfering ego comes between the instrument and the job to be done. This is why Zen puts so much store by what it calls 'spontaneity,' of 'being oneself' and thus not giving the ego a chance to 'paint legs on the snake.' Perhaps this is what T.S. Eliot had in mind when he spoke of the 'Shadow' in 'The Hollow Men':

Between the idea   Between the conception
And the Reality   And the creation
Between the motion   Between the emotion
And the act   And the response
Falls the Shadow.   Falls the Shadow.[324]

In the annals of Zen, two anecdotes survive to illustrate what is meant here in terms of human behaviour. The story is told of a wandering mystic in China who could perform miracles that were spectacular. This attracted a large crowd, to whom he preached on the banks of the river. Seeing a monk of the Zen sect on the other bank, he hailed him and asked whether he had a miracle to match his own. 'Our miracle,' replied the master, 'is that when we are tired we sleep and when we are hungry we eat.' He meant by this that there is nothing in Zen to come between feeling and response, that the Zen sect is not desirous to show how clever it is in exhibiting miraculous power acquired by some forms of meditation. In the case of the monk in question, this was a form of exhibitionism and, therefore, of egocentricity.

On another occasion, two monks were walking by the side of a fast-running stream when they encountered a young woman unable to cross. One of them accordingly picked her up and carried her across, whereupon the two continued their journey. After a few minutes, the other monk said: 'How could you have so brought yourself into contact with a woman. Don't you feel ashamed?' The other replied: 'I put her down some yards back but you are still with her.' This means that the first monk could forget the incident, not allowing concepts to be built up on what was for him, after all, simple assistance to the weak and, therefore, in keeping with his vows. For the other, this ingenuousness could not be understood. He thought more of the letter of the law of his brotherhood than of the incident in its simplicity.

In his *Essays in Zen Buddhism*, D.T. Suzuki says of the assertive state of mind of which Moran's is typical:

> While a man is attached to individualism (here the assertion of himself or his ego), asserting it consciously or unconsciously, he always has a feeling of oppression which he may interpret as sin; and while the mind is possessed by it, there is no room for the 'other power' (the power of the Unconscious) to enter and work, the way is effectively barred.[325]

Before Moran actually undertakes his quest and sets out with his son on the journey to find Molloy, we are confronted with numerous instances of his nervous irascibility and suspicion. In one such example, we find him first checking on the cook for suspected theft of his beer. He says:

> My weekly supply of lager, half-a-dozen quart bottles, was delivered every Saturday. I never touched them until the next day, for lager must be left to settle after the least disturbance. Of these six bottles, Gaber and I, together, had emptied one. There should therefore be five left, plus the remains of a bottle from the previous week. I went to the pantry. The five bottles were there, corked

and sealed, and the open bottle three-quarters empty.[326]

He then intrudes upon his son's innocuous enjoyment in looking at his stamp album. He effectively destroys this little pleasure. Such incidents only serve, however, to make things worse for him until he can say:

> The blood drains from my head, the noise of things bursting, merging, avoiding one another, assails me on all sides, my eyes search in vain for two things alike, each pinpoint of skin screams a different message. I drown in a spray of phenomena. It is at the mercy of these sensations which I happily know to be illusory, that I have to live and work. It is thanks to them I find myself a meaning. So he whom a sudden pain awakes.[327]

Yet, this creature describes himself as so 'meticulous' and 'calm in the main...'[328] However, now and again he communes with himself:

> Between the Molloy I stalked within me and the true Molloy, after whom I was so soon to be in full cry, over hill and dale, the resemblance cannot have been great.[329]

At this point the transformation begins whereby Moran is coalesced with Molloy.

Twelve-and-a-half pages follow with further arrangements for the journey and further confrontations with the other two inhabitants of the house. Moran sets off at last, turning for a last time towards 'my little all...in the hope of keeping it.' No doubt he has the feeling that something disastrous is about to take place, that, when he returns, if he returns, things will be irretrievably different. Characteristically, he locks the wicker gate. He has not gone many steps before he sees what he calls the 'slow tide of the faithful' going again towards Church. In doing so, he reveals how deep his religious feeling is. He refers to them as a 'docile herd going yet again to thank God for his goodness and to implore his mercy and forgiveness, and then returning, their souls made easy, to other gratifications.' Telling his boy to get behind him, he contemplates attaching the lad to himself by a rope (a figure which of course makes another appearance in *Waiting for Godot*).

Moran says a little later that he scorns his master, Youdi. He has only to carry out orders 'with hatred in his heart.' The 'paltry scrivening' he undertakes to complete his report is no more to him than that of a shuttle scuttling across the page to begin again on the other side. Still, at this point, he is sure of his identity. He knows himself to be Moran, the super-spy who will nose down Molloy wherever he may be. He will follow the voice within and be faithful though 'innumerable authorities speaking with one accord, enjoin upon me this and that, under pain of unspeakable punishments.'[330] Such is the vein at the outset, full of self-will and confidence.

While on the journey, Moran takes several precautions not to be seen on the highways, saying that it would be better really to travel at night and lie up by day.[331] One night, while sleeping, he is attacked by a tremendous pain as though he were kicked by a horse in the knee. This is a sign of the onset of the transformation into Molloy mentioned above. He can no longer walk without difficulty. After impugning his son with regard to an amount of money for the purchase of a bicycle, he sends him off to get one in the town of Hole, some fifteen miles away.

While he waits for his son to return with the machine he sees the figure of a man with his back towards him, standing motionless. He has a club-like stick. 'There was a coldness in his stare, and a thrust the like of which I never saw. His face was pale and noble.'[332] At first, we might take this for a beatific vision of Christ except that the narrator reckons the age of the stranger to be about fifty-five. No words are exchanged at first. Moran offers him a piece of bread that he was keeping for his son. The sad stranger breaks it into two and puts these pieces in his pockets, an odd gesture to Moran, who, as he admits himself, realizes that his son would be hungry when he returned. He asks if he might look at the stick that the stranger is carrying. He receives no reply. Placing his hand under the stranger's, he takes the stick gently from his enveloping fingers. He is surprised by its lightness. For a moment before this realization, Moran's old personality returns: 'Now it was I who held the stick.' This is short-lived, however. Soon the stranger goes, leaving him alone with the thought:

> I wished I could have stood there looking after him and time at a standstill. I wished I could have been in the middle of a desert, under the midday sun, to look after him until he was a dot, on the edge of the horizon.[333]

Left to his own thoughts, Moran pores over his condition, 'on me so changed from what I was. And I seemed to see myself ageing as swiftly as the day-fly.'[334] The stranger disappears with swift steps, his course uncertain and wayward, reminding one of the opening of the novel where A and C are seen from a distance. There is the same longing, here to watch the man disappear to a dot, there to overtake him and talk.

Moran's memory fails. He cannot think clearly anymore. He forgets what he has to do with Molloy when he finds him. He dismisses the thought and considers other 'unknowns.' His food rations gradually run out. He remains unperturbed. A day passes. He had lit a fire on the next day and was fully intent on kindling it when he hears a voice behind him. He finds a man of somewhat imperious manner speaking to him.

> Do you hear me? he said. But all this was nothing compared to the face which I regret to say vaguely resembled my own, less the refinement of course, same little abortive moustache, same little ferrety eyes, same pariphimosis of the nose, and a thin red mouth that looked as if it was raw from trying to shit its tongue.[335]

Moran kills this man, he does not know how. He has in effect killed himself, his old self. He loses his keys in the process but finds an ear (unconscious biblical reference?), 'which I threw into the copse.' A strange metamorphosis has taken place.

The third day of his waiting wears on. Finally, his son returns with the coveted cycle. Moran is critical.

> And you call that a bicycle? I said. Only half expecting him to answer me I continued to inspect it. But there was something so strange in his silence that I looked up at him. His eyes were starting out of his head. What's the matter? I said, is my fly open?[336]

The boy is incredulous. Moran brushes the matter off with the lame excuse that he has had a fall. The journey is continued with the boy for'ard and the father aft astride the carrier.

Although Moran has undergone an inward change, vestiges of his old self linger. What Suzuki called 'attachment to individualism' a moment ago and its accompanying sense of spiritual heaviness, which the individual feels must be expiated as sin, find outlet in other directions now that Moran is temporarily separated from his church. Proof of this is found a little later in the journey when, after many hazards, the two come upon a field of sheep together with their shepherd and his dog. Moran asks the way to Ballyba but his heart so overwhelms his intellectual faculties that he is utterly unable to converse with the shepherd. He describes himself as 'spellbound' and yearns to be free of himself.

> I longed to say, Take me with you, I will serve you faithfully, just for a place to lie and a little food.[337]

His question answered, he stays where he is, not knowing how to leave without 'self-loathing and sadness.' These feelings arise because he no longer believes in himself; he hates what he now sees himself to be. He is sad because he finds himself in the dilemma of not being able to follow the shepherd (this no less in the New Testament sense) and not wishing to continue his journey, which involves following a profession that he has come to detest.

The state of dilemma, as is well known, involves the individual very often in frustration. It is precisely this that now begins to boil over as, during the hours that follow, Moran has a furious row with his son. This is so tense that his son, hitherto obedient and co-operative, leaves him in the night, taking his possessions with him. Moran is alone. After such an outburst and after all that has happend, one would expect a reaction, in which indifference, or at least pretended indifference, dominates, This is exactly what we do find. 'For I had no illusions. I knew that all was about to end, or to begin again, it little mattered which, and it little mattered now, I only had to wait.'[338]

He watches the lights of the town with contempt, 'the foul little flickering lights of terrified men.' At the prospect of punishment at the hands of Youdi, he now shakes with laughter. This mood, too, passes and he prepares himself for death, contented at last that he has given up everything. Suddenly, Gaber is there. He has an order that Moran is to return instantly. Moran protests that he cannot walk, that he is a sick man, but Gaber does not seem to hear. He repeats that Moran is to go home immediately. Seeing that Moran has not a swig of beer about him, he turns to go. Moran is flabbergasted beyond words. He asks whether Youdi is angry but receives no satisfactory answer. He insists upon knowing what Youdi has said and again does not receive a proper reply. Finally, Gaber moves to go. Moran follows, screaming to know what Youdi has said. Despite his ailments, Moran succeeds in catching up with Gaber. He demands again to know what has been said. Gaber roughly shoves him aside and Moran falls to the ground. Gaber is moved by this. Finally, he is persuaded to talk. It breaks from his lips that the 'chief' has announced that 'Life is a thing of beauty, Gaber, and a joy for ever.' 'Do you think he meant human life?'[339] Moran breathes, beside himself with sheer astonishment, but Gaber is gone. Moran wakes from a moment of nightmare to see that he has been tearing up the grass in fistfuls.

With this incident, Moran's belief in himself and his relation to the world as he sees it receive a crippling blow. So

Youdi is a pompous nonentity. In time of distress Moran is cast aside with an empty platitude. He now knows where he stands at least:

> There are men and there are things, to hell with animals. And with God.[340]

On the way home, a journey that takes all winter, Moran has opportunity now and again despite his agony and despair to consider some rare theological chestnuts. This provides an opening for scathing satire. Coming as it does immediately after Moran's crushing disappointment in Youdi, it underlines once again the psycho-religious nature of the quest. The questions that Moran now poses are recognized by the reader, if not by Moran, as absurd:

> 7.   Does Nature observe the sabbath?

> 11.   What is one to think of the excommunication of vermin in the sixteenth century?

These and other questions concerning theology serve very clearly to show how deluded human beings can be when they seriously concern themselves with such spurious curiosities. Further, they highlight the importance of the questions asked, implicitly or explicitly, within the novel. One of these is the question of sin. Moran is weighed down by a sense of sin, stemming from a sense of inadequacy. Now that he has time to reflect, he considers the matter:

> 13.   Was Youdi's business address still 8 Acacia Square?[341] What if I wrote to him? What if I went to see him? I would explain to him. What would I explain to him? I would crave his forgiveness. Forgiveness for what?[342]

Forgiveness for what? And if Youdi is not inclined to forgive? What then? An avenging God? There is doubt about the question, and because there is doubt, there is chronic insecurity. The Christian belief in sin as it has developed over the centuries is challenged here by Beckett.

Buddhism does not presume to comment upon other religions. There is no authority, therefore, to appeal to but my own in saying that Christianity as we know it in its crystallized form as Church and theology is in one significant respect a perversion of the message of Christ from one of Faith and Love to Sin and Death.[343] Buddhism does not inflate sin to a way of life similar to that of the early Middle Ages in Europe where sin and death were the great sinews of Christian teaching. Furthermore, Buddhism does not thrust sin into the centre of its teaching. Instead, it sees sin as the result of ignorance. It likens wisdom to a candle lit in a cave; as more candles are lit, so the darkness recedes of itself. Our real concern, therefore, should be to give our minds to the task of dispelling the darkness rather than to dwell on how black the darkness is.

What this means in practical terms for one blighted by a sense of sin is illustrated in an anecdote from early Chinese Buddhism. It takes the form of an interview again, this time between Hui-K'e (sometimes Hui-K'o), who lived during AD 487—593, and Seng-ts'an, an earnest monk who threatened to take his life if his 'faults were not cleansed.' At first, Hui-K'e was unmoved by his pupil's protestations, but, seeing that the matter was ripe for dealing with, he asked him to step forward.

> What's the matter with you? he ordered.
> I would that my sins be cleansed, replied the monk.
> Then bring them here that I might be rid of them, said Hui-K'e.
>
> There was a moment's silence while Seng-ts'an considered this.
>
> When I consider, Your Reverence, indeed I cannot find them.
> Then I've done with cleansing them, retorted Hui-K'e.[344]

This is not so facile as it may at first seem. In the first place, the monk had a real problem, one to which, in the circumstances of those far-off times in Zen establishments, he had bent his mind night and day. We can say without exaggeration that he was 'eaten up' with his problem. What he could not see was that his problem, from which he suffered so intensely, was a conceptual one and entirely of his own making. In the same way that Hui-K'e himself had been asked by the Bodhidharma to 'bring his mind' before him and found himself unable to do so, he pulls the carpet from under the feet of Seng-ts'an. Seng-ts'an is said to have understood the meaning then of the master's utterance. His mind was ready for the 'turn about' that Hui-K'e was able to give it, that is, in the direction of *nirvanic* seeing. In short, he saw himself as a mere concept worrying about another concept at second remove. Historical detail does not indicate that he laughed but it is very likely that he did.

Moran, for his part, does not laugh although he is nevertheless relieved. Some of the grosser incrustations of his ego have dropped off with the suffering that he has had to undergo. He passes his hand over his face and remarks on the change that has taken place:

> Physically speaking it seemed to me that I was now becoming unrecognizable. And when I passed my hands over my face, in a characteristic and now more than ever pardonable gesture, the face my hands felt was not my face anymore...[345]

This does not disturb him unduly, however. He has found a truer identity than that of his old self, now that he has become half a Molloy.

> And to tell the truth I not only knew who I was, but I had a sharper and clearer sense of my identity than ever before, in spite of the deep lesions and the wounds with which it was covered.[346]

On the way home, this process of ego-erosion continues. Moran now begins to cast off his clothes, layer by layer (as Murphy had done in the relief that knowledge had brought him), especially the hard collars, which are outward symbols of inflexible egoism. Like Lear, he accepts his humiliation in all weathers. 'So I avoided as far as possible having recourse to proper shelters, made of boughs, preferring the shelter of my faithful umbrella, or of a tree, or of a hedge, or of a bush, or of a ruin.'[347] He has time to think with love of his bees and his hens and feels for their lot. Once at home in the darkness, he finds his bees reduced to an airy ball of wings and legs and can say:

Yes, now I may make an end.[348]

He sells his house and enjoys the passing summer in peace and consolation. 'I have been man long enough, I shall not put up with it anymore. I shall not try anymore. I shall never light this lamp again.'[349] Later he asks: 'Does this mean that I am a freer man now than I was?' He does not know. Certainly we can say that he knows himself better. His disturbed peace on that summer afternoon last year was the beginning of his journey 'backwards,' away from the successes he was to ascribe to his ego in being able to catch Molloy and towards failure and importunity. The inner voice 'telling me things' was becoming comprehensible, but the riddle of identity remains unsolved; he is no longer Moran but not yet Molloy. He is there to realize this, however. Who is there to realize? The dilemma is reflected in the novel's closing words: 'It is midnight. The rain is beating on the windows. It was not midnight. It was not raining.'[350]

9   *Desire for Freedom:* Malone Dies

Beckett began *Malone Dies (Malone meurt)* in the winter of 1947 and completed it in May of the following year. Like *Molloy*, it was written in French. Both novels were published in Paris in 1951 in March and October respectively. Beckett's English translation of *Malone Dies* was first published in New York in 1956 and in London two years later.

The idea of freedom found in Beckett's writing at this time could be interpreted as an autobiographical account of his desire to leave the values of middle-class Protestant Ireland despite his mother's constant wish that he settle down in that country with a regular income and an acknowledged position in society. This, as we can read from Bair's biography, was a continuing problem for Beckett from the time he left Ireland once and for all to settle in Paris. He felt himself quite naturally divided between maternal allegiance and natural inclination. However, as we have seen, the whole Beckettian gamut is about freedom, not in any social or political sense but with respect to inner freedom, the freedom to be, freedom from restricting, binding, interfering self. This, I have suggested, accounts for the attenuation of Beckett's characters and the economy of his dramatic presentation especially.

In the trilogy, there is progressive restriction of locomotor freedom. The inability of Molloy and Moran to walk properly, Malone's restriction to the hospital ward, and finally the Unnamable's incarceration in a jar are means whereby the narrator/character hopes to find more inner freedom. We have said that this elimination of external attribute promotes concentration. There is no attempt to deny this but the

motive perhaps for such a high degree of concentration
may well be an unconscious desire for the freedom we have
just mentioned. For example, Eugene Webb speaks of this
desire as a compulsion in his *Samuel Beckett, A Study of the
Novels*.[351]

> Human beings are in states of constant inner flux,
> but the patterns of flux vary little from person to
> person. All the patterns are repetitious of the same
> human compulsion: the compulsion to explain the
> inexplicable, to impose meaning on the meaning-
> less; the compulsion to be constantly active, in
> mind, in body, or in both and the compulsion to
> try futilely to escape into stasis, mental silence or
> nonbeing.

This futile escape into stasis constitutes the Beckettian
impasse. It is futile because, in effect, it is not a stasis and is,
therefore, unrewarding to the mind seeking it. It is, nevertheless, very important to bear in mind that the desire for
release is, in Buddhist terms and whether recognizable or
not, at the root of all human activity. It is also at the root of
all Beckett's writing and it is this fact among others, which
gives his work a universal character. The veritable tragedy
of his work is that no solution seems possible to the problems he enunciates. It is like the bee in Chinese Buddhist
tradition (*Ch'an*), which flies hither and thither in a room
and always collides with the window, a dilemma, which, for
the bee, must be appalling. Even when the window or part
of its surface is opened, it makes the same mistake and
crashes into it time and again. Sometimes it finds its way
out, more by chance than calculation we suspect, and flies off
into infinite freedom. Much the same is true for human
beings and their feelings of dilemma and restriction; the
freedom for them too is available, but to attain it there must
be a radical change of viewpoint.

Realizing that there seems to be no escape, Malone longs
for death. It will not be long, he informs us, 'perhaps I shall
survive Saint John the Baptist's Day and even the 14th of

July, festival of freedom.' But he doubts it. He could die today if he wished, but there seems no sense in 'rushing things.' He might just as well die quietly, without fuss. Malone is about to die, but he is not sorry to leave life. On the contrary, he is almost cheerful about it, if not vindictively so.

> Let me say before I go further that I forgive nobody. I wish them all an atrocious life and then the fires and ice of hell and in execrable generations to come an honoured name.[352]

This is the key to the rest of the novel. Throughout, there is a calculated indifference to the reader's sensibilities and a disgust with life that expresses itself in careless dismissal of anything that might 'descend' into literature or philosophical speculation. All that is so much 'ballsaching poppycock' despite the fact that it intrudes upon our lives from every quarter.

> I ought to be content with them (i.e. the pastimes of telling stories) instead of launching forth on all this ballsaching poppycock about life and death, if that is what it is all about, and I suppose it is, for nothing was ever about anything else to the best of my recollection.[353]

To pass the time before the onset of death, his 'throes,' Malone proposes to tell himself stories. The artless manner in which he addresses himself to this task is another expression, I contend, of his disgust. His exclamations of 'What tedium!' and 'This is awful!' as he goes along and the self-corrections '. . .no, that won't do,' and '. . .no, I can't do it,' not only effectively ruin the willing suspension of disbelief but, at the same time, project into the narrative a strong element of contempt for story-telling.

> I think I shall be able to tell myself four stories, each on a different theme. One about a man, another about a woman, a third about a thing and finally one about an animal, a bird probably.[354]

The triteness is clearly intentional. It is an echo of 'And if all muck is the same muck, that doesn't matter, it's good to have a change of muck, to move from one heap to another a little further on...'[355] As he goes on, the narrator stops to ask himself from time to time what can possibly be the point of this compulsive word flow.

> But I tell myself so many things, what truth is there in all this babble? I don't know. I simply believe that I can say nothing that is not the same thing but no matter. Yes that's what I like about me, at least one of the things, that I can say, Up the Republic!, for example, or, Sweetheart!, for example without having to wonder if I should not have cut my tongue out.[356]

But he continues writing, nevertheless, until the tension between writing and knowing that writing is a waste of time becomes so unbearable that the narrative breaks out into a fearful savagery, which ends everything. The dilemma is finally resolved by the intrusion of the irrational element, terrible and unforeseen, by a madman with an axe.

The dilemma of writing and yet being averse to writing, seeing that it is an artefact and yet being compelled to write, is the structure and the fabric of the novel. If we accept this, we have then to ask ourselves why writing should be such an object of contempt and why there should be the determination to write nevertheless; only then can we turn to the substance of the narrations themselves.

Is this aversion to writing simply a sympathetic response to Artaud and the battlecry of the French School of literary radicals that 'All literature is pigshit?' Perhaps not, for, strictly speaking, Beckett has never belonged to this coterie although it is possible of course that he may have adopted some of its ideas. Or is it the conscious rejection of old forms, the 'puny exploits' of his *Proust* and their replacement by new and more vital forms of composition? But can we speak of new and vital form in *Malone Dies* with its deliberate false starts, authorial interpolation and intrusion? Is it not more a parody or a deliberate travesty of the novel?

And is it not, therefore, more a destruction than a creation on new lines? Now, we can allow ourselves the point that this act of destruction is in itself a kind of creation as every such act is in a primitive sense. The argument is weak, however.

Form, if it exists at all in this novel, can occupy only a secondary place since a deliberate attempt has been made to rupture the sense of psychological continuity that the word implies. We are on much safer ground if we think in terms of a continued dialogue that intentionally misuses narrative technique to draw attention to the shortcomings of such a technique. There is ample support for this view throughout the novel. Two examples may serve here to demonstrate the point.

> And if I ever stop talking it will be because there is nothing more to be said, even though all has not been said, even though nothing has been said. But let us leave these morbid matters and get on with that of my demise, in two or three days if I remember rightly. Then it will all be over with the Murphys, Merciers, Molloys, Morans and Malones, unless it goes on beyond the grave.[357]

Later, Malone considers movement, even escape from his confinement.

> To be off and away. The dark is against me, in a sense. But I can always try and see if the bed will move. I have only to set the stick against the wall and push. And I can see myself already, if successful, taking a little turn in the room, until it is light enough for me to set forth. At least while thus employed I shall stop telling myself lies. And then, who knows, the physical effort may polish me off, by means of heart failure.[358]

At this point I believe we are given a clue to why 'literature' or the act of writing should be so distasteful. In the first quotation we are again confronted with what is now a familiar Beckettian contradiction. There is nothing more to be said; even though not everything has been said; and yet nothing has been said. The first two are not difficult to conjecture. Because Malone is a compulsive talker, if he ever stops talking there will be quite simply nothing more to say even though, of course, not everything has been said. Not everything can be said because such would be an impossibility. But he adds that nothing has been said (anyway), from which we may be at liberty to infer, in congruence with the blandness of the other two statements, that nothing of *significance* has been said. Whether anything has been said or not is, in any case, a 'morbid matter.' If we should pass to apparently less morbid matters like that of Malone's impending death, then all the talk of Murphy and the rest, including himself, will be over and done with.

What is probably meant here is that nothing new can be said, that, by extension, everything about human life has already been said before, that life repeats itself inexorably, that there is no escape from what Buddhism calls the painful 'round of birth and death.'[359] This view would seem to be supported by Beckett's *The Lost Ones*, surely one of the most depressing pieces of twentieth century literature. The author describes the existence of beings trapped in a huge, rubber cylinder. They are subjected to extremes of heat and cold in a yellow light, one body to one square metre with opportunity to climb ladders to niches high above this soundless world. Many of these stricken denizens climb the ladders in the hope of finding freedom but all the niches are blind. The beings are, therefore, doomed to frustration and psychological torture without the hope of death.

> From time immemorial rumour has it or better still the notion is abroad that there exists a way out. Those who no longer believe so are not immune from believing so again...[360]

The Lost Ones is one of Beckett's most succinct statements on this theme of there being no way out of the dilemma, which life (by inference) presents to human beings. Neither does literature offer a solution to the dilemma, but, as many critics have pointed out in connection with this point,

Beckett succeeds only in saying the same things again and again. As far as Beckett is concerned, these 'same things' are the description of suffering and the absence or failure to find meaning. Moreover, to imagine there could be a meaning is to deceive oneself, to tell oneself lies. We are doomed like the bee forever to crash against the window, but here with not the slightest hope of escape; it is a dream of escape along a road painted on a wall.[361] Because of this, to make judgements and draw conclusions about the quality of existence is, therefore, fallacious. One only makes oneself ridiculous. Beckett himself refrains from so doing.

Malone Dies, like much of Beckett's work, constitutes a dilemma; indeed, one is justified in saying that all his major work represents a series of dilemmas. They are dilemmas that Beckett the man has given serious thought to and perhaps also experienced as a personal crisis.[362] The dilemma that we speak of is made up of, first, the desire to be free from the limiting ego (in the Buddhist sense defined above), which is felt to be a burden, free from the realization that mental stasis is virtually impossible in this situation and, therefore, offers no relief, free from the compunction to act (hypothetical imperative, in this case the urge to write in search of the self); and, second, the sense of failure that this futile desire evokes, the frustration that failure, in turn, instigates, and a longing for death. The net result of these interacting forces is impotence.

The one solution, or seeming solution, death, is not conveniently at hand; one must go on with what is clearly a hopeless, joyless task. It becomes a 'mortal tedium.' What is the nature of this 'tedium'? In a superficial consideration of *Malone Dies*, this tedium concerns the actions of one Sapo and his relationship with his family and of a certain Mr. Lambert, who is a pigsticker by trade, and his family. Halfway through the novel, Sapo's name is changed by the narrator — 'I wonder how I was able to stomach such a name till now.'[363] Like the narrator himself, Sapo becomes the inmate of an institution, which is more clearly a mental hospital than Malone's place of confinement. As Sapo becomes Macmann, so Malone seems to coalesce with Macmann.

While in hospital, Macmann is cared for by Moll, a female attendant. Beckett has another opportunity to treat the reader to one of his notorious grotesqueries on the physical relationship between men and women. Finally, Moll dies and is succeeded by Lemuel. This particular attendant takes a group of patients for a sea outing. He kills four of his charges and goes out to sea with the rest. The novel ends in oblivion.

Up to the last few pages, the author, Malone, has been conspicuous as commentator and, one might say, as master of ceremonies. But despite this conscious supervision by the narrator, both character and meaning are deliberately obscured by the technique of beginning a story, breaking off, interposing a huge dilation in which triviality jostles with a modicum of astute observation. This in its turn is frequently neutralized by the author making some subversive remark such as: 'Very pretty' or 'I venture to hope that there will be no more of that depth'[364] (here referring to a well-formulated philosophical observation), and then resuming the story. This causes the reader to feel disorientated. The technique is meant to stimulate the 'mess' of existence, which is quite unaccountable. We are meant to read the book or the novel from beginning to end, not to gain satisfaction but to experience dislocation and mental unease.

Beckett is careful not to disinterest the reader entirely, however. There are sections which, with every justification, can be described as poetic:

> It helped here, when things were bad, to cling with her fingers to the worn table at which her family would soon be united, waiting for her to serve them, and to feel about her, ready for use, the lifelong pots and pans. She opened the door and looked out. The moon had gone, but the stars were shining. She stood gazing up at them. It was a scene that sometimes solaced her. She went to the well and grasped the chain. The bucket was at the bottom, the windlass locked. So it was. Her fingers strayed along the sinuous links. Her mind was a

press of formless questions, mingling and crumb-
ling limply away.[365]

Although the interruptions of the narrator are disruptive,
they are nevertheless a technical means of sustaining interest.
However, they do not ensure continuity, and Beckett hereby
risks frustrating his reader.

Neither is there any intellectuality. Whenever Malone discovers himself indulging in any form of intellectual activity,
this is soon cut off peremptorily and with unmistakable
relish:

> But it is gone clean out of my head, my little private
> idea. No matter, I have just had another. Perhaps it
> is the same one back again, ideas are so alike,
> when you get to know them.[366]
>
> And in the skull, is it a vacuum? I ask. And if I close
> my eyes...then sometimes my bed is caught up
> into the air and tossed like a straw by the swirling
> eddies and I in it. Fortunately it is not so much an
> affair of eyelids but as it were the soul that must
> be veiled, that soul denied in vain, vigilant,
> anxious, turning in its cage as a lantern, in the
> night without haven or craft or matter or under-
> standing.
> Ah yes, I have my little pastimes and they...
>
> What a misfortune, the pencil must have slipped
> from my fingers.[367]

This attack on intellectuality is everywhere in Beckett's
work. One frequently meets with such sentences as: 'Is
it convex or concave? I always forget. It doesn't matter.'
Or one comes across a misquotation or one that is half-
remembered. An example occurs in Act I of *Waiting for
Godot*. Vladimir musingly says: 'Hope deferred maketh the
something sick, who said that?' It remains unanswered in
the play. Occasionally, Beckett makes a satirical feast of his
opposition to pure intellect as in the interview with Mr.

Nackybal in the novel *Watt*. It is a parody of a viva voce conducted by university dons. It lasts for some fourteen pages.

The most well-known diatribe against intellectuality occurs in Lucky's long speech in *Waiting for Godot*. There is evidence that many of Beckett's tramps and narrators have also at one time been intellectually inclined, that they are well-read. However, virtually in every case where abstract ideas and the benefits of education are referred to, they are minimized or disparaged. Clov's scornful reply to Hamm's discomforting suspicion that the two might perhaps be beginning to 'mean something' in *Endgame* is a particularly clear example of this attitude. One asks why. Beckett perhaps realizes that the intellect, despite its good reputation, is, in the first place, only a part of the individual although it tends to be considered on its own merits and apart from the rest of the personality; and in the second place, it is apparently incapable of answering the kind of questions that Beckett exposes in his work. For those reasons, the intellect is of small importance and the acknowledgement accorded it a fit subject for ridicule.

That the intellect is only a part of the body-mind mechanism and in some situations not a very effective faculty for solving problems in certain dilemmas is easily illustrated. Were one to place an ordinary builder's plank on the ground and ask someone to walk along its length, he or she would not have the slightest difficulty in doing so. However, if this same plank were placed between two skyscrapers, the candidate would almost certainly refuse or declare himself quite incapable of the same action. No amount of practical information nor insistence on the illogicality of the candidate's reaction would have the slightest effect despite the fact that the information given is demonstrably true. Moreover, the person involved in such a venture knows that the information given is true. He is without doubt quite convinced that, essentially, the conditions for traversing the plank are the same. However, his intellectual faculty is no match against his instinct for self-preservation.

Consider another, less spectacular example, one which plays a part in our lives practically every day. It is a well-recognized fact that the process of learning is not only a conscious one but, perhaps much more importantly, an unconscious phenomenon. When we learn something hitherto quite unfamiliar, such as algebra or to play the violin, we use our mind under the auspices of the will. It frequently happens that we understand a point shown to us by our teacher (i.e. intellectually) but that we are unable to assimilate it or put it into practice. We then say that time is required for the new knowledge to 'sink in.' This 'sinking in' operation is carried out for us by what Zen Buddhism designates as the 'Unconscious.' It is distinct, as we shall see later, from psychology's definition of the word. Here we wish only to point out that the process of complete understanding takes place in another 'part' of the mind and is not directly under the control of the volition.[368] These 'instincts' as we choose to call them, this other part of the personality of the individual, is the area of the mind that most interests Beckett. It is also the object of Buddhist attention. The intellect is regarded as a useful tool but irrelevant to solving the problems, which, in English, we designate as the 'passions.'

Indeed, it is only in the last hundred years or so in the West that we have come to consider the mind scientifically at all. Even now, we have no satisfactory word corresponding to the Sanskrit *citta*. This refers to the processes of thought association plus the respective emotions of hate, desire and lust. We have not yet owned that these are the basic drives of the human animal. The word 'animal' is used advisedly and is not a term of derogation. Buddhism, without falling into the trap of hating, does not acknowledge us as finally human until we have succeeded in putting out the ego-centred fires of passion within us. Once the smoke of these has cleared, then we have our true humanity. As we have pointed out elsewhere, we need no additional proof of our 'animality' than our own social and political history or of our present condition than an average daily newspaper will supply.

We will not be honest with ourselves and admit that these three forces (hate, desire and lust) are the mainsprings of our human nature in its undeveloped form. The reason for this, in Buddhist terms, is that the passions or the Sanskrit 'mind-stuff' bring a degree of satisfaction, for a moment distracting us from what Beckett has called the 'boredom of living,'[369] or, more particularly for the Buddhist, the demands and disappointments of existence. Like children, once delighted, we crave for more. This perhaps is quite natural, but just as craving is not good for children, neither is it good for us. Sensation-seeking leads to attachment and attachment to ignorant enslavement. This way again also leads into a trap.

We would be free, however. This, as we have seen, is the desire and sustaining force behind Beckett's work. He 'would have done with it all' as soon as possible. Then indeed it will all be over with these Murphys, Merciers, Molloys, Morans and Malones and their accounts of what Beckett calls in sympathy their 'miserable existences,' but how? The exit from this 'issueless misery' is embodied in putting a stop to thought and implies ending both the natural associative processes of our everyday minds and the willed act of thinking, that is, intellection. In so doing, the mind and its passions are brought under control. This, however, has to be understood clearly. It is not an attempt to control by violence since the mind is not amenable to such a form of control. Violence implies willed assertion and is, therefore, egoistic. Neither can one subdue the passions with passion as many Christian saints have tried to do and which the Buddha himself attempted in the period of his experimentation with the meditative techniques of the Brahmins in the time prior to his great Enlightenment. He referred later to these as 'vain and unprofitable.' However 'holy' the passion, it remains passion. Attempts to mould the mind in this way are not only unsuccessful from the practical point of view but also warp the outlook of the possessor and thereby increase his suffering.

The means conceived by the Buddha's followers in order to obtain relief from the dilemma of being human was one by which the mind's activity is simply cut off by an act of inward looking, one of observation of the mind's content and movement. After a time, which may be months or even years of practice, the mind, like the fire of the comparison, undergoes something like a death, a 'going out'; its associative machinery comes to a halt and in the silence, in which there is Zen's 'no thing existing' (i.e. no concept of any kind), the One Mind (Sanskrit, *Prajna*) is apprehended.

Hui-Neng (638–713), one of the great patriarchs of Chinese Ch'an Buddhism, puts it thus:

> Turning thoughts on Self (i.e. inward-looking, concentrating on that which is before a thought arises) they are kept away from environing objects (within and without); thoughts are not raised on the environing objects.
>
> To raise thoughts towards (i.e. to think about them) and on these thoughts to cherish false views, this is the source of worries and imagination (fear and apprehension).
>
> What is *wu nien* (Chinese, lit. 'no mind', no-thought-ness)? Seeing all things and yet to keep your mind free from stain and attachment, this is 'no-thought-ness'.
>
> He who understands the idea of 'no-thought-ness' has a perfect thoroughfare through the world of multiplicities...attains the stage of Buddhahood'[370]

This, then, is the way out that Beckett's work very occasionally intimates but never explores. He is mainly concerned with the state of mind which is prior to the 'no-thought-ness' mentioned above. In *Malone Dies*, there is a marked shift from the outer quests of Molloy and Moran to the static, inner quest of old Malone. The novel is a record of his associative thought processes and those that are to be found in the extension of the thought processes, in the fictions that he invents for himself. The attempt to write fiction also provides a thread running through the novel, from which he digresses and to which he returns. In *The Unnamable,* even the thread disappears. The camera of Beckett's attention moves forward once again for a close-up on the associative process.

What is the nature of this associative process, this *'citta'*? Lord Acton once described memory as a place where we keep both our costliest treasures and our old shoes. So it is with our minds. It is like the candle of Hindu scripture that burns and sputters fitfully because of the impurities of the wax or because the wind drives the flame now one way and now the other. Zen Buddhism refers to the mind as a monkey and the word 'monkey-mindedness' is frequently to be found in its literature. It means that our minds, like the antics of a monkey, are always 'on the go.' They flit from one thing to another, fiddle with this and toy with that from the moment we are born until we die.

We must remember that the mind can be dangerously powerful too, especially when passion runs strong. For this reason, it is also likened to an ox, which must be tamed. It is a complex of different mental states, compounded of memories, perceptions, feelings and tendencies, both conscious and unconscious. Sometimes one aspect dominates, sometimes another, but there is always movement or seeking. It is this, primarily, that Beckett portrays in *Malone Dies* and *The Unnamable* in particular, the latter being a development of the former in this direction. Memory is sometimes the memory of facts, for example, when the narrator remembers by association the scenes painted by Caspar David Friedrich on looking out of the window at the tempest-torn sky, or when he recalls the famous ceilings in Würzburg, or that the word 'May' is derived from 'Maia' (*Maya* in Buddhism) and which he renders as 'hell.' Sometimes memory appears as the memories of childhood when, lying awake, the young Beckett listened to the dogs barking in the night or when by day he watched the hawk, now as Sapo . . .

> He would stand rapt, gazing at the long pernings, the quivering poise, the wings lifted for the plummet drop, the wild reascent, fascinated by such extremes of need, of patience and solitude.[371]

or he remembers the Dublin cabs of his youth:

> And you see the cabman too, all alone on his box
> ten feet from the ground, his knees covered at all
> seasons and in all weather with a kind of rug as a
> rule originally brown, the same precisely which he
> has just snatched from the rump of his horse.
> Furious and livid perhaps from want of passen-
> gers, the least fare seems to excite him to frenzy.[372]

Sometimes as something half-forgotten:

> I don't like those gull's eyes. They remind me of an
> old shipwreck. I forget which.[373]

which immediately leads to unconscious association and
perception:

> I know it is a small thing. But I am easily frightened
> now. I know those little phrases that seem so
> innocuous and, once you let them in, pollute the
> whole of speech. *Nothing is more real than nothing.*
> They rise up out of the pit and know no rest until
> they drag you down into its dark. But I am on my
> guard now.[374]

All the time there is the need to keep moving towards a
goal of some sort, but which is, as we have seen, simply the
desire for fulfilment. This becomes more evident as the book
draws to a close:

> We are getting on. On. On.

> A Stream at long intervals bestrid — but to hell
> with all this fucking scenery.[375]

Of feeling there is a great deal. The most prominent emotion
is restlessness and dissatisfaction:

> There is no use in indicting words, they are no
> shoddier than what they peddle. After the fiasco,
> the solace, the repose, I began again, to try and live,
> cause to live, be another, in myself, in another.
> How false all this is. No time now to explain.[376]

There is also pity, however, not for men so much as for animals. Lambert the 'bleeder and disjointer of pigs and greatly sought after,' receives unsympathetic treatment. He kills his pig on Christmas Eve, 'indignantly but without haste, upbraiding it the while for its ingratitude, at the top of his voice.'[377] There is a quiet aspersion cast in the direction of modern, inhuman pig-breeding inherent in Lambert's dread that exercise will thin the animal. There is the sympathy the narrator shows for hens that strut the yard and the kitchen of the Lambert property and for their favourite rabbit, Whitey, who, Lambert one day unfeelingly announces, must die. There is the poor donkey in the slaughter-house where Lambert buys his beasts. All this, with its overtones of death and mortality, occupies five pages.

There is disgust with the sexual act in the reference to the almost certain incestuous relationship between Lambert and his daughter and between Sapo and his sister. There is disgust or dissatisfaction with the body and its functions. Malone himself is old and ailing; neither the Saposcats nor the Lamberts are appealing physically; Moll is thoroughly repulsive. The body's decay and its susceptibility to disease is alluded to on serveral occasions, perhaps reaching its high point in the description of Moll's terminal illness, a theme that appears from time to time in Beckett's work from the Belacqua Shuah stories onwards.

Structurally, Beckett's *Malone Dies* is little more than a record of Malone's thoughts in commentary and narration, what we have chosen to designate as '*citta*,' recorded over a certain period of time. Its literary value lies in the insights this particular mind-flow exhibits from time to time, but, above all, in the fact that Beckett has represented the workings of the mind in such a way as to make us aware of its impotence as an instrument towards fulfilment. It seeks and seeks, trying to find its true identity among concepts. This, as we have seen, is impossible. To do so is to be like the denizens of the cylinder in *The Lost Ones*, to remain forever betrayed. Because the mind cannot be transcended in this manner, Beckett's assay is an assault on the impossible.

Live and invent. (i.e. find new methods of attack) I have tried. Invent. It is not the word. (Because it involves not only the resources of the intellect, but the spirit as well). Neither is live. (Because what kind of life is it that is spent in untiring search after something which, logically, must exist, but which is, or appears to be non-existent.) No matter. I have tried. While within me the wild beast of earnestness has padded up and down, roaring, ravening, rending.[378]

10 *The Inward Search:* The Unnamable

The Unnamable (L'Innommable), the last novel of what has come to be known as the 'trilogy,' took approximately nine months to write. Like the novels that precede it, it is characterized by first-person commentary, running to one hundred and twenty-five pages. This fact alone has led some critics to describe it as a 'bleak monograph' and a 'grey monotony' and yet others as something approaching 'unreadability,' if we may coin such a word. Properly understood, it is none of these things. As paragraphs go, it is, admittedly, somewhat long. However, this does not mean that the work should be regarded as lacking all invention, or, as has sometimes been suggested, as being some sort of collapse of the literary imagination.

The first mistake the reader can make in approaching *The Unnamable*, is to find the novel wanting in the conventions of traditional form. The second is to assume that the form that the novel in this case has taken is somehow an error of taste. On the contrary, the form, this extenuated paragraph, is quite deliberate and perhaps the only form that could sincerely express the author's viewpoint. Before we consider this viewpoint, let us first look at the characteristics of the material under consideration.

In the first place, the novel is not built upon the interplay of human activity. There are no characters worthy of the denomination 'character' as this is usually understood with respect to a novel. Except for Marguerite (once confused within the space of two pages with a 'Madeleine'), there are no palpable characters. Marguerite is barely described except in that she seems to tend to the narrator's needs out of pecuniary interest and is there more to lend a little credibility to *The Unnamable* perhaps than for any other reason. This is a one-man novel. But the 'man' is only a man's mind. The body is devoid both of limb and feature. The narrator refers to himself as 'a big talking ball,' a wedgeshaped, egg-like creature, whose eyes are 'streaming sockets'

> Stuck like a sheaf of flowers in a deep jar, its neck flush with my mouth, on the side of a quiet street near the shambles...at rest at last[379]

Neither is there a recognizable 'plot' in the sense we have briefly circumscribed on several occasions above. Such a writing form is now hardly to be expected. Here the pretence to any structure has been abandoned; there is not even the suggestion of a quest, for example. Central to everything is the author's voice.

Are we, in view of all this, justified in regarding *The Unnamable* more as a monologue than as a novel? Perhaps, but on the other hand one finds vigorous opponency between the narrator and an unidentified 'they' even although the novel does not correspond with the expected norms of a piece of 'fictitious prose narrative of sufficient length to fill one or more volumes, portraying characters and actions representative of real life in continuous plot.'[380] Some critics have maintained that the 'they' are the Mahoods and the Watts, Merciers, Molloys and Malones, of whom the author is so glad to be rid:

> All these Murphys, Molloys and Malones do not fool me. They have made me waste my time, suffer for nothing, speak of them when, in order to stop speaking, I should have spoken of me and me alone...Let them be gone now, them and all the others, those I have used and those I have not used...[381]

Although this is frequently the case, it is not consistently so.

At one point in the novel, the narrator recalls the incident of killing a family, presumably his own since he refers to his

mother and father, in an act of particularly savage mutila-
tion. These, too, are the 'they' to whom he is set against
throughout the narrative. Although this 'they' has no physical tangibility and although it does not concretely utter an
opinion, it is nevertheless a part of the novel similar to the
unseen wires that enliven the puppet. It would seem that
this 'they' has had its impact on the narrator in the past and
has been responsible for forming his concepts, which he
now entirely and contemptuously rejects. The juxtaposition
of the 'they' with its implied viewpoint is vital to the
coherence of the novel. Beckett rejects all its opinions and
beliefs and, thereby, substantiates his own position.

> They also gave me the low-down on God. They
> told me I depended on him, in the last analysis.
> They had it on the reliable authority of his agents
> at Bally I forget what, this being the place, accord-
> ing to them, where the inestimable gift of life had
> been rammed down my gullet.[382]

Neither the narrator's tacit conviction nor his contempt at
such times can be missed:

> Some of this rubbish has come in handy on occa-
> sions, I don't deny it. . . Low types they must have
> been, their pockets full of poison and antidote. . . [383]

The narrator has been the subject of its misinformation. He
has subsequently discovered that they were wrong, wrong
and irresponsible. It is a case of the blind leading the blind
and shall they not both fall into a ditch?

> What can you expect, they don't know who they
> are either, no, nor where they are nor what they're
> doing, nor why everything is going so badly, so
> abominably badly. . . So, they build up hypotheses
> that collapse on top of one another. It's human, a
> lobster couldn't do it.[384]

There is, therefore, a dialogue of sorts, in which the implied
values of the other, the 'they,' are denied. This, by further
implication, brings forth issues of serious import, which we
shall turn to shortly.

We have said that the novel has no structure in a recognizable traditional sense. Nevertheless, there are detectable themes. The novel opens with the words:

> Where now? Who now? Unquestioning. I, say I.
> Unbelieving. Questions, hypotheses, call them that.
> Keep going, going on, call that going, call that
> on.[385]

These words and the eleven pages that follow constitute what might loosely be called an 'exegesis.' The narrator questions himself on how to proceed:

> By aporia pure and simple? Or by affirmations
> and negations invalidated as uttered, sooner or
> later.[386]

He questions his motives for beginning, wondering in one place whether it would not be better not to begin at all, to remain silent, for:

> Can it be that I am the prey of a genuine preoccu-
> pation, of a need to know as one might say?[387]

At the same time he considers his position. He is in some kind of limbo apparently. At first, orientation is difficult —

> Did I wait somewhere for this place to be ready to
> receive me? Or did it wait for me to come and
> people it?
>
> Are there other places set aside for us and this one
> where I am with Malone, merely their narthex?[388]

There is the curious phenomenon of Malone passing and repassing with the punctuality of 'clockwork' before the narrator's eyes. Malone neither speaks nor shows any inclination to change his course. Many critics have assumed from this that the narrator throughout *Molloy*, *Moran* and *Malone Dies* is now dead and speaks from purgatory. It is possible but it is an assumption. One might well assume this from Beckett's interest in Dante, in his concern with Belacqua, who lazes under the rock before 'going up' to heaven. One could also assume this from the lack of all other geographical detail and persona, from the frequent reference to darkness, from the Unnamable's coffin-like immobilization. However, all this is difficult to reconcile with the jar and a Parisian street near the shambles and the corporate Marguerite, who comes every so often to empty his slops, and the people that use the restaurant opposite. The reference now and again to 'them' as 'up there in their world' would support the assumption that the narrator is in purgatory, but this is the only textual evidence we have for such an assumption. There is also some internal justification in that Beckett is now exploring the post-mortem experience suggested in the following:

> Then it will all be over with these Murphys, etc
> ...unless it goes beyond the grave.[389]

The temptation is great to think that the novel is set in purgatory. We are on firmer ground, though, if we consider the Unnamable's position to be an extreme expression of that tendency towards immobilization and attenuation that we can observe in the other novels and that here it has reached a final stage. In a situation of almost total atrophy, the reader is at liberty to hear the voice much more distinctly, undistracted by external circumstance. This is also borne out textually. The author speaks of scattering all that is extraneous to the winds:

> I shall have company. In the beginning. A few puppets. Then I'll scatter them to the winds, if I can. I flatter myself it will not take me long to scatter them, whenever I choose, to the winds...[390]

As part of the vestigial structure alluded to above, the novel has recognizable points of departure where there is a greater concentration on the theme. For example, after the approximately eleven-page 'exposition' referred to a moment ago, there follows what we might regard as a second section. It is true that one section passes without any kind of interruption into the other, but the second section is nevertheless identifiable. It can be recognized by its sudden, intense focus upon the subject of the narration. It gathers up the strands of disquisition, which have gone before, and leads them to a formal conclusion. Suddenly, there is a sense of orientation, which has been sought in the preceding pages:

> Nothing then but me, of which I know nothing, except that I have never uttered, and this black, of which I know nothing either, except that it is black, and empty. That then, is what, since I have to speak, I shall speak of, until I need speak no more. And Basil and his gang? Inexistent, invented to explain I forget what. Ah yes, all lies, God and man, nature and the light of day, the heart's outpourings and the means of understanding, all invented, basely, by me alone, with the help of no one, since there is no one, to put me off the hour when I must speak of me. There will be no more about them.[391]

It is one of the few 'tonic chords' in what Robin Lee, using a musical analogy in describing Beckett's work, calls writing that 'offers only a series of dominants.'[392] What does it mean? I suggest it means that Beckett has taken the one last step towards understanding the true self. Molloy and Moran go off in quest of themselves; Malone lies writing in bed and communes with himself; and finally, the Unnamable, quite unable to do anything else but think, turns the light of his questioning upon himself. His pseudo-selves, Basil and his gang, the Molloys and Merciers, Watts and Morans have been given up. What is left? There is nothing left that he can recognize but a blackness and an emptiness of which he knows nothing but which is himself. He is convinced of its ultimate reality because he says that everything else is lies. It is 'lies' because, as we have already shown above, all other matters are concepts and as such can only be projections of a mind. Here is the ultimate reality behind the concepts. The Unnamable describes his invention as base because it is a deception. It is a deliberate putting off of the 'evil' day when he must face himself, essentially cowardly, but typically human.

This is the stage at which the Zen master, ever on the lookout for such symptoms, comes to the aid of the struggling student. His search has brought him to the point where he has his back against the wall. This is the point where the master will deliver his *coup de grâce* of deliverance. He has to be quick to see the opportunity and also be nimble-minded because it is his responsibility to know precisely when to administer the slap or the right admonition, which will help the student to reach an immediate understanding of himself. It is possible, and very likely, that when the student has come this far, especially in the case where he has applied only his intellect to the problem and not his entire being, that he will retreat from this apparent spiritual cul-de-sac and seek solace among the familiarities of conceptual thinking. If he has worked alone up to this point, he can hardly be blamed for such a withdrawal because he will lack moral support to take the last step into the dimension that we have already discussed and that is called 'satori' in Buddhism. This, incidentally, is particularly true in those cases where, in western countries, the individual comes to this state and has no assurance that there *is* in fact a way out. He has neither background nor method, master nor reassurance. Having come so far, he sidesteps the issue in anxious trepidation.

The student familiar with Buddhist tradition will usually go on, not, however, without some fear and often under the influence of the strangest presentiments. Frequently, his passage towards Enlightenment is accompanied by peculiar physical sensations.[393] In his personal account in the Japanese *Orategama* of his experiences during this stage, Hakuin (1683–1768) says:

> When I was twenty-four years old I stayed at the Yegan monastery of Echigo. Here I assiduously applied myself to the *koan* Joshu's *Mu.*[394] I did not sleep days and nights, forgot both eating and laying down, when quite abruptly a great mental fixation (Japanese, *tai-i*) took place. I felt as if freezing in an ice-field extending thousands of miles, and within myself there was a sense of utmost

transparency. There was no going forward, no slipping backward; I was like an idiot, like an imbecile and there was nothing but Joshu's *Mu*. Though I attended lectures by the master, they sounded like a discussion going on somewhere in a distant hall...Sometimes my sensation was that of one flying in the air. Several days passed in this state, when one evening a temple bell was struck, which upset the whole thing. It was like smashing an ice-basin, or pulling down a house made of jade...Whatever doubts or indecisions I had before were completely dissolved like a piece of thawing ice. I called out loudly: How wondrous, how wondrous! There is no birth and death from which one has to escape, nor is there any supreme knowledge (Bodhi) after which one has to strive.[395]

To get the student into this state, which is the antecedent to Enlightenment, is the object and *raison d'être* of Zen. The *koan* is one such means (see note 194). Kao-feng Yuan-miao (1238–1295) has left posterity an account of its function:

The *koan* I ordinarily give to my pupils is: 'All things return to the One; where does the one return?' (in other words, what is the nature of the Ultimate, or What is the Ground of Being? or Who is God or What am I? or, not to be carried away by conceptual abstraction, we could put it into modern, colloquial terms: 'Is there really anything in this God-business?') I make them search after this. To search after it means to awaken a great enquiring spirit for the ultimate meaning of the *koan*. The multitudinous of things is reducible to the One, but where does this One finally return to? I say to them: Make this enquiry with all the strength that lies in your personality, giving yourself no time to relax in this effort. In whatever physical position you are, and in whatever business you are employed, never pass your time idly. Where does this One finally return? Try to get a

definite answer to this query. Do not give yourself
up to a state of doing nothing; do not exercise your
fantastic imagination, but try to bring about a state
of perfect identification by pressing your spirit of
enquiry forward, steadily and uninterruptedly.
You will then be like a person who is critically ill,
having no appetite for what you eat or drink.
Again, you will be like an idiot, with no knowledge of what is what. When your searching spirit
comes to this stage, the time has come for your
mental flower to burst out.[396]

Beckett's work is the incorporation of a spiritual journey.
The Unnamable is an account of the later stages of the *idée
fixe*, which is centred on the nature of 'I' and which is also
the preoccupation of students of Zen. The title itself at once
reveals the nature of the absorption of the rest of the novel.
In dismissing all the concepts current on God and His
Nature suggested by the dubious accounts disseminated by
the 'they,' Beckett suggests that the nature of 'I' is ineffable.
In short, he is concerned with that for which there is no
name unless one reduces it to a concept. It cannot be
spoken.

The book, therefore, begins with the basic questions
of identity as understood in the arguments we have put
forward above.

I, say I. Unbelieving. Questions, hypotheses.

In other words, the I-perceiving subject sees itself as an 'I.'
As we have shown, however, this cannot be accepted since
it is purely imaginary. Beckett cannot believe in it and
therefore the search continues. When one then asks about
the true nature of oneself, there is no reply on the intellectual,
ordinary mind-level and so one substitutes with hypotheses.
For Beckett, the old God of the Hebrews is defunct, unable
to help in what for him is the greatest of questions: What
am I?

I. Who might that be? The galley-man bound for
the Pillars of Hercules, who drops his sweep under

cover of night and crawls between the thwarts,
towards the rising sun, unseen by the guard, praying for storm. Except that I've stopped praying for
anything. No, no. I'm still a suppliant. I'll get over
it, between now and the last voyage, on this leaden
sea. It's like the other madness, the mad wish to
know, to remember one's transgressions. I won't
be caught at that again. I'll leave it to this year's
damned.[397]

A connection between common existence and the 'non-
existent' One Mind (i.e. not belonging to the realm of
samsara or to the existent world qualified and registered by
our senses) appears a few lines before and also in this
passage. It is clear that the 'they' are Beckett's pseudo-selves,
'Malone & Co.,' the vice-existers of his own imagining, the
superficial, fanciful figments of his own conceiving mind
and, moreover, recognized as such. Here, he hears his
'voices' again. These again are deceptive in that they are not
reliable carriers of information but also, probably, the phan-
toms of his own imagination:

> Faint calls, at long intervals. Hear me! Be yourself
> again! Someone has therefore something to say to
> me. But never the least news concerning me, (i.e.
> the real me) and beyond the insinuation that I am
> not in a condition to receive any, since I am not
> there, which I knew already. I have naturally re-
> marked, in a moment of exceptional receptivity,
> that these exhortations are conveyed to me by the
> same channel as that used by Malone & Co. for
> their transports. That's suspicious, or rather would
> be if I still hoped to obtain, from these revelations
> to come, some truth of more values than those I
> have been plastered with ever since they took it
> into their heads I had better exist.[398]

I-as-object does not exist and cannot exist except as our own
conception; this, too, is a figment of the imagination. Knowing this and rejecting this, who is it that knows and rejects?

Religion appears to offer no solution to the dilemma. Beckett spends a page and a half in examining the question. Although he does not specifically refer to God, the Hebrew and Christian God, it is clear from several broad hints that he is exploring this area. Now and again, he uses material from the Old and New Testament. In this instance he makes use of a reference to The Good Samaritan: 'They clothed me and gave me money' and to 'Moran's boss, I forget his name...':

> My master then, assuming he is solitary, in my image, wishes me well, poor devil, wishes me good, and if he does not seem to do very much in order not to be disappointed it is because there is not very much to be done, or better still, because there is nothing to be done, otherwise he would have done it, my great and good master, that must be it, long ago, poor devil.[399]

This, then, would be sufficient grounds for rejecting God. If he is omnipotent, he would have done something already about the dilemma Beckett (the Unnamable) finds himself in. The tone is patronizing and resigned − or at least it appears so. But this is merely a mask. The author affects that the whole thing is so boring that it is not worth serious consideration. The matter is clear; one can kill a little time by considering one or two 'suppositions':

> Another supposition, he (God) has taken the necessary steps, his will is done so far as I am concerned (for he may have other protégés) and all is well without me knowing it. Cases one and two. I'll consider the former first, if I can. Then I'll admire the latter, if my eyes are still open. ... There he is then, the unfortunate brute, quite miserable because of me, for whom there is nothing to be done, and he is so anxious to help, so used to giving orders and to being obeyed. There he is, ever since I came into the world, possibly at his

instigation, I wouldn't put it past him, command-
ing me to be well, you know, in every way, no
complaints at all, with as much success as if he
were shouting at a lump of inanimate matter...
What he wants is my good, I know that, at least I
say it, in the hope of bringing him round to a more
reasonable frame of mind assuming he exists and,
existing, hears me. In a word, let him enlighten me,
that's all I ask, so that I may at least have the
satisfaction of knowing in what sense I leave to be
desired.[400]

This is the dilemma. If only this God would *do* something.
One rejects Him only to find that He is on every hand; one
attempts to communicate with Him only to find that He is
incommunicable, apparently deaf and uncaring. The whole
thing smacks of senselessness. This God in His infinite
wisdom hath created a creature to resent His yoke. It is this
innate dilemma that supplies the energy to go on seeking.
The long paragraph that constitutes this novel is a form that
reflects this relentlessness, an uninterrupted determination
to bring the whole intractable business forward into the
light and to reveal it for what it is. Like the Hound of
Heaven Beckett goes on, half fearing that the affair is a
senseless waste of time, half being sure that the disappointments in God in the past are evidence enough of His
impassivity. His intention is blighted by doubt:

Keep going, going on, call that going, call that
on.[401]

One must continue the search as best one can. Is one getting
nearer? Is it a search that will find an end? And having
realized through intellect and experience that there must be
that which is unspeakable behind that which is (i.e.
phenomena), *how* is one to go on?

As we have seen, 'going on' in the spiritual sense would
mean being silent; words are the expression of concepts and
concepts are necessarily opposed to that which is unnamable. On the other hand, simply remaining silent is no

answer either and may be a sign of ignorance. In the early days of Chinese Buddhism, the monks in the Zen monasteries often retreated into silence in order to avoid saying the wrong thing and at the same time, of course, in order to escape the slaps and blows that the master might feel requisite to the occasion.[402] A good master would recognize this form of cowardice immediately. Yun-men, (Japanese, *Ummon*, d. AD 949) was one of many who used to deal with this problem by holding up his staff and demanding of his monks:

> What is this? If you say it is a staff, you go straight
> to hell, but if it is not a staff, then what is it?

Sometimes, as in the case of the Zen master Pi-mo, (Japanese, *Hima*), he would be approached respectfully by a monk. As the monk was bowing, the master would take a forked stick and catch him by the neck and press him slowly to the floor, much as an old-time schoolmaster collared erring pupils and, while demonstrating his physical superiority, subjected the scholar to an admonition. Here, the master, in forcing the monk to the ground would ask: 'What devil taught you to be a homeless monk, eh? What devil taught you to go a-begging (i.e. for alms, as was the custom for Buddhist monks in those days). Whether you can say something or not (i.e. whatever you say) you die under my stick.' Such an encounter should not be understood as some kind of malicious whim on the part of the master as in the case of the schoolmaster extracting a 'Yessir! yessir!' from a shrieking schoolboy taken by the ear. It was not an occasion such as that for half laughter, half pain. It was a deadly warning. The master certainly had no intention of injuring his monk. The 'You shall die under my forked stick' is not meant to be taken literally. The monk's mind, however, was brought to a sharp focus on such an occasion. His mind was suddenly cleared of all the associative 'clutter' with which it is usually filled. This was especially the case with a novice or a young monk. The experience was usually quite frightening. Sometimes it resulted in the experience of *satori* or awakening. To 'say something' would be to give expression to a concept and invite the pronouncement of 'death.' In other words, to speak is to go in entirely the wrong direction. To say nothing might be a trifle better but is still not the solution and, therefore, the monk is under 'sentence' anyway.

Similarly, to call Ummon's staff a 'stick' or a 'staff' is to conceptualize, to give a word to a thing and be content. There is no mystery about it; one remains in the world of *samsara*, in a world of purely relative values. For a monk who is aspiring to non-relative knowledge in a Buddhist community to remain content with such a view, existing, that is, at the expense of others, is plainly a betrayal of confidence. This is why Ummon says that he will 'go straight to hell.' On the other hand, what else can the monk say? Clearly, one cannot deny the fact that the staff is a staff, that is, what one sees in front of one's eyes: to deny this is manifestly to lie or to deceive oneself. What Ummon wants to hear is an utterance from his monks that comes from an understanding of the nature of the non-conceptual One Mind, the Unnamable.

Beckett does not bring us to an understanding of the nature of our true self, but he does apprehend the nature of the dilemma Ummon's monks found themselves in. His speaking, that is, his novel, is described as 'this futile discourse which is not credited to me and brings me not a syllable nearer silence.'[403] It is in a sense 'futile' because it will not bring him nearer to the understanding to which we have been alluding. However, from the point of view of a work of art, we can see that the discourse has value for the reader when properly understood because it is an exposure. It demonstrates that 'thinking' cannot bring one a syllable nearer the silence of the Unnamable and, by implication, that such as the Unnamable exists.

Realizing this, Beckett often catches himself being carried away by his thoughts. He stops himself with an abrupt reconsideration such as in the following:

> I mean while floundering through a ponderous
> chronicle of moribunds in their courses, moving,

clashing, writhing or fallen in short-lived swoons, with how much more reason should I not hear it (referring here to music) now, when supposedly I am burdened with myself alone. But this is thinking again. And I see myself slipping, though not yet at the last extremity, towards the resorts of fable. Would it not be better if I were simply to keep on saying babababa for example, while waiting to ascertain the true function of this venerable organ? Enough questions, enough reasoning.[404]

Or:

Deplorable mania, when something happens, to enquire what.

Or:

No, I must not try to think, simply utter.[405]

There are frequent allusions to the sense of going on and to whether there is any point attached to this activity:

So I have no cause for anxiety. And yet I am anxious. So I am not heading for disaster, I am not heading anywhere, my adventures are over, my say said, I call that my adventures. And yet I feel not. And indeed I greatly fear...[406]

I hope this preamble will soon come to an end and the statement begin that will dispose me. Unfortunately I am afraid, as always, of going on.[407]

Thought is impossible as a solution: 'Dear incomprehension, it's thanks to you I'll be myself, in the end. Nothing will remain of all the lies they have glutted me with.' This, Zen would conclude, is the gateway to wisdom. It is the first step to the realization that we are erring. It is a vital step for 'all our long vain life long. Who is not spared by the mad need to speak, to think, to know where one is, where one was, during the wild dream, up above, under the skies...'[408]

In all this, of course, there is room for the reader to conclude that perhaps this talk of identity in its Buddhistic sense is a little far-fetched, that it is all very well as an interesting perspective on Beckett's work with, possibly, some truth, that, Beckett's *œuvre* is so complex and so packed with innuendo that, like the Bible, we can take from it whatever interpretation we will and leave the rest. We can argue that the term 'The Unnamable' refers only to the being in the jar. It is neither man nor animal, nor anything to which we can give a name. In other words, we can dismiss any other associations that the word might have. In so doing, however, we still have to ask ourselves why Beckett should choose such a medium and why he is disposed to concentrate on the thought processes that issue from this creature of his imagination. In short, why the reduction?

We can maintain that the novel is an extravagant pot-pourri, a colourful pastiche, which need not necessarily have the meanings we have attributed to it. Here we may feel safe under the authoritative pronouncement of the author himself with regard to his work: 'It means what it says.' In this case it would be little more than a literary experiment. We should probably be obliged to ask whether, in judging it at this level, it is a successful experiment and what the intent of such an experiment might be. In these terms, could we say, for example that the book has a universal appeal? We would have to be scrupulously honest in the matter of such riddles as the following:

> I am on my way, words bellying out my sails, am also that unthinkable ancestor of whom nothing can be said. But perhaps I shall speak of him some day, and of the impenetrable age when I was he, some day when they fall silent, convinced at last that I shall never get born, having failed to be conceived . . . Yes, perhaps I shall speak of him, for an instant, like the echo that mocks, before being restored to him, the one they could not part me from.[409]

Even contextually, that is to say, taken as an integral part of that preceding and succeeding this passage, it is extremely

difficult to rationalize. Moreover, could we with impunity
conveniently ignore all the references to God and religious
tradition, both directly expressed or inferred, or in the
rhythmic suggestion of the lines and the snippets from
hymnal and liturgy?

> ...the soul being notoriously immune from
> deterioration and dismemberment...[410]

> adeste, adeste, all ye living bastards[411]

> ...the daily round the common task...[412]

> The essential is never to arrive anywhere, never to
> be anywhere...The essential is to go on squirming
> forever at the end of the line, as long as there are
> waters and banks and ravening in heaven a sport-
> ing God to plague his creature...[413]

All this makes little sense if it is to be regarded simply as
entertainment. Seen as a 'squirming' spiritual predicament,
it assumes meaning. And why is life a predicament?
Because the sensitive mind before Enlightenment can quite
clearly discern the pain and the struggle inherent in existence, the blind, chthonic forces that hold the world together
and that are just beneath the surface of man's mind. The
sensitive mind can perceive the infinite duality in the relative, *samsaric* world, its transience, its tragedy; it apprehends
all too clearly the evanescence of joy and the tenuousness of
human relationships and all about, the imminence of death
and disease. Through all this is the awareness of our own
personal transience and the sadness that accompanies us in
looking back on our lives, especially to moments of happiness enjoyed with those we shall never see again. There is
the gnawing sadness that there is no abiding place. It is not
suprising that in view of all this men take refuge in their
religions in search of security. A few, like Beckett, take a
hard, long look at what he describes as the 'chaos' and, like
the Buddhist, has traced its origin to the thought-to-thought
movement of the human mind. Here dwells the reason, in
the Buddhist view, for the lack of satisfaction in existence.

In concluding this section on the trilogy, I propose to consider three statements occurring towards the end of *The Unnamable* in order I hope, to expel any remaining doubts that may be harboured with respect to Beckett's intention to lay bare the nature of his own identity. We have spoken of the transitions that occur in *The Unnamable*. We have noticed that they do not take place by any formal convention such as the use of the paragraph or chapter. The whole telescopes together neatly, but even so the sections, like the extensible parts of the telescope itself, are recognizable. The comparison is a coarse one, however. These subtle changes of mood are not nearly as mechanical as suggested but are much more like the play of the sun over water or the changes of key in music. The following is an example of one of those changes. In order that the passage be apprehended in context, I have taken the liberty of quoting at length:

> This will never end, there's no sense in fooling oneself, yes it will, they'll come round to it, after me it will be the end, they'll give up, saying, It's all a bubble, we've been told a lot of lies, he's been told a lot of lies, who he, the master, by whom, no one knows, the everlasting third party, he's the one to blame, for this state of affairs, the master's not to blame, neither are they, neither am I, least of all I, we were foolish to accuse one another, the master me, them, himself, they me, the master themselves, I them, the master myself, we are all innocent, enough. Innocent of what, no one knows, of wanting to know, wanting to be able, of all this noise about nothing, of this long sin against the silence that enfolds us, we won't ask any more, what it covers, this innocence we have fallen to, it covers everything, all faults, all questions, it puts an end to all questions.[414]

When Beckett refers to 'this' never ending, are we to think that 'this' is the novel, the 'going on' in the literal sense with which he uses it at the beginning of the work and in its idiomatic sense? Is he, in other words, referring to his text?

Yes, certainly, and it is a technique that we have seen employed before.[415] The question is whether he is not also alluding to a state of being at the same time, whether the 'this' is not the experience of existence. There is no reason why it should not be synonymous with the other. We suggest that the 'this' here refers to what Buddhism, in describing human existence, calls 'the eternal round of birth and death' or sometimes 'life's deathly ocean.'

The import, both in Beckett's work and in Buddhism, is that of enslavement. We are not free. We are under the duress of our own conditioning, brought about partly by ourselves and partly by others. We believe these injunctions imposed on us by such conditioning and act upon them as if they were valid, sometimes long after the circumstances, in which they arose, have ceased to exist. We believe, moreover, that the accretion produced from these influences is also real or true. Our borrowed plumage we take for our own and imagine ourselves as something we are not. This identification with what we have acquired, knowingly or unknowingly, over the years is a deception. If it were not so, we would not be able to recognize it as such. The fact that we can do so is proof of the existence of another, perceiving self than the one we recognize.

To paraphrase Beckett then: It seems that it will go on for ever; the powerful forces governing life are too strong; there seems no way out (the whole process seems to be self-fertilizing and self-propagating). Let us cease deceiving ourselves, therefore, and give up. Yes, it can cease; one day they (the conditioned beings) will see it at last. I now so reduced that I have given up all human feature except my mind and that too I see is an illusion made up of these Malones and Mahood and the rest. I have even traced the origin of it all for you in Worm). Then, when they realize this, they'll give up and see that it's all a bubble and that all of us have been thoroughly betrayed. It's all lies (a fabrication of concepts).

Who is to blame for this extraordinary situation — the everlasting third party (God). He is the one responsible for the mess, the suffering and the creation of a cock-eyed world. No human is to blame, not even the master (Christ?), nor even they, nor I, least of all I. When we look at the matter like this, then none of us can blame ourselves for the semi-hell in which we find ourselves. That would be foolishness. We are all innocent of blame; we are God's innocent victims. But then, if we think about it, innocent of what? What have we done to be innocent of exactly? Are we innocent of wanting to know (about God and creation), of being able to find out? What kind of 'innocence' is that? Is it then a crime to want to know? What kind of a damn silly situation is that? The whole business is too absurd for comment. We are innocent of this long 'sin' against the silence. Our 'innocence' is our justification against this tyrannous God and against all the sin ascribed to us and all our questions. Seen in this way, there are no more questions. We are as we are.

This is all very well but it lands us in a spiritual vacuum. Moreover, it does not solve the problem. To rid oneself of conditioned concepts and to recognize them for what they are is an excellent start but what is the use of clearing the ground for vacuity? Taking away the identity we once possessed, our ego-identity, is a necessary preliminary but the voidness that is left is uncomfortable, totally unsatisfactory and, from the Buddhist point of view, a whistling in the dark.

To the root problem of why the world is constructed as it is and why the human mind must struggle to win its emancipation from a dominating ego, the Buddha himself declined to provide an answer.[416] In our scientific way today, we may well interpret this reticence as a lack of knowledge or perhaps a disinclination to commit oneself on the point. However, the historical fact (insofar as we can rely on the Buddha's biographers) is that he insisted that such knowledge was not necessary to our mental and spiritual well-being. We are not, he maintained, required to know the nature of the genesis of our problem as long as we are aware of its mechanics. He urged that we have a practical problem to work out and that it is in the interests of our own happiness to solve it. When it is finally solved, we shall look at things differently. It is as it is. This is Beckett's conclusion without the accompanying aspersion cast against God. The Buddhist answer differs also from Beckett's in that it says that the cause of the existential malaise is in ourselves and not to be sought in third-party irresponsibility. As Heinrich Zimmer states:

> The craving of nescience, not knowing better (*avidya*), is the problem — nothing less and nothing more. Such ignorance is a natural function of the life-process, yet not necessarily ineradicable; no more ineradicable than the innocence of a child. It is simply that we do not know that we are moving in a world of mere conventions and that our feelings, thoughts and acts are determined by these. We imagine that our ideas about things represent their ultimate reality and so we are bound in by them as by the meshes of a net. They are rooted in our own consciousness and attitudes; mere creations of the mind; conventional, involuntary patterns of seeing things, judging and behaving; yet our ignorance accepts them in every detail, without question, regarding them and their contents as the facts of existence. This — this mistake about the true essence of reality — is the cause of all the sufferings that constitute our lives.[417]

As we proceed with *The Unnamable*, there is no relief from the fervour of the search for meaning. The voice continues. The moments where it becomes earnest are more frequent as the novel draws to its conclusion. Beckett's earnestness becomes like the thrashing of a great hooked fish. He may well say that he delegates responsibility to an errant God and rests in his 'innocence' — at least intellectually — but the drive for an answer leaves him not a second's peace. He begins to refer to it as a thirst.

> No point, either, in your thirst, your hunger, no, no need of hunger, thirst is enough, no point in telling yourself stories, to pass the time, stories don't pass the time, nothing passes the time...in

your thirst, trying to cease and never ceasing, thirstier than ever, seeking as usual...seeking once more, any old thing, thirsting away, you don't know what for, ah yes, something to do, no no, nothing to be done, and now enough of that, unless perhaps, that's an idea, let's seek over there, one last little effort, seek what, pertinent objection ...cursing man, cursing God, stopping cursing, past bearing it, going on bearing it, seeking indefatigably, in the world of nature, the world of man, where is nature, where is man, where are you, what are you seeking, who is seeking, seeking who you are, supreme aberration...prattling along, ...who is talking, not I, where am I, where is the place where I've always been...[418]

After such a declaration, it is no longer possible for us to say that Beckett's work has nothing to do with the metaphysical condition of human beings. It would be difficult to imagine greater evidence of Beckett's concern with the human condition than this passage affords.

Beckett's thirst here is distinguished in one aspect from the Buddhist *tanha* in that it is not for sensation but for understanding; it is the 'thirst for righteousness' of the Sermon on the Mount, for the knowledge of God. This, no doubt, is why some critics have referred to Beckett as a mystic; he has the true mystic's indefatigable ardour. There is no need to hunger, 'thirst is enough,' he says. On a deeper level, the thirst for sensation and the thirst for this particular knowledge have the same origin in that of the need for fulfilment, as we have shown. Fulfilment is not found in telling stories, nor do these 'pass the time,' for, to 'pass the time' is to be temporarily preoccupied until the desire to seek re-asserts itself. It represents a temporary, comfortable distraction from the main issue of restoring our true identity. Thus, nothing really satisfactorily passes the time since, for those earnestly seeking to know the true nature of their personality, there is always the uncomfortable incumbency of knowing that they are indulging in an illusion. Furthermore such people are set upon a mental rack where constant questioning tortures them, where they would gladly cease from all their seeking but cannot; where they are past bearing the strain that such investigation entails and yet continue to endure. This, one might say, is Beckett's *koan*. The *koan*, it will be remembered, is basically neither a riddle nor a means to induce concentration but it is a means by which our faculty for rationalization is exhausted and through which we come to the end of our resources. The question: 'Who am I?' is in fact a *koan*, both existentially and as one officially entered in the list of Zen *koans*.

The Venerable Hsu Yun (1840—1959), who is acclaimed by Chinese Buddhists as the successor to the Ch'an tradition that stretches back into ancient times, always made a point of inculcating the spirit of this *koan* (Chinese, *hua t'ou*, lit. 'word-head' or 'coming before words') into the minds of those students under his charge.

> All these *hua t'ous* have only one meaning which is very ordinary and has nothing peculiar about it. If you look into him 'Who is reciting a *sutra*?', 'Who is holding a *mantra*?'... 'Who is taking a meal?', 'Who is wearing a robe?', 'Who is walking on the road?', or 'Who is sleeping?', the reply to 'Who?' will invariably be the same: 'It is Mind.' Word arises from Mind and Mind is head (i.e. 'ante-' word.) Thought arises from Mind and Mind is head of thought. Myriad things come from Mind and Mind is head of myriad things. In reality, a *hua t'ou* is the head of a thought (i.e. ante-thought). The head of thought is nothing but Mind. To make it plain, before a thought arises, it is a *hua t'ou*. From the above we know that to look into a *hua t'ou* is to look into the Mind.[419]

We may well ask the question: What is meant in this context by 'to look into the Mind.' How are we to understand the spirit of the 'Who' here? This is important. The Zen practitioner is required to cultivate a mind which 'has no abiding place,' that is, a mind which does not settle anywhere or does not give rise to thinking and which is fixed. It is a mind that is soon wholly overtaken by the one question: 'Who?' There is literally no room left in it for anything else. There is, therefore, a state of great concentration and great doubt (about the nature of the 'Who' in question). This spirit of self-enquiry leaves no room for any kind of discursive thought whatsoever. If, at a very deep level of such self-immersion, a thought does enter the mind, it is likely to be disruptive and sometimes can be of great power in overthrowing the mental balance of the meditator.

Beckett's spirit of enquiry is both sustained and deep. His observations here show him to be utterly committed to the purpose of finding out the nature of what is called the Real Self. Such commitment is rare. Incidentally, one of the principal problems for the Zen masters of the last three hundred years or so has been to implant just this spirit. When this kind of will prevails, Enlightenment is bound to follow. Hsu Yun, commenting on this stage at well over the age of a hundred, said:

> Ancestor Kao Feng said: 'When a student looks into a *hua t'ou* with the same steadiness with which a broken tile when thrown into a deep pond plunges straight down 10,000 changs to the bottom, if he fails to become awakened in seven days, anyone can chop off my head and take it away'. Dear friends, these are the words of an experienced master.[420]

However here, as elsewhere in Beckett's work, there is doubt. There is doubt not only about the phenomenal reality of the self necessary to progress in meditation but also about the possibility of such transcendence. This, however, is indispensable for true Enlightenment. In Beckett, only suffering is detectable, not the state of Enlightenment. He is like a man overboard, struggling to catch the line thrown to him, now so near and now so far away. The pain in the words is easily recognizable in the short, desperate sentences (pointed up by the excessive punctuation and reminiscent of the 'panting' of the next novel, *How It Is*) and their insistent questioning.

> ...what have I done to them, what have I done to God, what have they done to God, what has God done to us...[421]

Although he answers his own questions with 'nothing,' there is no comfort in the conclusion and so the search continues. Because the search is carried out among the objects of the mind, its furniture of concepts, memories, aspirations, discriminations and feelings, there cannot be any return to its pristine emptiness, its true nature. There is only sorrow and frustration.[422]

The third and last statement to be considered appears towards the conclusion of the novel. Beckett is still talking in terms of 'fault,' that is, who is to blame for the state of affairs (his term, see p.389) with which we are confronted, the 'How It Is' of being:

> ...it's the fault of the pronouns, there is no name for me, no pronoun for me, all the trouble comes from that, that, it's a kind of pronoun too, it isn't that either, I'm not that either, let us leave all that, forget about all that, it's not difficult, our concern is with someone, or our concern is with something, now we're getting it, someone or something that is not there, or that is not anywhere, or that is there, here, why not, after all, and our concern is with speaking of that, now we've got it, you don't know why, why you must speak of that, no one can speak of that, you speak of yourself...[423]

Here, in a rare moment, Beckett reveals the heart of his concern unequivocally. There is, he is saying, no name for the real 'me' (my true nature) and he is right. Any reference to 'me' is a reference to the fabricated ego I have formed for myself over the years. All the trouble, he says (wrongly) comes from that for which there is no name and that which he has indicated from time to time as an abyss or a great void. He wrestles with the idea. He knows it is there but cannot bring forward a word to encompass it. 'It's a kind of pronoun too,' he quickly asserts but then immediately corrects himself by contradiction. So it is not a pronoun. Dilemma. He changes direction: 'I'm not that either.' The phenomenal 'I,' the 'me' of the above is not the real self or true self. This, he sees at once, is going to complicate matters. Let's not bother about that, he hastens to suggest. Our concern, he maintains is with 'someone,' ...no, he's not too sure about that either,...with a 'something.' Now he feels closer to describing what he senses is right: 'something that is not there.' This 'something that is not there' is not 'there' in the sense of the phenomenally 'existent,' like a tree or a glass of water, and yet must...Here words break down. Clearly, if it is not 'there,' it cannot exist; if it does not exist, then what can we say about it? Again, he finds himself embarrassed and changes tack — again in contradiction.

Since we cannot imagine 'not there,' we must speak of a 'there' and 'why not after all?' Here, of course, is where the danger lies for the author, the Mr. Beckett behind the pages. Although the 'thing' has been brought into focus, we are back in the world of concepts and, consequently, as far as Enlightenment goes, off again down a blind alley. However, for the purposes of this short exposition, it will be sufficient to unfold the object of his contemplations. '...you don't know why,' he continues, 'you must speak of that,' and again contradicts himself by saying, rightly, that one cannot speak of it. In doing so, one speaks of oneself, that is, of the phenomenal self.

If this does not unequivocally point to that movement of the mind which we have referred to for convenience as 'Enlightenment,' it shows us, nevertheless, how perspicuous Beckett's understanding of the mind is, and, moreover, how near he is to apprehending the 'No-mind' and 'Mind' of Zen Buddhism, and, indeed, his own 'Unnamable.' However, it is difficult to attain precisely because we see it as 'attainment,' that is, something to be grasped. Once all the grasping is forgotten, it — the comprehension — is there. It is what Hubert Benoit, in his remarkable book, *The Supreme*

Doctrine,[424] calls that which can 'neither be affirmed or denied, up-stream of all duality':

> At the centre of myself, in this centre which is still unconscious today, resides the primordial man, united with the Principle of the Universe and through it with the whole of the Universe, totally sufficient unto himself, One from the beginning, neither alone nor not-alone, neither affirmed nor denied, up-stream of all duality. It is the primordial Being, underlying all egotistical 'states' which cover it in my actual consciousness.
>
> Because I am ignorant today concerning what are in reality my egotistical states, these states constitute a sort of screen which separates me from my centre, from my Real Self. I am unconscious of my essential identity with the All and I only consider myself as distinct from the rest of the Universe.

We are so near and yet so far. This, from the Zen point of view, is the sum of Beckett's three great novels. This, too, is the nature of the dilemma they present. They constitute one man's utterly sincere re-assessment of his religious outlook, not from the moral and ethical point of view, but from what we might call absolute principles. These question God's existence and his relationship to his creature, scorn his apparent impotence and upbraid his apparent cruelty. He hints that Christ was deceived and doubts whether the God of the Hebrews exists or ever existed. Despite this, however, he cannot accept his conclusious. He cannot entirely get rid of the old God and his appurtenances. Somewhere, somehow, there must be a vestige of purpose, of sense in the creation and maintenance of man and the world. His mind is a cacophony of 'Ayes and Noes,' for on the one hand there is everything that speaks for His existence and on the other for His non-existence. Beckett's novels are the expression of that dilemma.

As in all religious activity, more is needed than intuitive speculation in understanding that which has no name. A practical step has to be undertaken; there must be a 'doing,' not simply and only a 'thinking.' For if thinking alone could have held the clue to the nature of man, his existential dilemma would have been solved centuries ago. No, to know Beckett's 'something' or 'someone,' that centre of ourselves, which is our true identity or our true home where we shall at last feel on an even keel, the fires of the old mind, the monkey-mind of Zen, must once and for all be extinguished, obliterated. When the smoke of this has cleared, we shall be able to see without hindrance.

11 *Abandoning the Ego:* How It is

There is a remarkable museum in Frankfurt am Main called the Senckenberg Museum. Freely exhibited there, without showcase or railing, are the fossilized remains of prehistoric plant and animal life. In the basement of the museum, there lies the reconstructed skeleton of an anatosaurus[425] or 'beaked dragon,' which flourished some seventy to a hundred million years ago in the swamps of the land-mass that is now the American continent. The accidence of circumstance attending the creature at death, such as the sterile mud and the hot, dry air of the region, constituted an ideal situation for this beast of several tons to become mummified. One notices with interest the vestiges of the rod-like sinews, which once propelled the animal, and above all, the immense claw, which is not unlike the human hand and which, to the sensitive observer, even now after the incredible chemistry of petrification seems ready to spring to life and resume its functions of seeking and grasping. None but the most dull onlookers, observing this hand, could fail to be aware of its purpose. Not a few will be struck by the imperative behind its construction, the will, that is, underlying its design and informing its use.

The Buddhist observer, for his part, will quietly note that even in those far-off times passionate grasping was as much an intrinsic part of the world's essential pattern as it is today. The forms of its expression have changed with time but not the primordial instinct itself; this continues to find expression as much in the world of man as in that of the animal. Throughout the 'vast tracts of time,' which is inconceivable for most of us, the instinct to go out and search, to find and, one way or another, to grasp has held its own and is, we may say, as old as the very foundations of the world itself. This is how it was then and how it is now.

Before discussing the ideas implicit in Beckett's *How It Is* (*Comment c'est*), it would be well to consider the structure of the novel. In the first place, we find that, after completing *The Unnamable*, Beckett had found himself in a literary cul-de-sac. He expresses this in the following words in a letter to his friend Israel Schenker in 1956:

> The French work brought me to the point where I felt that I was trying to say the same thing over and over again. For some authors, writing gets easier the more they write. For me, it gets more and more difficult. For me, the area of possibilities gets smaller and smaller... In the last book *L'Innommable* — there's complete disintegration. No 'I', no 'have', no 'being'. No nominative, no accusative, no verb. There's no way to go on.
> The very last thing I wrote — *Textes Pour Rien* — was an attempt to get out of the attitude of disintegration, but it failed.[426]

Thus, *How It Is* marks a change in content and, in addition, a change in presentation. There is no punctuation; the writing is in blocks which, at a pinch, we might describe as paragraphs although some of the blocks consist of only two lines. Occasionally, only one line marks off one block of writing from another. Everything that is not absolutely essential is abandoned. The novel is in three parts. It is laced with repetition, the most prominent expressions of which are as follows:

> ...I say it as I hear it...I murmur it as I hear it...

> ...vast stretches/tracts of time...

> ...movements of the lower face...

> ...something   wrong   here/there...something missing here...

...when the panting stops...

...they are good moments...

...the voice on all sides quaqua...bits and scraps...

The repetition occurs, like an incantation, from one end of the novel to the other and has to be considered as an important component of the work.

Each of the blocks or paragraphs is only very loosely connected with that preceding or succeeding it. There is a very general coherence in that sometimes more emphasis is put on a particular theme than at other times, but at no time is there development of any one topic. To avoid complete chaos and perhaps also to ensure that the reader will exert himself against all odds, the whole is held together by the movements of the nameless narrator. He struggles in the mud:

...right leg right arm push pull ten yards fifteen yards halt...[427]

He drags a coal sack full of tinned food behind him. He has a tin opener, which he also uses as an instrument of attack. There is the element of anticipation. Just as in *Waiting for Godot*, the audience is kept waiting in the hope of a denouement. This never comes. Perhaps this would be a mean gesture on the part of our author were it not for the fact that Beckett, convinced as he is that there is no coherence or meaningful pattern in human existence, is attempting to mirror this conviction in his novels.

The structure of the novel is extremely simple. It involves the movement of the narrator through the mud towards Pim, another creature presumably like the narrator. This arduous passage is accompanied by a variety of reflections, many of which are concerned with the past. This constitutes Part I of the book. Part II covers the narrator's encounter with Pim and his attempt to make him communicate with him. It consists of a 'say-after-me' training, which is conducted in a desperately determined manner and results in grievous bodily harm.

> first lesson theme song I dig my nails into his
> armpit right hand right pit he cries I withdraw
> then thump with fist and skull his face sinks in the
> mud his cries cease end of first lesson...[429]

> with the handle of the opener as with a pestle bang
> on the right kidney...cry thump on skull silence
> brief rest jab in arse unintelligible murmur bang on
> kidney signifying louder once and for all cry thump
> on skull silence brief rest...[429]

On another occasion, the speaker scores the letters of his
questions deep into the back of the other.

In Part III, the narrator moves away from Pim and the
novel ends. Before this is achieved, however, Beckett resorts
again to the device of exploding all that has gone before.

> can't go on...Pim is finished Pim has finished me
> now part three not Pim my voice not his saying
> these words can't go on and Pim that Pim never
> was and Bom whose coming I await to finish be
> finished have finished me too that Bom will never
> be no Pim no Bom and this voice quaqua of us all
> never was only one voice my voice never any
> other...[430]

There is then only one voice, Beckett's voice, which invests
the novel. It is this voice that sets the tone of the novel, if, in
view of the above, we can still regard the work as a novel.
Strictly speaking, it is not a novel in the usually accepted
sense, any more than *The Unnamable* is. Like that work, it
is more a monologue which, during its outpouring, describes
certain mental preoccupations. The tone of the novel or
monologue is conveyed by its rhythm. The reader will
probably be immediately struck by the frequent use of the
short sentence — apprehended despite the absence of punctuation — and syntactical simplicity. The whole has the
rhythm of 'panting,' a word that appears throughout the text
in the phrase 'when the panting stops.' In this interval the
narrator hears what is told to him 'by the voices on all sides.'

> ...all that once without scraps in me when the
> panting stops ten seconds fifteen seconds all that

> fainter weaker less clear but the purport in me
> when it abates the breath we're talking of breath
> token of life when it abates like a last in the light
> then resumes a hundred and ten fifteen to
> the minute when it abates ten seconds fifteen
> seconds...[431]

This form strengthens the sensation gained from the absence of all words that are not absolutely essential to the conveyance of meaning. Only the absolutely essential is being said. It is as though Beckett were saying: There shall be only those words and nothing to distract the reader from them. No character is to be defined, no relation shall exist between characters other than the most primitive of exchanges; there shall in addition be no incident other than this and there is to be no background other than a homogeneous, monochromatic, featureless sea of mud. The narrator, just detectable in this sea, pulls and pushes his way through his viscid medium, murmuring what he hears with 'brief movements of the lower face' to the pervading mud. Pim is little more than an object within it while Krim and Kram are mere vaporous wraiths upon its surface.

If we thought, wrote Maurice Nadeau in the *Express* in 1961, that we have reached the ultimate in 'derision and suffering' — and we may add 'attenuation' to this — then

> We were mistaken. The narrator of *How It Is*, even
> if he still possesses his arms and legs, has lost
> the habit of a vertical position, even through the
> artifice of a jar. He is stretched out in the mud, his
> face half buried, and if he manages to move by
> crawling...he has lost the use of an audible voice;
> his 'brief movements of the lower face' give him
> the vague consciousness of a murmur that he alone
> hears, of an interior voice (he is not sure that it is
> his) which forces a way for itself every ten or
> fifteen seconds through the endless panting...[432]

This, I suggest, is the structure, tone and substance of Beckett's last novel. There remains a great deal more to be said on these issues alone but our concern here is to confine our attention to what we have alluded to as the 'content' of the novel. We cannot suppose that the absence of punctuation and the abandonment of the conventions of syntax and paragraphing as well as the denudation of the literary landscape in themselves constitute a literary masterpiece. There must, I suppose, be some purpose behind such radical effacement. The questions we might ask ourselves in what follows could be: Why this 'paring to the bone?' What does the voice in the monologue say that is of relevance to the reader, or are we here confronted with an internal dialogue, the content of which is only relevant to the experience of the author?

We might do well to begin with the title, '*How It Is.*' What springs to mind first is 'How *what* is?' Knowing that Beckett's titles are almost always indicative of the nature of the work or its content, we may justifiably assume that the author is suggesting that the novel's substance contains parallels with human existence. He is not seriously suggesting, however, that our life bears any comparison with the muddy homogeneity, which he described[433] – or is he? And can we really be compared with the narrator or his creature, Pim? Neither are we tormentors nor tormented. Only a few of us envisage life as a perfect round of torture *ad infinitum.* That is not how it is with us.

On the other hand, there is struggle. There are life's vicissitudes, which every individual experiences. They crop up in all lives with more or less the same distribution throughout the social structure. Perhaps to mention a few among the main ones are impecuniosity, death, disease and personal relationships.

It will be quite clear that the first three are a cause of mental distress; the last perhaps is not so immediately clear. We can concur that our relationships with others are of the highest importance to us. Not infrequently, they involve us in hatred, envy, fear and disappointment. They also teach us self-control, tolerance, love and understanding. The 'other' is a challenge to the assessment of ourselves for good or for ill from the time we first become conscious of these things until we relinquish them at death. We must reckon with the 'other,' knowing well that we cannot live in isolation. At root, however, is the problem of self-fulfilment. We cannot have what we want because the other is in the way or is deliberately obstructive or dangerous or cannot return in kind what we give him or her. When the union is close,[434] as for example in marriage or between a child or young person and parents, frustration may arise owing to the dilemma patent in a situation where desire on the one hand conflicts with need on the other. A child, for example, may wish to fulfil a desire but is not able or not allowed to do what it wants because its parents forbid it. The child cannot circumvent its parents and act independently because it needs them.

But in *How It Is* the problem is deeper than the need for self-fulfilment; it is the need to know whether the self exists at all. In every step towards self-fulfilment in our daily lives, the self, consciously or unconsciously, is taken for granted. There is no doubt or confusion arising about the 'I.' To this end, Beckett envisages a situation for his character that obviously lacks all the attributes which are associated with the self and by which it is usually identified. There is, to begin with, no individual body or face — or at least none that is described. The narrator tells us that he swims in the mud. He is, to all intents and purposes, one with the mud. Mud, unlike water, is not transparent. An object imbued in it does not, therefore, appear in space relative to other objects, which might also occupy the mud. Mud, moreover, like snow, is an effective hindrance to identification even when an object is withdrawn from it. Passage through it cannot have the same sense as passage through water, where, because of its transparency, locomotion can be easily recognized relative to objects that remain stationary, and where, in the act of locomotion, there arises the sensation of progress. Added to this, the narrator speaks in a murmur to the mud, moving only the lower half of his face. He relates only what he hears:

> I say it as I hear it brief movements of the lower
> face which I murmur to the mud[435]

The rest of the circumstance surrounding the narrator is an apparently limitless sea of mud, which is set in 'vast unimaginable tracts of time.'[436] Since the idea of time, especially of this nature, is difficult to represent, the author repeats the phrase frequently. The only accoutrements that this lonely warrior in space and time has are his sack of tinned provisions and an opener. Neither of them, oddly enough, are essential to his encounter with Pim (he has his nails). They contrast strangely with the stark monodism of the rest of the landscape. The conditions are almost similar to those we associate with outer space, of . . .

> monster silences vast tracts of time perfect nothingness[437]

The contrasted spectacle of the world as we know it is something exterior to this conception and referred to as 'life up above.'

All this seems very strange to the reader. Privately, we ask ourselves whether Beckett is not going too far, whether he has exaggerated technique at the expense of intelligibility. Beckett's view, however, is like that of the meditator. True meditation, like true prayer, is an act of abandonment, the abandonment of self. In the first place, the body is settled and forgotten; all current preoccupations, problems and obligations are shelved. There is no thought of even the nearest and dearest of associations. Home, family, job, interests, worries, ambitions, affiliations, likes and dislikes, friends and enemies are all temporarily laid aside like our clothes before retiring. The mind of the meditator is turned inward. What does the meditator discover there? He discovers an inner voice, not the voice of God or of the meditator's conscience necessarily, but something much larger and more insistent, his own thought-stream. This seems to rise incessantly, like the water from an unnamable spring in undiscoverable infinity. Watching it, we see that it is an ever-moving stream, seeming to pass the observer's contemplation with its emotionally charged moods and desires, its debris of memories and recollections, the passing eddies of its day-dreams, its currents of will together with its vast undercurrent of fears and needs.

This, too, is what we observe in *How It Is.* A few examples suffice to illustrate the point. Illustrative of mood:

> ...what can one say to oneself possibly say at such a time a little pearl of forlorn solace so much the better so much the worse that style only not so cold cheers alas...

> I'm often happy God knows but never more than at this instant never so oh I know happiness unhappiness I know I know...[438]

and desire:

> life above life here God in heaven yes if he loves me a little if Pim[439] loved me a little yes or no if I loved him a little in the dark the mud in spite of all a little affection find someone at last someone find you at last live together...[440]

The mood of reminiscence is frequent:

> next another image yet another so soon again the third perhaps they'll soon cease it's me all of me and mother's face I see it from below it's like nothing I ever saw[441]

> we were on a veranda smothered in vebena the scented sun dapples the red tiles yes I assure you the huge head hatted with birds and flowers is bowed down over my curls the eyes burn with severe love I offer her mine pale upcast to the sky whence cometh our help...[442]

> the satchel under the arse the back against the wall raise the eyes to the blue wake up in a sweat the white there was then the little clouds...the jersey striped horizontally blue and white...[443]

and continued...

> ...papa no idea building trade perhaps some
> branch or other fell off scaffolding on his arse
> ...must have been him or the uncle God
> knows... [444]

> ...mamma none either column of jade bible
> invisible in the black hand the edge red gilt the
> black finger inside psalm one hundred and
> something oh God may his days as grass flower
> of the field wind above in the clouds the face of
> ivory pallor muttering lips all the lower it's
> possible... [445]

Here and there he dreams for a moment:

> ...and yet a dream I am given a dream like some-
> one having tasted of love of a little woman
> within my reach and dreaming too it's in the
> dream too... [446]

and occasionally will and day-dreaming are together:

> ...an oriental my dream he has renounced I too
> will renounce I will have no more desires...

Sometimes reminiscence of the sea and the harbour are
found linked with the desire for freedom, the spiritual
freedom alluded to above, to be eternally released from the
demands existence makes upon one:

> ...sea beneath the moon harbour mouth after the
> sun the moon always light day night little heap in
> the stern it's me all those I see are me all ages the
> current carries me out the awaited ebb I'm look-
> ing for an isle home at last drop never move again
> ... [448]

There is the recurring image of the galley slave:

> he falls I fall on my knees crawl forward clink of
> chains perhaps it's not me perhaps it's another...
> what isle what moon you see the thoughts some-

times that go with it it disappears the voice goes
on. . .[449]

The question that Beckett asks himself in all this and that
underlies the novel as structure-in-depth is: Can this voice
really be me? For most of us, as with Descartes, the fact that I
think proves axiomatically that I am, that I exist, but Beckett
here entertains a dreadful doubt about this. This thinking
comes from somewhere, for if I can observe myself thinking,
I cannot be the stream of thought which I observe since that
is an object to the perception of the observer. Thus, we have
the fundamental epistemological question about the 'who-
ness' of the observer. Daisetz Suzuki, in considering the
father of modern philosophy's dictum, has this to say:

> . . .*Cogito ergo sum*, but we have to reverse it. *Sum*
> comes first. By asserting that "I am", I think as I say
> it. I separate 'I' from 'not I'. When I say 'I am', I am
> going out of myself. "I am" is the starting point,
> but we come out of this to 'cogito', "I think". This
> is a part which is difficult to explain, for no intellec-
> tion will solve the problem. When we leave this life
> there will be no problem, and before consciousness
> was awakened there was no problem. Plants do not
> think. The trees grow, shed their leaves, grow them
> again, and die, but they have no problem. Dogs eat
> and take whatever is given them. They never
> murmur or complain that the next dog is better fed.
> This is a human characteristic, but human beings
> divide themselves up into "I am here and the
> world is there, and not merely 'there' but against
> me".[450]

This, too, is a sentiment which permeates all Beckett's work,
including the work under present scrutiny. With Beckett we
may add that he feels that the gods as well are 'against' him.
In the early part of *How It Is*, there is a reference to Belacqua,
with whom perhaps Beckett compares himself on occasion.
Beckett, too, has searched and waited in vain for the answer

that must be there but does not materialize. There is dissatisfaction with the 'them,' with God and His elect, who sit in
glory and do nothing:

> ...I see me asleep on my side or on my face...the
> sack under my head or clasped to my belly...
> the knees drawn up the back...the knees curled
> round the sack Belacqua fallen over on this side
> tired of waiting forgotten of the hearts where
> grace abides asleep...[451]

However, this beautiful poetic thought gives way to
violent, gnashing anger later in his encounter with Pim,
on whom he can take revenge and so vent his pent-up
frustration.

> bloody him all over with Roman Capitals...dig
> my nails into his armpit...
>
> ...rummaged in the mud between his legs I bring
> up finally what seems to me a testicle or two...
>
> ...in the gloom HERE HERE to the bone the nail
> breaks quick another in the furrows HERE HERE
> howls...good try again HERE HERE to the
> marrow howls...[452]

Alternatively, he sneers at the universe as it appears to go on
aimlessly yet on iron ways of physical law, almost, it would
seem, with delighted malignity:

> God's old clapper old mill threshing the void or in
> another mood as though it changed great shears of
> the black old hag older than the world born of
> night click clack clack two threads a second...[453]

Now, all this has a purpose other than the expression of
frustrated energy; it is the desperate attempt to confirm his
own being now that there is doubt about the reality of the
'I.' If the source of the 'voice,' the stream of consciousness,
cannot be found, then the only confirmation according to
simple logic is to have one's existence confirmed in the eyes
or the presence of another. If this other cannot acknowledge

you, as Pim does not seem to be able to do in an independent way, then one can resort to torture. If your victim cries out in pain, then there must be an agent there to inflict the pain. The agony of the situation is that there seems to be no other way, no other alternative than this primitive method to be sure about the matter. The other, in his turn, will do the same, for he too, being in the same position presumably, will also be in doubt about his identity. And this, in Beckett's opinion, is 'how it is.'

However it may be, it is not satifactory. It is this note of frustration which runs through the novels and the plays and which, in addition, is responsible for the tension underlying all that Beckett writes. This tension is the statement of a dilemma, the horns of which are the need to know God and the conviction that there is no God. The element of required decision usually inherent in situations of dilemma is given here by the rejection of the former because of the validity of the latter, and the rejection of the latter in view of the urgency of the former. In other words, there is no need to go searching for something that does not exist. On the other hand, however, there is so much evidence for a creative intelligence in the world that we feel it must be realizable in some form or other, and so the search continues. Knowledge of our true identity, which we may here equate with a knowledge of God, can only be acquired by this primitive resort to violence. Despite this, on departure from Pim, the narrator is not less dissatisfied than when he first encountered him.

We can look at the matter another way. We can accept John Updike's suggestion that Pim can be equated with Christ. The values are the same inasmuch as we have a dilemma where a human being (the narrator) is searching for confirmation of the existence of God. The existence of such a God as that described in our religious literature would revolutionize our assessment of ourselves. We would have a frame of reference, a point of orientation; our lives would then assume meaning and we would become identifiable as His subjects. If for some reason, however, we become dissatisfied with traditional religion, and, as Beckett has done, reject its tenets,[454] we may, on the one side, have undoubtedly cast off a great quantity of dross acquired through the centuries, but we shall also have thrown away valuable insights.

The problem of whether there is a God or not still remains. We have to find other means for reaching an answer to this question. Beckett's work can be thought of as the artistic expression of an impelling need to find such an answer. As we have seen, up to *How It Is*, there has been no answer forthcoming. *How It Is* itself seems to be an act of resignation. Hence the furious attack on the figure in the mud, the deep cuts in the back, the desperate, end-of-tether demonstrations of anger and frustration directed against one who professed to know God and called himself the 'Son of God.' From this person, Beckett's narrator will have an answer and to the devil with all the deference and respect with which such a figure should be approached. Either he is a Saviour or he is not.

> . . . but he can't affirm anything no deny anything no things may have been different yes his life here pause YOUR LIFE HERE good and deep in the furrows howls thump face in the mud nose mouth howls good . . . [455]

With this root dissatisfaction, Part II of the novel closes. The narrator finds himself alone again to plan the next move:

> . . . that one day come back to myself to Pim why not known not said from the nothing come back from the nothing the surprise to find myself alone at last no more Pim me alone in the dark the mud end at last of part two how it has with Pim leaving at last only part three and last and how it was after Pim before Bom how it is that's how it was with Pim.[456]

If the hypotheses set out in this essay are accepted, that is, that Beckett's work is primarily concerned with finding the 'I' within ourselves or the true God that is said to be within us, the obvious question is why should our author be so tenaciously committed to his quest. In part, it is the very insolubility of the questions he asks himself that provide the driving force and that lead him again and again into a re-assessment of the situation. This irresolvable dilemma arises from an intellectual observation and conclusion, which can be illustrated in a very simple way. We might, for example, consider an onion. As an object of our horticulture, it is quite simply recognized by its size, shape, colour, smell and taste and perhaps by other attributes such as the scaly leaves that often accompany it. We are in no doubt about its existence and we are free to relish it and look for more without further reflection. However, when we begin to ask ourselves about its essential 'onion-ness,' we might feel tempted to peel it. As we remove layer on layer of the onion, we find that we have nothing when we have finally removed the last of its covers. What we have then is not an onion anymore but something else. The onion was only the sum of its parts; there is no essential 'onion-ness.'[457]

According to Buddhist philosophy, the same is true of the 'soul' (Sanskrit, *atman*) or essential 'self.' The 'self' is only the sum of its parts (the Buddhist 'aggregates') and when these are dissolved at death, the self also disappears. In Buddhist terms, we are the expression of 'becoming,' the arising and passing away of a phenomenon like waves on water. It is at this point that the phenomenal self, which we have alluded to, becomes desperate, like a drowning person clutching at a straw in order to justify itself as something substantial. We totally resist the idea, but analysis demonstrates that it is true. On the other hand, nothing arises from nothing; every phenomenon can be traced to a cause and this cause too can be traced and so on to unthinkable extremes. There is, for example, water and the molecular components of this in ever decreasing smallness of particle until we have an extreme, which is inconceivable. On the other hand, there cannot be a 'nothing' for a nothing would posit a something as we have seen and so we come to the borders of irrationality. The mind cannot leave the matter there, however. Such a state of affairs is wholly unacceptable, especially to those of an intellectual bent. The search is taken up again. A new investigation is made with the result that more 'phenomena' are discovered but no essence is found that is quantifiable and intelligible to the rational mind. 'Not in a million aeons will you ever find as much as a fraction of a self, no matter how hard your search,' warns a Buddhist saying.

The situation is made more complicated and more depressing by the contemplation of time past. None of Beckett's novels is free from autobiographical detail. In *Krapp's Last Tape*, Beckett develops the theme of reflection. In reflection we can see quite clearly that everything is a matter of coming into existence and passing away. To anyone of normal sensibility, this is always a distinctly saddening experience. Among other things, we can see the vanishing of self, the self of childhood, for example, or the self of passions long since cold and we wonder where that self can be. Even of old photographs we ask: Can that really be me? There is incredulity. We observe the changes in the body and are cognizant of the modifications to our thinking that experience brings. Quite clearly, we are not what we were, and yet we are always what we were.[458] Again, the past is irretrievable, irredeemable; what joy it contains can never be recaptured in quite the same way. Some of the actors in our little personal drama have gone for ever; some of the places are no more; names escape one. Very often, the whole is no more than an image in one's mind like that of seeing a star, which disappeared two thousand years ago. It is there and yet it is not 'there' in any real sense, any practical, everyday sense; it exists and yet does not exist.

The deep sadness, which overwhelms us at times of reflection, is well conveyed by Robert L. Stevenson's 'Home no more Home to me,' to cite just one poet among a great many who have dealt with the same theme. Perhaps it might be more correct to say that no truly great poet fails to represent the sentiment at some time or other in his career. For its depth and pathos, and because it so well illustrates the feelings we entertain about the past, we may perhaps quote part of it here:

> Fire and the windows bright glittered on the
> moorland;

Song, tuneful song, built a palace in the wild.
Now, when the day dawns on the brow of the
    moorland,
Lone stands the house and the chimney-stone is
    cold.
Lone let it stand, now the friends are all departed,
The kind hearts, the true hearts, that loved the
    place of old.
Spring shall come, come again, calling up the
    moorfowl,
Spring shall bring the sun and rain, bring the bees
    and flowers;
Red shall the heather bloom over hill and valley,
Soft flow the stream through the ever-flowing
    hours;
Fair the day shine as it shone on my childhood —
Fair the day shine on the house with open door;
Birds come and cry there and twitter in the
    chimney —
But I go for ever and come again no more.[459]

The keen sense of sadness, which invests reflections such
as these, is awakened by a subliminal awareness that there
is, essentially, nothing to grasp, that our life passes away in
unfulfilment, that, as children, we were nearer to understanding in the Buddhist sense than we are now in our
maturity. No one has better expressed this feeling perhaps
than Thomas Hood in his famous poem 'I remember, I
remember.' He quite unambiguously asserts that he is 'no
nearer heaven than when I was a boy' and, as he recalls
watching the swallows diving, he remarks with poignant
remorse that 'My spirit flew in feathers then/That is so
heavy now.' There is a sharp pang of loss. Not only have the
circumstances of our childhood changed with the knowledge that fleeting happiness can never be recovered, but we
ourselves have changed.

In truth, however, Buddhism asserts, nothing has been
lost. Especially is this true of those deep, compassionate
feelings we have had for others, or those moments in our

lives that have involved love and understanding. What has apparently been lost can be rediscovered. In this case it is the ability to act naturally as a child does, to accept experience without 'filtering' it through our meddling intellects and without reducing it to something graspable. Thus, when Ryokan, the eighteenth century Japanese Zen wanderer and poet, returned to his hut to find that it had been burgled, he did not fall to speculation and hard thoughts but sat down in his empty hovel and reflected:

> The thief
> Left it behind
> The moon at the window.

A mind such as this could never feel remorse at that which is past because there is no loss in what is past. Ryokan's life was lived in the eternal present. Whoever concerns himself with this need never have regrets about the past. His life, we might say, was the embodiment of Buddhist teaching, a person for whom no teaching is relevant any more. He has never lost, as we who look back have lost, that childlike spontaneity and whole-hearted response to all that experience offers.

For Ryokan, both past and future were alike in their meaninglessness. In other words, he enjoyed the 'life eternal' of Christian teaching. Christianity, properly understood, is akin to Buddhism in that it is a release from the burden of *samsaric* thinking. Both are concerned with putting us into contact with a new way of thinking and helping us to experience a new outlook on the world. Both teachings are a means to re-orientate our minds so that we may be unaffected by life's vicissitudes while at the same time to create in us compassion for those who are afflicted by such changes. Just as Christianity would be dead without Christ risen, so Buddhism would be nothing without this re-orientation (*satori*). Hugh Latimer's cheerful words of encouragement to his companions at the stake and the sixteenth century samurai's spoken *haiku* on the evanescence of cherry blossom in succumbing to a hail of swords are declarations of the same disinterested insight and compassion.

Unfortunately, Beckett's work never rises to this sublimity, for the past is always a part of his work, sadly interwoven as reminiscence:

> . . .my life we're talking of my life
>
> my life above what I did in my life above a little of everything tried everything then gave up no worse always a hold a ruin always a crust never good at anything. . .[460]

The future is contained in the quest, the search, the hope to encounter that which has been lost. Locomotion itself is a means towards satisfaction, but it is not blessed with satisfaction very often. It is as if one were on a monorail, able to move in two directions only, the one distance travelled being an extension of the other. Looking back, we view the way we have come; looking forward, we are faced with a similar perspective. To one in this state of mind, the present too looks disconcertingly familiar. There seems to be a cheap, irritating familiarity about the experience as a whole except for what Beckett calls the 'good moments,' sometimes in contemplation of the past and sometimes in the hope of death. These moments, recalled now to memory, are the points in time where the buddhic mind impinges on that of the *samsaric.* For a very short duration, there is a liberation from time.

This phenomenon was often recorded by the poets of the nineteenth century and in our time notably by T.S. Eliot in his *Four Quartets.* Time here can be regarded as the 'monorail' to which the 'intersecting' moment, as Eliot calls it, is tangential and therefore outside it. In this state of mind, time ceases to be. Time belongs to the world of *samsara.* Buddhism's concern is to inculcate this 'timeless mind,' asserting at the same time that it is attainable for anyone willing to invest a little effort towards its acquisition. Buddhism can, therefore, be called a teaching that has as its objective the release from time and the exploration of that area of experience at 'right angles' to the monorail of our illustration.

The tragedy of Beckett's work is that it is doomed to failure as both his interviews assert and his work attests. The monorail appears to stretch to infinity in both directions, an infinity of space and time, those 'vast stretches of time' which promise no change, no deviation from the 'mortal tedium' of the past. The length, monotony and insistence of his novels, especially the later ones, would seem to be a palpable reflection of this viewpoint. The failure here is not artistic failure but a failure to break out of this mental incarceration or even to see that there is a means to escape from the impasse, in which he has declared himself to be. Qualitatively, this experiene is that of watching life being consumed, like observing water vanish down a hole. It is the agony of observing oneself grow older without the hope of pardon from the tyranny of Time. It recalls the words of a dying friend of mine who said: '*Das Leben is ein Verlustgeschäft und schließlich verliert man alles,*' (i.e. 'Life is a losing game and finally one loses everything.')

The tragedy is that it need not be so. But for the dweller in *samsara*, or, rather, the samsaric thinker who holds this view, there is only one solution — death. Death shall put an end to the agony:

> ...so things may change no answer end no answer I may choke sink no answer sully the mud no more no answer the dark no answer trouble the peace no more no answer the silence no answer die no answer DIE screams I MAY DIE screams I SHALL DIE screams good
>
> good good end at last of part three and last that's how it was end of quotation after Pim how it is.[461]

But will it? Hamlet's doubt is Beckett's doubt and an uncomfortable bedfellow. On what grounds are we at liberty to assume that the insubstantial mind will perish along with the substantial body? An end of sorts there certainly is, but is this also the end of mind? Beckett himself is not wholly satisfied with such appearances nor with accepted belief in such matters. 'It' may indeed go on beyond the grave. This is the reason for the persistence of the idea in his work that he cannot die and the aporia contained in the lines quoted above. There is no definitive answer to his anxious questions. Line by line, the tension mounts until finally, in unspeakable desperation he screams, 'I MAY DIE!' hoping desperately that the possibility of death exists.

The book, for practical reasons, must come to an end, and this is a suitable cadence on which to bring it to a close. The doubt that has been entertained throughout Beckett's work, in this work as well as elsewhere, is sustained here with consummate artistry. The reader closes the book with the feeling that an insecure compromise has been arranged and that the doubt once made explicit in *Malone Dies*:

> Then it will all be over with the Murphys, Merciers
> . . .But sufficient unto the day, let us first defunge,
> then we'll see.[462]

has now become more ominous. Apart from the question of the body and mind alluded to a moment ago, there is also the question of relationship between birth and death, or life and death. We commonly regard the one as the pole of the other and in manifest opposition to one another. We think, for example, of life moving towards death, death as the inevitable termination of life. In this we are not wholly deceived, for the relationship when seen in this way can be proved. Once the flower has bloomed it dies, but does it die forever? In one sense, yes, if we regard that particular flower. Yet the species lives on and not only as a physical entity but also as an idea contained in the seeds of the flower that has died. Experience, moreover, teaches us that everything, every relationship in our samaric world, is a relative one, that there is nothing that exists with absolutely no reference to anything else; there are no absolutes, and if there were, we would not be able to understand them any more than we can understand an absolute like mathematical infinity, beginningless Time or the First Cause. Such comprehension is beyond intellect since to understand anything with the intellect there must be relationship.

It is possible then not to think of death as an entity as we think of 'life' but rather as a point of transformation after which another relationship is formed. We in the West are now becoming more aware of this as a result of the advances made in parapsychological and physical research[463] so that one of the world's most distinguished physicists, Wernher von Braun, could say a few years ago: 'Nature knows no extinction; all it knows is transformation. Everything science has taught me, continues to teach me, strengthens my belief in the continuity of our spiritual existence after death.' If we were to put this in negative terms, we could say that it is highly unlikely that the transformation we speak of could be a total eradication since nothing is ever totally eradicated.

This too has always been the Buddhist view. The 'aggregates' we have spoken of disintegrate at death and the personality or the creature we once knew cannot for this reason continue to exist. However, the forces that worked to bring the so-called aggregates together and that maintained them do not and cannot disappear. One can look at the matter another way: the forces we speak of pre-exist, or, if we like, they 'exist' *nirvanically* that is, *non-samsarically* or non-relatively. Adopting the Buddhist viewpoint, we can imagine them as 'desiring expression' in *samsara*. When the circumstances are ripe for this expression, they come into being in recognizable form, that is, recognizable to the human senses.[464]

It is perhaps correct to say that some of these ideas are not new to us in the West. What is divergent is that Buddhism[465] holds that at death these forces seek re-creation in another individual body and that the sum of the first individual's mental and moral make-up is taken into this new body. This is the doctrine of *karma*, or cause and effect. The process is known in Buddhism loosely as the doctrine of 'rebirth' or, more precisely, 'dependent origination.'

If this is true, as parapsychological and psychological research would seem to affirm, Beckett's worst suspicions are also confirmed, that is, from Beckett's point of view, the whole dreadful business goes on endlessly. But there are compensations. Having arrived at such a view is itself grounds for seeking refuge from such a situation. Being weary of the world is just cause to retire from it by some means or another. One may retire from it physically and live in a cave or one may simply renounce its values and thus retire from it mentally. In any case there will be a search for other values. One may find these on the *samsaric* plane or find them, as in Buddhism, by totally withdrawing into the dimension of *nirvana*. When this happens, the inquirer is said to have passed beyond the 'triple world' (i.e. of past, future and present and their concomitants of earth, heaven and hell) and to stand outside its influence. In our example, this would be akin to stepping off the monorail—at right angles to it.

From this new point of view, we would see the system in its entirety, the extension of Time, the deception under which human beings labour (by either looking forward or backward), and the veritable bondage to which they are committed. For the individual having thus 'stepped off' [466] there would be a degree of freedom (the freedom that Beckett's characters yearn for) hitherto unimagined by those bound to the rail. Also, there would be natural compassion for those in their plight on the monorail. Conceivably, such an individual would be moved to offer assistance by removing the delusion to which they are subjected. Such an individual Buddhism calls a *Bodhisattva*, that is, one who has knowledge of the '*bodhi*' or *nirvanic* mind and who is devoted to helping others.

Unless one can 'step off' in this way, Buddhism holds, there will be no end to the round of *samsara*, of dying and being born and of suffering. This echoes the teaching of the ancient Vedas as summed up in the *Bhagavad Gita*, where Sri Krishna, the incarnation of the deity, exhorts Arjuna to action on the battlefield. He points out that the fear of death is an attribute of *samsaric* existence and for that reason ego-centred. Arjuna, a valiant bowman, hesitates, not out of cowardice but pity for those whom he must kill. Krishna plies him again:

> Death is certain for the born. Rebirth is certain for the dead. You should not grieve for what is un-avoidable. Before birth, beings are not manifest to

our human senses. In the interim between birth
and death they are manifest. At death they return
to the unmanifest again. What is there in all this to
grieve over?[467]

Krishna's exhortation is not to the spirit of belligerent
hatred, as some commentators have concluded, but to a
disposition of mind that can perceive the abiding Mind
amid manifest change, involving birth and death and all its
attendant circumstance. It is the Unmanifest which Sri
Krishna wishes Arjuna to apprehend. This, he feels, is of
vital importance and, whatever the cost, must be sought:

This Atman cannot be manifested to the senses, or
thought about by the mind. It is not subject to
modification. Since you know this, you should not
grieve.[468]

The emphasis is not on death, which is samsaric and therefore relative, but on trying to understand death from the
nirvanic standpoint so that it can be seen as it really is, not
as the 'end of all,' but as an incident in a process.

No one would maintain that this point of view is easy
to acquire. No one who is enjoying a healthy state of mind
wishes to lose his life. There is nothing unnatural about this
but this is not what is urged. What is urged with the utmost
cogency is that resistance to death is in fact an expression —
albeit a very natural expression — of egocentricity. In death
our sense of individuality is lost. The ego sees this as the
one catastrophe that must be strenuously avoided. When
this strategy of the ego is realized, we can change our point
of view without the need to die physically. When the time
for physical death comes, we will find that we can dispense
with this mortal coil as easily as laying ourselves down to
sleep. What has taken place is the death of the ego, the last
barrier to acquiring the *nirvanic* viewpoint that we have
described in these pages. Through this barrier Beckett's
heroes fail to emerge.

Lest we incline to the conclusion that all of this is theological conjecture, we may take a leap of some three thousand

years from Vedic India to nineteenth century Japan. In the first half of this period, the art of swordsmanship (Japanese, *kendo*) was still assiduously practised in some training establishments as it had been in feudal times. The training in such places was earnest; accidents were common and death not infrequent. It was into one of these training centres that a passing traveller came on his way to another town and, as was the custom in some places, asked for a night's lodging. While taking tea with the master of the school, shortly before retiring, the traveller was asked whether he knew anything of the art of swordsmanship. He modestly replied that he had had some experience but was no great hand at it. A pause ensued during which the master's curiosity was aroused. Finally, he asked the guest with the ceremonial politeness of the times whether he would be interested in a round the next day before he re-commenced his journey. The guest knew what this might mean and looked at the assembled pupils sitting quietly around him. To refuse would be dishonourable and also be a slight to his host's hospitality. To accept, on the other hand, might mean death and the last sojourn on an import-ant journey. He thought for a while and then accepted, saying that he was quite unworthy of doing his host honour by such participation.

The next morning, the school assembled at an early hour to watch what they expected to be a model combat round between their master and the guest. The first few strokes showed the traveller to be no mere novice and within a few minutes the master himself was obliged to resort to his reserves in order to maintain his footing and save himself from injury. After a few more minutes, the master cried 'Hold!' and the traveller bowed and put up his sword. 'Ah, indeed you are yourself a master of the sword,' exclaimed the master somewhat reproachfully.

'With all respect, your Honour, I am no such thing, but an ordinary man with some little experience.'

The master was not quite satisfied with this answer although he felt that he was being told the truth. 'How is it then,' he asked, 'that such an "ordinary man" can wield a sword so well?'

'I know not, Your Honour, unless it be that I have never feared death. Perhaps it is that Your Honour enquires into?'

'That's it to be sure,' said the master, 'For forty years I have laboured within these walls to implant into these young people just that fearlessness that I detect in you and in all those forty years there have been many who have been able swordsmen but none that has attained to your rank and that is why I have no follower.'[469]

Such were the acid tests of non-egoicity among the Zen exponents of swordsmanship in days gone by.[470] Here there is no thought of theological i-dotting or scholastic cheese-paring but a matter of life and death. Nor has Beckett any time for academic nicety, valuable though this may be on occasion. He knows only too well that death is the touch-stone of inner freedom, not the death of the body, for this, he tells us, may not be an answer but only an interruption. True death must be the death of the clamorous, chattering ego. This is what stands in the way of true understanding of oneself, preventing one from attaining the perfect freedom the human psyche so desires. We have already referred to Buddhism's solution to the problem as a starvation of the fires of passion; where there is no fuel to burn, there cannot be a fire. This is the 'ablation of desire.'

Beckett, too, has tried this means of restriction. In *Murphy* (in which the hero's physical demise solved none of his problems), there is an attack on the means of being able to go out and grasp (Murphy is strapped to a chair). In *Molloy*, we find this character slowly reduced to a pained figure in a ditch, unable any more to carry on his journey to his mother (the return to his true self). Moran follows Molloy into physical and spiritual poverty. In *Malone Dies*, the story begins with a supine invalid, and the journey is all inward. Finally, in *The Unnamable*, there is utter destitution, the giving up of everything other than thought. *How It Is*, if anything, is even more attenuated since it is a tale told at second remove. After this, there could only be silence. This is the quest that seeks to know itself by what Ross Chambers calls 'a constant movement inward and downward,' which, by 'ablation' finally arrives at nothing:

but a nothing that insistently and desperately proclaims itself something. Through the labyrinth, a
single Ariadne's thread: the pursuit of self.[471]

In truth, there is only one desire and that is the desire to
know. However, the desire to know always leads Beckett
into an impasse. He is, therefore able to say only that this is
'how it is,' a trackless, hopeless dead-end. The nearer he
comes to his goal, the self, the louder the 'voice on all sides'
becomes until, like the Odyssean sailors, he can hear nothing
but its insidious tones. Finally, his questing skiff breaks up
on the rocks of disillusion.

Beckett's greatness as an author lies in his attempt to
explore the mind, an expanse that is practically uncharted.
We can be certain that few have journeyed so far without
the lode of a religious tradition of some kind. Beckett, with
commendable courage, ingenuity and perseverance as
well as independence of mind has come almost, from the
Buddhist's point of view, within sight of land.

1 *Bibliography: The Works of Samuel Beckett*

The following lists the works of Samuel Beckett referred to in this essay.

PUBLISHED IN ENGLISH

1929 *Dante...Bruno. Vico...Joyce. Our Exagimination Round his Factification for Incamination of Work in Progress*, (Faber & Faber, London, 1972).

1930 *Whoroscope*, poem of seventy-four lines appearing in *Transition*, (June 1930).

1931 *Proust* and *Three Dialogues with Georges Duthuit*, (Calder & Boyars, London, 1965).

1932 *Sedendo et Quiescendo*, short story, appearing in *Transition*, edited by Eugene Jolas.

1934 *More Pricks than Kicks*, short story collection, (Caldar & Boyars, London, reprinted 1973).

1938 *Murphy*, novel, (originally published by Routledge, London and later as a 'Picador' edition [used here] in 1973).

1949 *Three Dialogues* (I Tal Coat, II André Masson and III Bram van Velde; originally published in *Transition* in December 1949 and later with the *Proust* edition above).

1953 *Watt*, novel, (originally published in Paris by Olympia Press and later by Calder & Boyars, London, as 'Jupiter Book,' [the edition used here] in 1972).

1956 *From an Abandoned Work*, unfinished novel, (originally in *Trinity News, A Dublin University Weekly*, June 1956).

1957   *All That Fall*, radio play, (originally published by the Grove Press, New York and later by Faber & Faber, London, 1957, the edition used here).

1958   *Beckett's Letters on Endgame.* His correspondence with his director, Alan Schneider, (dated December 27th, 1955 and occurring in New York's *Village Voice*, March 19th, 1958, pp. 8 and 15).

1958   *Krapp's Last Tape*, play in one act, (Faber & Faber, London, 1973).

1961   *Happy Days*, play, (first published by the Grove Press, New York and later reprinted by Faber & Faber, London, 1973).

1964   *Play*, play in one act, (Faber & Faber, London).

PUBLISHED IN FRENCH

1945   *La Peinture de van Velde, ou: le monde et le pantalon*, criticism, (Cahiers d'Art, Paris).

1948   *Peintures de l'empêchement*, criticism, (Derrière le miroir, Galerie Maeght, Paris).

1951   *Molloy*, novel, (Editions de Minuit, Paris. Edition used here appearing as a trilogy of novels: *Molloy; Malone Dies; The Unnamable*, Calder & Boyars, London, 1959).

1951   *Malone meurt*, Malone Dies, (Editions de Minuit, Paris and above).

1952   *En attendant Godot*, Waiting for Godot, play, (Editions de Minuit, Paris. Edition used here: *Samuel Beckett: Warten Auf Godot* etc. in three languages, Suhrkamp Verlag, Berlin & Frankfurt/Main).

1953   *L'Innommable*, The Unnamable, (Editions de Minuit, Paris and as a trilogy above).

1955   *Textes pour rien*, Texts for Nothing, short stories, (Editions de Minuit, Paris and by Calder & Boyars, London, translated by the author, 1974).

1955   *Henri Hayden, homme-peintre*, criticism, Cahiers d' Art − Documents, 22 (November 1955).

1957   *Fin de Partie*, suivi de Acte sans paroles, Endgame, play and mime respectively, (Editions de Minuit, Paris;

later published by Faber & Faber, London, and reprinted in 1973).

1961 *Comment c'est*, How It Is, novel in three parts, (Edition de Minuit, Paris and by Calder & Boyars, London, 1964).

1970 *Premier Amour*, First Love, prose piece, (Editions de Minuit, Paris and Calder & Boyars, London, 1973).

1971 *Le Depeupleur*, The Lost Ones, prose piece, (Editions de Minuit, Paris and Calder & Boyars, London, 1972).

OTHER PUBLISHED WORKS

1973 *Not-I*, play, (Faber & Faber, London).

1972 *Film*, written in 1963, (Faber & Faber, London).

2 Bibliography: Criticism of Samuel Beckett's Works

Adorno, Theodor, *Noten zur Literatur II*, "Versuch das 'Endspiel' zu verstehen,"(Frankfurt am Main, 1961).

Alvarez, A., *Beckett*, (London, 1973).

Bair, Deidre, (biography) *Samuel Beckett*, (London & New York, 1978).

Birkenauer, Klaus, (biography) *Beckett*, (Hamburg 1971).

——, *Samuel Beckett in Selbstzeugnissen und Bilddokumenten*, (Hamburg, 1971).

Bowles, Patrick, *The Listener*, 'Waiting for Godot,' (June 19th, 1958, p.1011ff).

Coe, R.N. *Beckett*, (Edinburgh, 1964).

Cohn, Ruby, *Back to Beckett*, (New Jersey, 1973).

Delye, Huguett, *Samuel Beckett ou la philospophie de l'absurde*, (Aix-en-Provence, 1960, dissertation de La Pensée Universitaire).

Doherty, Francis, *Samuel Beckett*, (London, 1971).

Dreysse, Ursula, *Realität als Aufgabe: Eine Untersuchungen über Aufbaugesetze und Gehalte des Romanwerks von Samuel Beckett*, (Berlin, 1970).

Driver, Tom, *Beckett by the Madeleine*, (Columbia University Forum, Vol. IV, No. 3, 1961).

Duckworth, Colin, *Samuel Beckett 'En attendant Godot,'* (London, 1966).

——, *Angels of Darkness. Dramatic Effect in Beckett and Ionesco*, (London, 1972).

Esslin, Martin, ed. *Samuel Beckett: A Collection of Critical Essays*, (New York, 1966).

Fletcher, John, *The Novels of Samuel Beckett*, (London, 1960).

Fletcher and Spurling, *Beckett: A Study of His Plays*, (London, 1972).

Fletcher, Smith & Bachem, *A Student's Guide To Samuel Beckett*, (London, 1978).

Finney, B., 'Assumption to Lessness,' *Beckett the Shape Changer: A Symposium*, ed. K. Worth, (London, 1975).

Graver & Federmann, *Samuel Beckett, The Critical Heritage*, (London, 1979).

Gregor & Stein, *The Prose for God*, 'Samuel Beckett: The Unalterable Whey of Words,' (London, 1973).

Hayman, R., *Samuel Beckett*, (New York, 1973).

Harvey, Lawrence E., *Samuel Beckett, Poet and Critic*, (New Jersey, 1970).

Hesla, David, *Samuel Beckett, The Shape of Chaos*, (Minnesota, 1971).

Hobson, Harold, *The Novels of Samuel Beckett*, (London, 1964).

Hoffmann, F.J., *The Language of Self*, (New York, 1962).

Jacobsen & Mueller, *The Testament of Samuel Beckett*, (New York, 1964).

Kenner, Hugh, *A Reader's Guide to Samuel Beckett*, (London, 1976).

————, *Samuel Beckett: A Critical Study*, (London, 1962).

————, *The Cartesian Centaur*, (*Perspective* No. XI, autumn 1959).

Kermode, Frank, *Beckett, Snow and Pure Poverty*, (occurring in *Encounter*, 15th July, 1960, pp.73−7).

————, *A Critic's View*, (London, 1962).

Kern, Edith: 'Drama Stripped for Inaction: Beckett's Godot' Yale French Studies, No. 14, (New York, 1965, pp.41−7).

————, 'Beckett's Knight of Infinite Resignation,' Yale French Studies, No. 29, (New York, Spring-summer, 1962, pp.49−56).

Laass, Werner, *Samuel Beckett: Dramatische Form als Medium der Reflexion*, (Bonn, 1978).

Lee, R., 'The Fictional Topography of Samuel Beckett,' occurring in *The Modern English Novel, The Reader, The Writer and The Work*, edited G. Josipovici, (London, 1976).

Leventhal, J., 'The Beckett Hero,' occurring in *Samuel Beckett, A Collection of Critical Essays*, (op. cit.) delivered as a lecture at Trinity College, Dublin in June 1963.

Mayoux, Jean-Jacques, 'Samuel and the Universal Parody,' occurring in *Samuel Beckett, A Collection of Critical Essays*, (op.cit.) p.77ff.

Metman, Eva, 'Reflections on Samuel Beckett's Plays,' *The Journal of Analytical Psychology*, (January, 1960).

Nobokov, Vladimir, *The Novel, A Forum on Fiction*, spring, 1971, remarks on Beckett in interview; reprinted in *Strong Opinions*, (London, 1978, pp.159–76).

Nadeau, Maurice, Article on Beckett's novel *How It Is*, appearing in the *Express* on the January 26th, 1961 (No. 25) and appearing also in *The Critical Heritage*, (op. cit.) p.224ff.

New York Times, Beckett's correspondence with his friend, Israel Schenker some of which was published on May 6th, 1956, section 2, pp.1 and 3.

Pearson, Gabriel, 'The Monologue of Samuel Beckett,' occurring in *The Spectator*, April 11th, 1953, p.446ff.

Pilling, J., *Samuel Beckett*, (London, 1976).

Porter-Abbott, H., The Fiction of *Samuel Beckett: Form and Effect*, (London, 1973).

Radke, J., 'The Theatre of Samuel Beckett: "Une Durée à Animer," Yale French Studies, No. 29, (New York, 1962, pp.57–64).

Reid, A., *All I Can Manage, More Than I Could: An Approach to the Plays of Samuel Beckett*, (Dublin, 1968).

Robinson, M., *The Long Sonata of the Dead*, (London, 1969).

Rosen, S., *Samuel Beckett and the Pessimistic Tradition*, (New Brunswick, 1976).

Ross Chambers, 'Beckett's Brinkmanship' occurring in *Samuel Beckett, A Collection of Critical Essays* (op. cit.) p.152.

Ross-Chambers, 'Samuel Beckett and the Padded Cell,' taken from the *Meanjin Quarterly*, (December 1962, p.451ff).

Scott, Nathan, *Samuel Beckett*, (London, 1965).

Schenker, Israel, 'Moody Man of Letters,' *New York Times* for May 6th, 1956.

Schneider, Alan, Beckett's friend, who quotes part of a letter from Beckett which subsequently appeared in the *Village Voice*, New York, March 1958.

Selz, J., editor of Beckett's essay on *Henri Hayden*, appearing in Geneva, 1962.

Sontag, Susan, *Against Interpretation and Other Essays*, (New York, 1966).

Szanto, G.H., *Narrative Consciousness*, Part II, 'The Form of Consciousness': Modified Patterns, (Austin, Texas, 1972).

Updike, John, Article appearing in *The New Yorker* on December 19th, 1964 and parodying Beckett's style, pp.165–6.

Webb, E., *Samuel Beckett: A Study of His Novels*, (London, 1970).

———, *The Plays of Samuel Beckett*, (London, 1972).

3 Bibliography: Works on Zen Buddhism and Related Material

Benoit, H., *The Supreme Doctrine: Psychological Studies in Zen Thought,* (New York, 1955).

Bhagavad Gita (classical Hindu poem) translated by Prabhavananda and Christopher Isherwood, first published in 1947 and reprinted in 1960 from which publication the quotations are taken.

Blofeld, John, *The Zen Teaching of Huang Po on the Transmission of Mind,* editor and translator, (London, 1968).

Dogen, *The Shobogenzo* part of which appears in English translation in Philip Kapleau's *Three Pillars of Zen.* See pp.297–8 of that work below.

Eliot, T.S., *Collected Poems, 1909–1962,* (London, 1963).

Fontein & Hickman, editors, *Zen Painting and Caligraphy,* Museum of Fine Arts, (catalogue), (Boston, 1970).

Foster, Paul, *The Buddhist Elements in T.S. Eliot's 'Four Quartets'* (Frankfurt am Main, 1977).

Fraser, J.T., *The Voices of Time,* (London, 1968).

Fromm, Erich, (in conjunction with De Martino and D.T. Suzuki) in *Zen Buddhism and Psychoanalysis,* (London, 1960).

Goddard, D., editor, *A Buddhist Bible,* (Boston, 1970).

Herrigel, Eugen, *Zen in the Art of Archery,* (New York, 1953).

Huang Po, Chinese Zen master. See Blofeld, John, above.

Huxley, Aldous, *The Human Situation,* (London, 1937).

——, *Ends and Means,* (London, 1937).

——, *The Perennial Philosophy,* (London, 1946).

James, William, *Some Problems of Philosophy,* (New York, 1948).

Kapleau, Philip, *The Three Pillars of Zen,* (New York, 1966).

Luk, Charles, *The Secrets of Chinese Meditation*, (London, 1964).

———, *Ch'an and Zen Teaching*, First Series, (London, 1960).

———, *Ch'an and Zen Teaching*, Second Series, (London, 1961).

———, *Ch'an and Zen Teaching*, Third Series, (London, 1962).

Menninger, Karl, *Man Against Himself*, (London, 1938).

Merton, Thomas, *Elected Silence*. (London, 1949).

———, *Seeds of Contemplation*, (London, 1949).

Nyanatiloka, (Buddhist monk and writer) *The Word of the Buddha*, (Kandy, Sri Lanka, 1968).

Suzuki, D.T., *Essays in Zen Buddhism*, First Series, (London, 1958).

———, *Essays in Zen Buddhism*, Second Series, (London, 1958).

———, *A Manual of Zen Buddhism*, (London, 1957).

———, *The Zen Doctrine of No-Mind*, (London, 1985).

Story, Francis, *The Four Noble Truths*, (Kandy, Sri Lanka, 1968).

Tsung Kao, Buddhist Zen master, *The Practice of Zen*, translated Chang Chen Chi, (London, 1953).

Watts, Alan W., *The Way of Zen*, (London, 1957).

Wei Wu Wei (pseudonym), *Ask the Awakened*, (London, 1963).

Wienpahl, Paul, 'Ch'an Buddhism, Western Thought and the Concept of Substance' appearing in *Inquiry*, No. 14 (Universitetsforlaget Oslo, 1971).

———, 'Spinoza and Mental Health,' *Inquiry* No. 15 (op. cit.)

Zimmer, Heinrich, *The Philosophies of India*, (New York, 1971).

OTHER

Ayer, A.J., *The Problem of Knowledge*, (London, 1978).

Calder, John, *Beckett at Sixty: A Festschrift*, (London, 1967).

Federman & Fletcher, *Samuel Beckett, His Works and His Critics*, (London, 1970).

Grossvogel, D. *The Blasphemers: The Theater of Brecht, Ionesco, Beckett, Genet*, (New York, 1962).

Khayyam, Omar, *The Rubaiyat of Omar Khayyam*, translated by E. Fitzgerald, (London).

Prayers and Hymns for Use in Schools, (Oxford, 1928).

Rolph, C.H., *Personal Identity*, (London, 1957).

Spinoza, Baruch, *Ethics*, Vol. II, text and commentary by Carl Gebhardt, (Heidelberg, 1925).

Notes

CHAPTER ONE: THE NATURE OF THE IMPASSE

1   Quoted from a letter written to Beckett's friend, Alan
    Schneider, and printed in the New York *Village Voice*
    in March 1958.
2   Quoted by John Fletcher in *The Novels of Samuel
    Beckett*, (London, 1960).
3   Israel Schenker, 'Moody Man of Letters,' *New York
    Times*, June 5th, 1956.
4   Quoted from an interview with Professor Colin Duck-
    worth and appearing in his book *Samuel Beckett 'En
    Attendant Godot,'* (London, 1966, p.xxv).
5   John Fletcher and John Spurling in *Beckett, A Study of
    His Plays*, (London, 1972, p.20).
6   Ibid. p.34.
7   Ibid. p.70.
8   *Waiting for Godot*, p.34
9   This remark of Beckett's occurs throughout the work
    of his critics, but see Rosen, S., *Samuel Beckett and the
    Pessimistic Tradition*, (New Brunswick, USA, 1976,
    p.55).
10 Tom Driver in the interview with Beckett entitled
    Beckett by the Madeleine, Columbia Univ. Forum, Vol.
    IV, No. 3, 1961.
11 Rosen (see above) p.55. My brackets.
12 With regard to the 'fundamental sound,' it is interest-
    ing to cite a remark made by Beckett to Harold Pinter.
    I give the whole of the incident here since it puts the
    matter in context. The extract is taken from Deidre
    Bair's biography of Samuel Beckett (so entitled) and

published in London in 1978. The following is to be found on p.528 of the work. All brackets are mine:

When they (Beckett and Pinter) talked about Beckett's own work, he (Beckett) insisted repeatedly that none of his writing possessed any form, as if he wanted Printer to challenge the statement. Pinter disagreed, saying that Beckett's writing seemed to him a constantly courageous attempt to impose order and form upon the wretched mess mankind had made of the world. 'If you insist on finding form, I'll describe it to you,' Beckett replied. 'I was in hospital once. There was a man in another ward, dying of throat cancer. In the silence I could hear his screams continually. That's the kind of form my work has.'

13   Op. cit. p.23.
14   Op. cit. p.10.
15   The phrase occurs in *The Prose for God*, (London, 1973).
16   *Endgame*, p.45.
17   Ibid. p.38.
18   Ibid. p.12.
19   Ibid. p.13.
20   Ibid. p.13−14.
21   Sontag, S., *Against Interpretation and Other Essays*, (New York, 1966 p.14).
22   See in particular: Szanto, G.H., *Narrative Consciousness*, pt. II, 'The form of consciousness: Modified Patterns,' p.71. (Austin, Texas, 1972).
23   Robinson, M., *The Long Sonata of the Dead*, (London, 1969, p.26).
24   Ibid. p.26.
25   Rosen, S., op. cit. p.66.
26   Fletcher and Spurling, op. cit. p.34.
27   Among others, the philosophies mostly referred to have been those of: Parmenides, Zeno, Heraclitus, Pythagoras, Georgias, Aristotle, Augustine, Kant, Descartes, Geulincx, Malebranche, Hume, Berkeley, Schopenhauer, Spinoza, Mauthner, Heidegger and Wittgenstein.
28   See Pilling, J., *Samuel Beckett*, 'The Intellectual and Cultural Background to Beckett,' (London, 1976), and

allusion throughout in Hesla, D., *The Shape of Chaos, an Interpretation of the Art of Samuel Beckett,* (Minnesota, USA, 1971).

29   But see Metman, Eva, 'Reflections on Samuel Beckett's Plays,' *Journal of Analytical Psychology* (USA), V, (Jan. 1960), pp.41–63.

30   For confirmation, see Bair, op. cit. p.177.

31   Ibid. Bair notes throughout that Beckett is susceptible to depression.

32   London, 1970.

33   As an example of such turgidity, see the work of Huguette Delye, *Samuel Beckett, ou la philosophie de l'absurde,* Aix-en-Provence, 1960, Ph.D. publication, La Pensée Universitaire.

34   References to the 'human condition' or the 'human situation' are so numerous and so thoroughly disseminated in the body of Beckett criticism that it is impossible to cite all of them. It has simply become universally applied and it would be easier to say that one can hardly take up a work of criticism without coming across it. Among the most prominent are the following:
Jacobsen and Mueller, *The Testament of Samuel Beckett,* (New York, 1964), where, incidentally, a whole chapter is devoted to the subject; Reid, A., *Samuel Beckett, An Approach* etc., (Dublin, 1968, p.54); Cohn R., *Back to Beckett,* (New Jersey, 1973), Foreword and elsewhere; Laass, H., *Dramatische Form* etc., (Bonn, 1978), p.9 and elsewhere; Pilling, J., *Samuel Beckett,* (London, 1976), p.131 and elsewhere; Fletcher/Fletcher, Smith and Bachem, *A Student's Guide to Samuel Beckett.,* (London, 1978), p.33 and elsewhere; Coe, R.N., *Beckett,* (Edinburgh, 1964), pp.1 & 5 and elsewhere; Hesla, D., *Samuel Beckett,* op. cit. Foreword and elsewhere; Rosen, op. cit. p.129 and elsewhere; Robinson, op. cit. p.32; Hayman, R., *Samuel Beckett,* (New York, 1973), pp.50–53; Szanto, G.H., op. cit. p.105; Finney, B., 'Assumption to Lessness' from *Beckett the Shape*

Changer, A symposium, ed. K. Worth, (London, 1975), p.58; Scott, N., *Samuel Beckett*, (London, 1965, pp.91, 123, 127 and elsewhere; Fletcher, J., *The Novels of Samuel Beckett*, op. cit. p.226; Webb, E., *Samuel Beckett, A Study of His Novels*, (London, 1970), pp.25, 31—32 and elsewhere; Webb, E., *The Plays of Samuel Beckett*, (London, 1972), p.86. Hoffmann, F.J., *The Language of Self*, (New York, 1962), p.148 and elsewhere; Duckworth, C., op. cit. (London, 1966), p.xxxvi and throughout the chapter: 'What are Beckett's Works About?' Duckworth, C., *Angels of Darkness*, etc., (London, 1972). 'The Mortal Coil' ff.; Dreysse, U., *Realität als Aufgabe* etc., (Berlin, 1970), p. 13. See also *Samuel Beckett, The Critical Heritage*, ed. Graver and Federman, (London, 1979), a compendium of reviews of Beckett in the years between 1931 and 1977, and also *Samuel Beckett, A Collection of Critical Essays*, (New York, 1965).

35 Op. cit. pp.3 and 24ff.

36 Op. cit. p.158.

37 *Hayden*, ed. J. Selz, (Geneva, 1962), pp.40—1.

38 Here we are not using the word in any definitive psychological sense, but simply to mean 'the awareness of the "I" here that suffers.'

39 The word *dukkha* is almost universally translated into English as 'suffering.' Literally however, it means 'sour,' its antonym *sukkha* in Sanskrit meaning 'sweet' or agreeable. Hence, *dukkha* signifies 'not sweet,' 'unsatisfactory.'

40 This, bare as it seems here, is of the most profound importance. It redeems man from a condemnation to automatism or, in its worst aspect, from being simply a devil; it is, coupled with the fourth truth, a practical solution for the dwellers in Plato's cave.

41 The actual Path is generally summarized as: Right understanding, Right intention, Right speech, Right action, Right livelihood, Right effort, Right mindfulness and Right concentration.

42   The Philosophies of India, (New York, 1971), p.4. My brackets.

43   Except in Tibet where there are certain superficial correspondences.

44   See page 15 of this essay.

45   It should be pointed out here that for our immediate purposes the two can be separated. For the Zen student however, there is no such division.

46   This includes all Beckett's reviews, his *Hommage à Jack Yeats*, his essays, *La Peinture de van Velde, Peintres de l'Empêchement* and his essay on Henri Hayden.

47   In *Samuel Beckett, Poet and Critic*, (New Jersey, 1970).

48   In his conversation with Gabriel d'Aubarède.

49   Webb, Eugene, *The Plays of Samuel Beckett* (London 1970, p.132).

50   *Proust*, p.65.

51   3rd edition, (Oxford, 1970), p.510, cols. 1—2.

52   *Three Dialogues*, (here Tal Coat; Calder & Boyars edition, London, 1970), p.103.

53   *Waiting for Godot*, p.124 and elsewhere.

54   In *Molloy*, the death of the shepherd (Moran?); in *Malone Dies*, in the bloodbath which punctuates Lady Pedal's boat excursion; in *Watt*, the contemplation of Nature by Sam and Watt.

55   Samuel Beckett: *How It Is*, translated from the French by the author, (London, 1964), p.159.

56   Watts, A., *The Way of Zen*, (New York, 1957), p.137.

57   It may not be out of place here to draw the reader's attention to the autobiographical elements in the first paragraph of the quotation from *How It Is*. That which is 'all balls,' i.e. the business (of a heaven) above; 'the women' (his outwardly pious mother in particular), the 'blue Kerry bitch' much beloved by the family at Caldrinagh; the sad pointlessness of memory; 'the prayers,' presumably those he learned at his mother's knee; Beckett's two homes in Ireland with their associated memories. This is made absolutely clear by reference to Bair's biography, op. cit.

58   For a thorough account of the extent of Time's impingement on our lives, see Fraser, J.T., *The Voices of Time*, (London, 1968).

59   *Happy Days*, p.38.

60   *Watt*, p.78.

61   The complete scenario with illustrations, production an essay on directing *Film* (with Alan Schneider as Director) has been published by Faber & Faber, (London, 1972).

62   *Watt*, pp.78–9.

63   It is a shock because, at one stroke, it lays an axe to our carefully nurtured idea of ourselves through the years, an idea buttressed by memory and supported by society and generally reinforced by all whom we meet and all that we do.

64   Zen experienced its heyday in the T'ang period (AD 618–906).

65   The anecdote is a condensed version of that given by D.T. Suzuki in his *Essays in Zen Buddhism*, Second Series, (London, 1950), p.204.

66   Op. cit. p.8.

67   It will be recalled that while the word 'metaphysics' is used here for the sake of convenience and because it loosely refers to that which is under consideration, it is netheles a word which has suffered demotion, especially since the rise of science. However, it is interesting to observe now that, just because of this development, there is a desperate need to re-establish those values which once had their origin in metaphysics.

68   *Watt*, p.89.

69   The phrase was first used by Vivian Mercier.

70   Op. cit.

71   *Endgame*, p.41.

72   *Waiting for Godot*, p.230.

73   *How It Is*, p.95.

74   *Three Dialogues*, op. cit. p.103.

75   *Molloy*, p.152.

76   *Endgame*, p.29.
77   Beckett to John Gruen in 1970.
78   *Samuel Beckett, A Study of the Novels*, (London, 1970), p.21.
79   My brackets.

CHAPTER TWO: WHAT THE CRITICS SAY

80   This percentage was arrived at by considering the titles and content of all those works on Beckett listed in Federman & Fletcher's compendium, *Samuel Beckett, His Works and His Critics*, (Berkeley, 1968), taking the phrase 'human condition' or 'human situation' etc. as a guideline and finding the percentage of discussion committed to the subject. The figure is an approximate one.

81   Lee, R., 'The Fictional Topography of Samuel Beckett,' occurring in *The Modern English Novel, the Reader, the Writer and the Work*, ed. G. Josipovici, (London, 1976).

82   Kermode, F., 'Beckett Country,' occurring in *Modern Essays*, (London, 1971), p.215; Kermode's italics.

83   *Yale French Studies*, (New York, 1965). No. 14, pp.41−7.

84   *Molloy*, p.31.

85   Published by Thames and Hudson.

86   Kennes, Hugh, *Samuel Beckett, A Critical Study*, (New York, 1961), p.109.

87   Ibid.

88   (New York, 1963), p.88.

89   Beckett to the director of *Endgame*.

90   We say 'apparent' here because there is in fact a solution to the problem, one however lying outside the clutch of ratiocination and not within the consideration of this essay except in passing.

91   See also John Pilling op. cit., and the chapter on 'The Literary Background to Beckett', p.132; and Szanto, op. cit.

92   Op. cit. p.126.

93   Reid, A., *All I Can Manage, More Than I Could do* etc.,

(Dublin, 1968). Reid does not say where these quotations of Beckett's come from; one must accept their authenticity in good faith.

94　Ibid. p.61.
95　Ibid. pp.61−2.
96　Ibid. p.63.
97　Ibid. p.63.
98　Ibid. p.80.
99　Ibid. p.128.
100　June 19th, 1956.
101　Ibid. p.1011, col.1.
102　Ibid. p.1012, col. 1.
103　Scott, Nathan, *Beckett*, (London, 1955), p.22.
104　Op. cit. p.31.
105　Ibid. p.81.
106　Ibid. p.90.
107　Ibid. p.91.
108　Ibid. p.126.
109　Ibid. p.126.
110　Taken from the *Meanjin Quarterly*, (December, 1962), p.451.
111　Ibid. p.453.
112　Ibid. pp.453−4. My brackets.
113　Alvarez, A., *Beckett*, (London, 1973), p.50.
114　*Malone Dies*, p.289. My brackets.
115　Op. cit. p.459. Author's italics.
116　Samuel Beckett in a letter to Israel Schenker, later published in the *New York Times*; see 'Moody Man of Letters,' op. cit. above.
117　Op. cit. p.459.
118　Ibid. p.460. My brackets.
119　Op. cit. p.124.
120　Ibid. p.127.
121　Ibid. p.129.
122　Quoted by one of Beckett's biographers, Bair, op. cit. p.386 'Christianity is a mythology with which I am perfectly familiar, and so I use it.'
123　The following books are recommended to those

interested in interpretations of Beckett's work with reference to their allusion to Christianity:

(a) Anders, Günther *Die Antiquiertheit des Menschen: über die Seele im Zeitalter der Zweiten industriellen Revolution*, (München, 1956), pp.213–31.

(b) Mailer, Norman, *Advertisements for Myself*, (New York, 1959), 'A Public Notice on Waiting for Godot' pp.320–5; originally published as 'Reflections on Waiting for Godot.'

(c) Hudson, D., *English Critical Essays: 20th Century*, 2nd series. (London, 1958) (Ed. Hudson) G.S. Fraser 'Waiting for Godot,' pp.324–32.

(d) Scott, Nathan A., Jr. *Modern Religious Frontier*, (New York, 1958), 'Heckett,' pp.324–32.

(e) Beckett, Jeremy, 'Waiting for Godot,' *Meanjin Quarterly* XV, no. 2, (1956), pp.216–18.

(f) Ionesco, E., 'There is no Avant-Garde Theatre,' trans. R. Howard, appearing in the *Evergreen Review*, I, no. 4 (1957) 101–5.

(g) Vahanian, G., 'The Empty Cradle,' appearing in *Theology Today*, No. XIII, (January, 1957), pp.521–6.

(h) Chadwick, C., 'Waiting for Godot: A Logical Approach' appearing in *Symposium*, XIV, (1960), pp.252–7.

(i) Cohn, R., 'Endgame: The Gospel According to Sad Sam Beckett' appearing in *Accent*, No. XX (1960), pp.223–34.

(j) Cohen, R.S., 'Parallels and the Possibility of Influence between Simone Weil's *Waiting for Godot* and Samuel Beckett's *Waiting for Godot*, occurring in *Modern Drama*, VI, (1964), pp.425–36.

124   Jacobsen and Mueller, op. cit. pp.138–9 and elsewhere.

125   Coe, R.N., *Beckett*, (Edinburgh, 1964), p.1.

One dictionary definition of the word 'absurd' is as follows: '2. Out of harmony with reason or propriety; in modern use, plainly opposed to reason and hence ridiculous, silly 1557.' (*The Shorter Oxford English Dictionary*, 3rd Edition, 1970, p.8, col. 3). We have already mentioned Kenner's example of the circus clown, Emmett Kelly, attempting to sweep a circle of light into a dustpan and doing so with the utmost dignity and resolution. This is an illustration of absurdity. We know that it cannot be done because it is against all reason and propriety. Because it is incongruent both with our conviction that it cannot be done and with normal, human behaviour it causes laughter. Indeed, the object here in the circus is nothing more than to evoke laughter. Absurdity is comic. But, with regard to the theatre, the comic is not necessarily absurd; the springs of comedy are incongruency and surprise in a situation which might be absurdly plausible. In other words, such a concatenation of circumstances could possibly arise in real life or may indeed also have happened to real people in a historical situation, (this can quite easily be imagined in the theatrical situations Molière or George Bernard Shaw create for example, but much less so in *The Importance of Being Earnest* perhaps since, for this highly evolved congruence of accident and intention to take place in real life would need something little short of a miracle.) Even less 'realistic' in this sense — highly unlikely situations — are some of the situations presented in the modern theatre and here Beckett might number among the 'absurdists' if we recall his players in their vases and dustbins. However, merely to create laughter by presenting an absurd situation is not Beckett's intention, but rather to draw the audience's attention to Pascal's assertion (in the *Pensées*) that the 'solution to man's problems and the satisfaction of his hopes' cannot be solved by rational means. As we have insisted elsewhere, thinking (rationalization, ratiocination) is a useful tool for solving problems exterior to ourselves, but rather ineffectual when it comes to solving the problems touching our inner life.

Thus the idea of absurdity can be widened to encompass the realization that life itself is 'absurd' in that it seems to have no definite objective. Religion purports to fill this vacuum. But for those lacking this stay, or who remain unconvinced for some reason or another, the 'absurd' in this sense poses a real problem. Only in this sense can Beckett's work be linked to the idea of the absurd.

126   Ibid. p.3.

127   Ibid. p.18.

128   Ibid. p.18.

129   See also at ibid. pp.24ff and 46ff.

130   London, 1966.

131   Ibid. 'What are Beckett's Works About?', p.xxxiii

132   Ibid. p.xxxvi.

133   Quoted here by Prof. Duckworth, ibid. p.xlIII.

134   By 'mechanics of mind' we mean, primarily, the activity of the self or ego in the subject-object relationship as described above. If, for example, we consider the problem as outlined by Chambers in the passage above, and if it is seen that the I-supposed-subject and supposed object are functions of an antecedent Subject (Buddhist 'Mind') and if, further, these are regarded as unreal as we have seen from preceding arguments, then their removal (the removal of the one implies the removal of the other) leaves only a condition of I-am-not. Apprehension of this is the objective of Buddhist teaching. This is the logical crux of the matter which is generally left unconsidered by practically every critic.

135   To assert, as some critics do, that the dilemma is irresolvable is at once correct and incorrect; correct if they mean rationally, but incorrect if they imply thereby that it cannot be solved by the intuitive 'leap' practised by the Buddhist.

136   *The Long Sonata of the Dead*, (London, 1969), p.25.

137   'Hither' is neither 'here' nor 'there,' but within.

138   *The Long Sonata of the Dead*, (London, 1969), p.25.

139   Ibid. p.26.

140   Ibid. p.26.
141   *Beckett*, (London, 1964), p.310.
142   *The Long Sonata of the Dead*, (London, 1969), p.30.
143   Ibid. p.56.
144   *Samuel Beckett Another Pessimistic Tradition*, (New Brunswick, 1976), p.5.
145   Ibid. pp.154–5.
146   Ibid. p.155.
147   Nagarjuna: 14th patriarch of Zen (*Ch'an*), active during the first half of the 3rd century AD.
148   Ibid. p.158. Author's italics.
149   Ibid. p.160. My brackets.
150   *Watt*, p.46.
151   *Samuel Beckett*, (New York, 1973), p.25.
152   Ibid p.25.
153   Op. cit.
154   *Samuel Beckett, The Shape of Chaos,*(Minnesota, 1971).

CHAPTER THREE: TIME, HABIT AND MEMORY: PROUST

155   See Federman and Fletcher, *Samuel Beckett, His Works and His Critics*, (London, 1970), p.9 (7.2).
156   But see Beckett's poem *Whoroscope*.
157   *Murphy*, p.101.
158   Op. cit. p.17.
158a Wei Wu Wei, (pseudonym) *Ask The Awakened*, (London, 1963), p.251 (Section 108).
159   This translation from Dogen's *Shobogenzo* is taken from Philip Kapleau's *The Three Pillars of Zen*, (New York, 1966), pp.297–8.
160   The Japanese word 'Zen' is derived from the Chinese 'Ch'an,' which in turn is the Chinese rendering of the Sanskrit *dhyana* meaning 'meditation.'
161   *Proust*, op. cit. p.13.
162   'The Countess Cathleen.'
163   T.S. Eliot, *Collected Poems* (1909–1962), 'The Dry Salvages' II. 133–43.

164 *Waiting for Godot* p.26.
165 Ibid. p.220.
166 Ibid. p.222.
167 *Proust*, p.18.
168 *Proust*, p.19.
169 *Proust*, p.21.
170 This anecdote is well-known in Zen, but a version of it appears in Charles Luk's *Ch'an and Zen Teaching*, First Series, (London, 1960), p.123.
171 *Molloy*, pp.66—7.
172 *How It Is*, pp.107—8.
173 *Proust*, p.21.
174 Luk, Charles, *Ch'an and Zen Teaching*, Third Series, (London, 1962), p. 189.
175 Huang Po, *The Zen Teaching of Transmission of Mind*, translated by J. Blofeld, (London, 1968), p.44.
176 *Proust*, p.23.
177 Ibid. p.30.
178 Ibid. p.33. All brackets mine.
179 Ibid p.33.
180 *Krapp's Last Tape*, p.15.
181 Ibid. p.15.
182 Ibid. p.17.
183 Ibid. p.20.
184 Pr. p.35 *Proust*, p.35.
185 Op. cit. pp.218—19. All brackets mine.
186 *Proust*, pp.17—18.
187 *Molloy*, p.78.
188 *Happy Days*, p.142.
189 *Endgame*, p.27.
190 *Waiting for Godot*, pp.230—1.
191 *Malone Dies*, p.226.
192 *Proust*, pp.36—7.
193 For an account of the phenomenon, see Suzuki, D.T., *Essays* etc., (op. cit.) Vol. II, (1950) p.189ff.
194 The *koan* is an irrational problem set for the meditator. It is what we would call a riddle the answer to which does not lie in the rational domain of thinking however. An example of such a *koan* is, for example: What

is the sound of one hand clapping? or: What was your face before you were born? neither of which yields to the grappling of the ratiocinative mind. In other words, it is non-intellectual. There *is* an answer, but this lies in the field of spiritual experience. Once the mind's mechanism has been understood, then the *koan* can be answered.

It is incident to us all, having received such a problem, to go at it with might and main in order to solve it by the only means we know, i.e. by thinking. After a time however, our thinking becomes exhausted. There is no answer that satisfies and finally we give up. At this point, having come to the end of our resources, we are ripe for an apprehension of what precedes intellect; another, quite unsuspected area of our mind opens up, and this is said to be Enlightenment.

The *koan* as it was dispensed to aspirants to Enlightenment in ages past and as it continues to be given to monks today in Japan is, admittedly, to place them in an artificial state of dilemma and had its origins at a time when Zen Buddhism became popular and when the monasteries were crowded with students of the well-to-do who were anxious for their sons to acquire something of traditional religious culture. Zen was obliged to defend itself from such mass invasion and from the deterioration of standards which invariably accompany such developments and therefore introduced the *koan* exercise. We should not forget however that, originally, there was no need to resort to an artificial dilemma; life itself provided the problem. The text here is from Suzuki's *Essays*, Vol. II, op. cit., (1955) p.131. All brackets mine.

195   *Proust*, p.33; Beckett actually uses the word 'explosive.'

CHAPTER FOUR: THE OBLIGATION TO EXPRESS: THREE DIALOGUES
196   *Proust*, p.90.
197   *Three Dialogues*, pp.102—3.

198   From *The Practice of Zen*, (London, 1953), his words translated by Chang Chen Chi. Brackets are mine. We should also bear in mine though that the great Chinese painters always had the 'Void' in mind and this is the reason for the ample representation of space in their work.
199   Blofeld, op. cit. p.107.
200   Wei Wu Wei, *Ask the Awakened* etc., (London, 1963), p.45; my brackets.
201   *Three Dialogues*, p.110 (II Masson).
202   For an excellent introduction to this aspect of eastern painting, the reader's attention is drawn to Fontein & Hickman's *Zen Painting and Caligraphy*, (Museum of Fine Arts, Boston, 1970).
203   What this means in practical terms is recorded by Eugen Herrigel, onetime professor of philosophy at the University of Heidelberg, in his *Zen in the Art of Archery*, (*Die Kunst des Bogenschießens*) translated by F.F.C. Hull, (New York, 1953).
204   *Proust*, p.113.
205   *Proust*, p.113.
206   *Proust*, pp.120−1.

CHAPTER FIVE

207   *Man Against Himself*, (London, 1938), p.3. My brackets.
208   Ibid.
209   *Beckett by the Madeleine*, Columbia Univ. Forum, Vol. IV, No. 3, 1961.
210   First published in 1946 by Chatto & Windus in London; republished 1972.
211   Ibid. p.260.
212   Ibid. p.260.
213   We shall not of course attempt a definition of literature in this connection but simply adopt Shakespeare's generalization that it 'holds the mirror up to Nature.' Alvarez, (op. cit. p.50) is certainly speaking in such

terms in regretting the fact that Beckett has withdrawn
from these traditional patterns of literary expression.
He does not see that this is Beckett's avowed intention.
While we neither condone nor endorse M. Antonin
Artaud's arrogant assertion that 'All writing is
pigshit,' we can perhaps understand the insight behind the condemnation, for he goes on to say. . .'all
those for whom words have meaning; (i.e. in the
relative sense). . .are pigs.' My brackets.

214 'The only possible spiritual development is in the
sense of depth' — Beckett in *Proust*, p.64.

215 Fromm, E., De Martino, R., & Suzuki, D.T., *Zen
Buddhism and Psychoanalysis*, (London, 1960), p.145.

216 Ibid. p.144.

217 Ibid. p.146.

218 Ibid. p.147.

219 Jalal-uddin Rumi.

220 This does not mean that Zen has no use at all for the
sutras as a source of study and edification, but that
Zen is not something 'studied' in the purely intellectual use of the word. It is a discipline to be learned in
daily activity.

221 This does not deny for a moment that self-enlighten-
ment is possible. On the contrary, countless millions
of human beings have found their own way out of the
mortal labyrinth in which we find ourselves. An
element in the will to find such a path is the belief that
it exists and this is tacitly assumed in the East. The
quoted passage above is taken from p.148 of De
Martino.

222 The *raison d'être* of the traditional Zen master.

CHAPTER SIX: A QUEST FOR INNER PEACE: MURPHY

223 *Murphy*, p.53.

224 In an interview with d'Aubarède in 1961, op. cit.

225 Op. cit.

226 See Bair, D., op. cit. p.352.

227   This phrase, often erroneously attributed to Beckett,
       was first used by William James in his *Some Problems
       of Philosophy*, (New York, 1948), p.48.
228   *Murphy*, p.67.
229   *Murphy*, p.127.
230   *Murphy*, p.29.
231   Op. cit. p.31.
232   *Murphy*, p.112.
233   In his discussion of the novels, op. cit. p.52.
234   *Proust*, p.18.
235   *Murphy*, p.148.
236   That is, 'nothing is more real than Nothing.'
237   *Murphy*, p.140.

CHAPTER SEVEN

238   Bair; op. cit. p.308.
239   *Watt*, p.41.
240   Later, he was able to leave this establishment and live
       in a small house not far away with his wife Suzanne.
241   Op. cit. p.328.
242   Op. cit. p.331.
243   *Watt*, p.28.
244   Huxley, A., *The Human Situation*, (London, 1937), p.138.
245   *Watt*, p.6.
246   *Watt*, p.7.
247   *Watt*, p.8.
248   *Watt*, p.15.
249   *Watt*, p.16.
250   *Watt*, p.16–17.
251   *Watt*, p.16.
252   *Watt*, p.22.
253   Op. cit. p.79. Brackets mine.
254   *Watt*, p.32.
255   Since Beckett is fond of word-play, this word too might
       have a double meaning. Apart from the obvious 'cross,'
       it could also possess the meaning of 'a thing that it
       puzzles one to interpret or explain,' and, according to

the *Shorter Oxford English Dictionary*, 3rd Edition p.432, col. iii it could mean 'a conundrum or riddle,' (1718).

256 *Watt*, p.26ff.

257 *Watt*, p.27.

258 *The Shorter Oxford English Dictionary*, op. cit. p.1974, col. i.

259 *Watt*, p.25.

260 *Watt*, p.26.

261 *Watt*, p.61.

262 Op. cit. p.39.

263 Ibid. p.46.

264 Ayer, A.J., *The Problem of Knowledge*, (London, 1956), p.133.

265 *Watt*, p.69.

266 *Watt*, p.76.

267 *Watt*, p.77.

268 *Watt*, p.71.

269 *Watt*, p.69.

270 *Watt*, p.69—70.

271 *Watt*, p.70.

272 *Watt*, p.71.

273 *Watt*, p.73.

274 *Proust*, p.66.

275 *Watt*, p.70.

276 *Watt*, p.70.

277 Blofeld, op. cit. pp.51—3ff. Brackets mine.

278 *Watt*, p.73.

279 Op. cit. p.46.

280 *The Rubaiyat of Omar Khayyam*, translated by Fitzgerald.

281 *Watt*, p.147.

282 *Watt*, p.147.

283 *Watt*, p.147.

284 It should be mentioned here that both the 'aged sixty-four years' and the 'church announcements' refer essentially to English practice and custom. The first is a convention to be seen on English gravestones to the present day and the second occupies a place

somewhere in the middle of the Church of England service, usually immediately before the sermon.

285   *Watt*, p.98ff.
286   *The Rubaiyat of Omar Khayyam* op. cit.
287   *Watt*, p.153ff.
288   *Watt*, p.157.
289   *Watt*, p.166. My brackets.
290   Op. cit. p.201.
291   *Watt*, p.244.

CHAPTER EIGHT: THE DILEMMA OF IDENTITY

292   Reid, A., *Beckett/Beckett*, op. cit. p.161.
293   Cohn, *Back to Beckett*, (New Jersey, 1973), p.119.
294   *Molloy*, p.10.
295   *Molloy*, p.40.
296   The French text has A and B. It is likely that Beckett included himself in the English translation. In this way, he would be the observer.
297   *Molloy*, p.13.
298   *Molloy*, p.17.
299   Beckett's mother, with whom he experienced a tense relationship throughout life, if we are to rely on Bair's account, was called May.
300   *Molloy*, p.18.
301   The Buddhist sutra *Anguttara-Nikaya*, III, 35.
302   This reads: 'I undertake to abstain from killing all living beings.' (Sanskrit, *Pamatipata veramani sikkha padam samadiyami*).
303   *Molloy*, p.29.
304   *Molloy*, p.21.
305   *Molloy*, p.23.
306   This, too, might be a flavour of autobiographical experience entering into *Molloy* since Beckett frequently had problems during his residence in France, especially during the war years, because of his Irish passport.
307   *Molloy*, p.31.

308 Interesting reading on this point is C.H. Rolph's *Personal Identity*, London, 1957. On a deeper level, Spinoza's *Ethics* deals with the same problem. (See Proposition V especially where he contends that there is only one substance, God), all other phenomena being 'modes' of that substance.

309 It is interesting in passing to note that some American banks today do not verify their customers' identity by signature anymore, but rely on an electronic device which identifies the individual's manner of speaking.

310 For this purpose *A Buddhist Bible*, edited by D. Goddard, (Boston, 1970) is to be recommended, or, for a scientific treatment: *The Word of the Buddha*, with a commentary on the *Pali Canon* by the monk Nyanatiloka is suggested, and obtainable from the Buddhist Publication Society, (Sri Lanka, 1968).

311 From the second recommendation above, p.8.

312 Story, Francis, *The Four Noble Truths*, (translation and commentary) (Kandy, Sri Lanka, 1968).

313 *Molloy*, p.31–2.

314 *Molloy*, p.49.

315 Cf. Buddhism's 'Suchness'; Hinduism's 'Thatness' and the 'Quiddity' of the European medieval mystics.

316 This 'knowing nothing' is the last but one stage of Han Shan's objective. See Luk, C., *The Secrets of Chinese Meditation*, 'Han Shan Meng Yu Chi,' (London, 1964), p.56ff.

317 *Molloy*, p.64.

318 For an understanding of this from the Hindu standpoint, one might refer to the *Bhagavad Gita*, sometimes, though not quite correctly, called the 'Bible of Hinduism.'

319 *Molloy*, p.92.

320 There may also be a little autobiographical detail here too. In most of the pictures taken of Bill Beckett, Samuel's father, a hearty, robust man who had a surveyor's business in Dublin, he is wearing a bowler. The young Beckett must have been very familiar with

his father's idiosyncrasies with regard to this particular form of headgear.

320   *Molloy*, p.98.
321   *Molloy*, pp.101−2.
322   *Molloy*, p.102.
323   *Molloy*, p.106.
324   'The Hollow Men,' T.S. Eliot, *Collected Poems 1901−
       1962*, (London, 1963) p.24.
325   Op. cit. Second Series, p.270. My brackets.
326   *Molloy*, pp.108−9.
327   *Molloy*, p.111.
328   *Molloy*, p.114.
329   *Molloy*, p.115.
330   *Molloy*, p.132.
331   This form of travel may also be an autobiographical
       touch when we recall that Beckett in escaping to
       southern France slept by day and travelled by night.
332   *Molloy*, p.146.
333   *Molloy*, p.147.
334   *Molloy*, p.149.
335   *Molloy*, p.151.
336   *Molloy*, p.156.
337   *Molloy*, p.159.
338   *Molloy*, p.162.
339   *Molloy*, p.165.
340   *Molloy*, p.166.
341   Knowing Beckett's disposition for the ambiguous
       proper name, it is a temptation here to construe the
       'eight' as the sign for infinity, an 'eight' on its side,
       and 'Acacia' as 'Arcadia'! But perhaps this is a
       quibble. On the other hand, there are interesting hints
       of an autobiographical nature such as the word 'Yerk'
       mentioned on p.138 of this edition as among the
       'rabble' of moribunds and which, if inverted, gives
       'kery' and may refer to the beloved 'Kerry Blue bitch'
       of the Beckett household, (for reference, see Bair, D.,
       op. cit., p.249). Definite reference of autobiographical
       nature occurs in the allusion to the Elsner sisters on

p.105 of *Molloy*. These were two elderly German spinsters who ran a private academy in Stillorgan and were the first to educate Beckett at kindergarten age, (See Bair, p.24).

342   *Molloy*, p.168.

343   For a full treatment of this theme the reader is referred to the works of the Christian monk, priest and writer, Thomas Merton.

344   This anecdote mirrors Hui-k'e's interview with the Bodhidharma, the first Indian monk to bring Buddhism to China and now recognized in Ch'an Buddhism (Zen) as the First Patriarch.

345   *Molloy*, p.170.

346   *Molloy*, p.171.

347   *Molloy*, p.172−3.

348   *Molloy*, p.175.

349   *Molloy*, p.176.

350   *Molloy*, p.176.

CHAPTER NINE: DESIRE FOR FREEDOM: MALONE DIES

351   Op.cit. p.31.

352   *Malone Dies*, p.180.

353   *Malone Dies*, p.225.

353   *Malone Dies*, p.181.

355   *Molloy*, p.41.

356   *Malone Dies*, p.236.

357   *Malone Dies*, pp.236−7.

358   *Malone Dies*, p.255.

359   Cf. T.S. Eliot's *Four Quartets*, 'East Coker,' Movement V, lines 184ff. for a similar thought.

360   *The Lost Ones*, p.17−18.

361   So it appears to the author, but we must bear in mind that Beckett has not finally closed his mind to the possibility of release.

362   It is interesting to note that Mrs. Bair, Beckett's biographer, on page 352 of her work, records that once in a bitter moment, Beckett confessed himself 'doomed

to spend the rest of my days digging up the detritus of my life and vomiting it out over and over again.'

363 *Malone Dies*, p.229.

364 *Malone Dies*, p.194.

365 *Malone Dies*, p.217.

366 *Malone Dies*, p.225.

367 *Malone Dies*, p.222.

368 Perhaps the most appalling testimony of the juxtaposition of intellect and instinct is provided for us by the contemporary arms race and the kind of weaponry this includes.

369 *Proust*, p.19.

370 D.T. Suzuki, *The Zen Doctrine of No-Mind*, (London, 1958), p.126. All brackets mine.

371 *Malone Dies*, p.191.

372 *Malone Dies*, p.231.

373 *Malone Dies*, p.193.

374 *Malone Dies*, p.193. Author's italics.

375 *Malone Dies*, pp.193, 279, 281–2.

376 *Malone Dies*, p.195.

377 *Malone Dies*, p.201.

378 *Malone Dies*, p.195. My brackets.

CHAPTER TEN: THE INWARD SEARCH: THE UNNAMABLE

379 *The Unnamable*, p.329.

380 *The Concise Oxford Dictionary*, 4th edition, 1951, republished 1954, p.808.

381 *The Unnamable*, p.305–6.

382 *The Unnamable*, p.300.

383 *The Unnamable*, p.300.

384 *The Unnamable*, p.375.

385 *The Unnamable*, p.293.

386 *The Unnamable*, p.293.

387 *The Unnamable*, p.293.

388 *The Unnamable*, p.295.

389 Op.cit. p.237.

390 *The Unnamable*, p.294.

391   *The Unnamable*, p.306.

392   Lee, R., in 'The Fictional Topography of Samuel Beckett,' op.cit. p.209.

393   That these odd occurrences are not simply isolated historical facts, but part of the experience of Mind has been exemplified in modern Zen studies to be most clearly witnessed perhaps in Kapleau's *The Three Pillars of Zen*, op.cit. p.204ff.

394   'Joshu's *Mu*' refers to the great Chinese Zen master Chao-chou, who being asked one day whether the Buddha nature was in a dog (i.e. whether a dog also possesses or is part of the great One Mind) gave the surprising answer 'No!' Since there is no reason for a dog to be excluded from the One mind of creation, the questioner was left astounded and at once thrown back on his own resources to enquire into the meaning of the remark. (Chinese, *Chao-chou*; Japanese, *Joshu*.)

395   Hakuin was the founder of the modern Rinzai school of Zen and a famous Zen master. The text is taken from Suzuki's *Essays in Zen* Buddhism, op.cit. First Series, pp.254−5. My brackets.

396   Suzuki, D.T., *Essays in Zen Buddhism*, op.cit. Second Series, pp.121−2. My brackets.

397   *The Unnamable*, p.339.

398   *The Unnamable*, p.339. My brackets.

399   *The Unnamable*, p.314.

400   *The Unnamable*, p.314. The first set of brackets is mine.

401   *The Unnamable*, p.293.

402   It must not be imagined that these blows were in any way sadistic. Nothing of the kind was intended, but they were earnest and kept the mind of the aspirant strictly applied to the central issue of the training.

403   *The Unnamable*, p.309.

404   *The Unnamable*, p.310. My brackets.

405   *The Unnamable*, p.302.

406   *The Unnamable*, p.304.

407   *The Unnamable*, p.304.

408   *The Unnamable*, p.349.

409   *The Unnamable*, p.356.

410   *The Unnamable*, p.333.

411   From the famous Christmas carol, 'O Come all Ye Faithful' etc.

412   From the hymn book. It occurs for example in the well-known hymnal used in English schools, entitled *Prayers and Hymns For Use in Schools*, OUP, first printed in 1928, p.218, verse iii. Correctly, it reads: The *trivial* round, the common task, etc.

413   *The Unnamable*, p.341.

414   *The Unnamable*, p.379.

415   See for example the employment of the idea of 'ending' in *Molloy*. p.175, in Malone Dies, p.207 or *Endgame*, p.41 as random illustrations.

416   Whatever the origins of this problem may be, it is interesting here to recognize that Hinduism possesses the same concept in likening our existence to being bound on a cosmic wheel. In some Buddhist configurative paintings, too, (Sanskrit, *mandala*, meaning place or abode) one can see the abodes of earth, heaven and hell supported by the demon Mara who has often been likened in his turn to the Greek god Chronos in his omnipotence. In each of the abodes in the Buddhist representations there appears a Boddhisattva symbolizing the fact that, among other things, Buddhist Enlightenment transcends even the highest abodes of heaven and the blackest depths of hell. In Enlightenment, we can say that these things are annihilated at one stroke. Thus, in one sense, Buddhism stands outside traditional religion in a realm beyond all concepts whatsoever.

417   Op.cit. pp.467–8.

418   *The Unnamable*, pp.388–9.

419   Upsaka Lu K'uan Yü, *Ch'an and Zen Teaching*, First Series, (London, 1969), p.23. My brackets.

420   Ibid. p.24. My brackets.

421   *The Unnamable*, p.389.

422 This is exactly the kind of frustration we find at the heart of the next novel, *How It Is*.

423 *The Unnamable*, p.408.

424 Benoit, H., *The Supreme Doctrine*, (New York, 1955), p.83.

CHAPTER ELEVEN: ABANDONING THE EGO: HOW IT IS

425 The animal is known as a *trachedon*.

426 From *The New York Times*, CV, Sunday, 6th May, 1956, Section II, pp.1—3.

427 *How It Is*, p.68.

428 *How It Is*, p.69.

429 *How It Is*, p.75.

430 *How It Is*, p.95.

431 *How It Is*, p.145.

432 26th January, No. 25, here in the translation given in *The Critical Heritage* edition, op.cit. p.224ff.

433 It is of passing interest to speculate on where the idea of 'mud' comes from. One possibility which suggests itself is Beckett's frequent reference to his house at Ussy (near Meaux, north-east of Paris) among his friends as his 'hole in the Marne mud' (see Pilling, op.cit. p.10 and Bair, op. cit. p.413ff.) Another possibility might be the image of the lotus flower and its associations in eastern literature, especially the Hindu and Buddhist, where the flower begins to grow from its bulb in the mud and aspires to the light of day through ever lighter regions, until it breaks through the surface and there unfolds completely. This parallels the development of man, beginning in the 'mud' of ignorance and, on hearing of the teaching of a great master, developing through purification to Enlightenment. It is certain that Beckett is familiar with the parallel. There is also a short but trenchant reference to Buddhist teaching in *How It Is*, occurring on page 62 of the edition used in this work.

434   The composer Haydn — and Beckett quotes this somewhere — once spoke of marriage, for example, as 'parallel thirds'!

435   *How It Is*, p.15.

436   *How It Is*, p.115.

437   *How It Is*, p.89.

438   *How It Is*, p.48.

439   John Updike, writing in the *New Yorker* (pp.165—6) on December 19th, 1964, and parodying Beckett's style in *How It Is*, makes the interesting observation that the letters of which 'PIM' are formed correspond to the name of Christ in Greek, '...chi, rho, iota looks XPI, take away X, and 'M'...Beckett's favourite letter...'

440   *How It Is*, p.82.

441   There is a famous picture of Beckett at his mother's knee and one that appears in several books on Beckett, notably on p.64 of the 'Festschrift' *Beckett at Sixty*, (London, 1967) and it is almost certain that this is what Beckett is referring to here.

442   *How It Is*, pp.16—17.

443   *How It Is*, p.50.

444   Beckett's father was a quantity surveyor and as such was very often on the scaffolding of newly-erected buildings.

445   *How It Is*, p.86.

446   *How It Is*, p.14.

447   This again is evidence of Beckett's acquaintance with Buddhism and its teaching of the 'ablation of desire,' *How It Is*, p.62.

448   *How It Is*, p.94.

449   *How It Is*, p.95.

450   Suzuki, D.T., *The Field of Zen*, (New York, 1970), p.18 and originally published by *The Buddhist Society*, London in 1969.

451   *How It Is*, p.26.

452   *How It Is*, p.60, 69, 105.

453   *How It Is*, p.114.

454   Beckett has frequently alluded to Christianity, for

example, as a 'myth.' See also Beckett's satirical observations on Christianity in *Watt*.

455   *How It Is*, p.107.

456   *How It Is*, p.108.

457   The classical Buddhist formulation is that of the wheel which in design and function is only the sum of its parts.

458   This sentiment is expressed almost in these words in *Happy Days*, p.38.

459   Stevenson, Robert, 'Home no more Home to me.'

460   *How It Is*, p.86ff, p.140.

461   *How It Is*, p.160.

462   *Malone Dies*, p.237.

463   For very interesting reading on this subject, the reader is referred to the journals of the British Society for Psychical Research which was set up to look into paranormal phenomena a hundred years ago, (1880).

464   This doctrine, which in Buddhist theology is a highly evolved thesis, can be followed up in any authoritative study of the Buddhist canon.

465   This view also obtains for Hinduism too.

466   It would be wrong to imagine that Buddhism is the only means towards such emancipation. It is emphasized again that there are other methods and other means but none so comprehensive as yet as Buddhist teaching.

467   *Bhagavad Gita*, p.42.

468   Ibid. p.43

469   This anecdote is a well-known Zen story.

470   See also Eugen Herrigel's *Zen in the Art of Archery*, originally published by Herrigel in German as *Die Kunst des Bogenschießens*, (London, 1959).

471   Chambers, op.cit. p.462.

Other Wisdom East-West Books